Conflicts of Interest

Challenges and Solutions in Business, Law, Medicine, and Public Policy

Edited by

DON A. MOORE

Carnegie Mellon University

DAYLIAN M. CAIN

Carnegie Mellon University

GEORGE LOEWENSTEIN

Carnegie Mellon University

MAX H. BAZERMAN

Harvard Business School

CAMBRIDGE
UNIVERSITY PRESS

CAMBRIDGE UNIVERSITY PRESS
Cambridge, New York, Melbourne, Madrid, Cape Town, Singapore,
São Paulo, Delhi, Dubai, Tokyo

Cambridge University Press
32 Avenue of the Americas, New York, NY 10013-2473, USA

www.cambridge.org
Information on this title: www.cambridge.org/9780521143462

First published 2005
This digitally printed version 2010

A catalog record for this publication is available from the British Library

Library of Congress Cataloging in Publication data
Conflicts of interest : challenges and solutions in business, law, medicine,
and public policy / edited by Don A. Moore . . . [et al.].
p.   cm.
Some of the papers were prepared for presentation at the Conference on Conflicts
of Interest in Organizations.
Includes bibliographical references and index.
ISBN 0-521-84439-8 (hardback)
1. Business ethics.   2. Legal ethics.   3. Medical ethics.   4. Professional ethics.
5. Conflict of interests.   I. Moore, Don A., 1970–   II. Title.
HF5387.C6614   2005
174′.4 – dc22   2004017666

ISBN 978-0-521-84439-0 Hardback
ISBN 978-0-521-14346-2 Paperback

Contents

List of Contributors

Mahzarin R. Banaji
Harvard University

Max H. Bazerman
Harvard Business School

Daylian M. Cain
Carnegie Mellon University

Dolly Chugh
Harvard Business School

Jason Dana
Carnegie Mellon University

Robyn Dawes
Carnegie Mellon University

Baruch Fischhoff
Carnegie Mellon University

Robert H. Frank
Cornell University

Samuel Issacharoff
Columbia Law School

Jerome P. Kassirer
Tufts University School of Medicine

Scott Y. H. Kim
University of Michigan

George Loewenstein
Carnegie Mellon University

Robert J. MacCoun
University of California, Berkeley

David M. Messick
Northwestern University

Dale T. Miller
Stanford University

Don A. Moore
Carnegie Mellon University

Mark W. Nelson
Cornell University

Andrew Stark
University of Toronto

Ann E. Tenbrunsel
University of Notre Dame

Tom R. Tyler
New York University School of Law

Peter A. Ubel
University of Michigan

Acknowledgments

We are grateful to many people who have made this book possible. First, we want to thank the organizations that contributed financial support. This book and the conference that spawned it are based on work supported by the National Science Foundation under Grant No. 0302715. It is, however, incumbent on us to point out that the opinions, findings, conclusions, and recommendations expressed in this material are those of the author(s) and do not necessarily reflect the views of the National Science Foundation.

We also are grateful for the generous support of the Carnegie Bosch Institute at Carnegie Mellon University. In addition to providing financial support, CBI hosted the conference. Mike Trick, Cathy Burstein, Cynthia Chemsak, and the staff of the CBI were essential to making this project a success. We also should thank Sam Swift for helping with the logistical work that made the conference a success. We are further indebted to Scott Parris and Simina Calin at Cambridge University Press for their patience and support.

The conference was improved by the work of several other people whose names do not appear in this book. In particular, keynote addresses by John Coffee, the Berle Professor of Law at Columbia University, and by Lynn Turner, former Chief Accountant at the Securities and Exchange Commission, were important contributions to our discussion. Both of them have a great deal of firsthand experience dealing with conflicts of interest in particular industries. We also appreciated the other attendees at the conference whose sharp questions and enthusiastic participation helped us develop our ideas.

Introduction

Don A. Moore, George Loewenstein, Daylian M. Cain, and Max H. Bazerman

Many professionals face a conflict between their professional responsibilities to protect the interests of their constituents, shareholders, patients, clients, or students, and their own self-interest. Under the best of circumstances, they stumble along, making implicit tradeoffs that represent some kind of rough compromise between these competing motives. The auditor may give clients some breaks but blow the whistle on cases of egregious corruption. The doctor accepts trinkets from a pharmaceutical company and may even prescribe that company's drug when it is perfectly equivalent to the competition's. The academic serving as an expert witness tries to craft her argument to satisfy the side she is working on but avoids saying anything that she vehemently disagrees with.

At times, however, this fragile equilibrium seems to break down, either within a single profession or more broadly. Exactly why this happens is not well-understood, but it is clear that we are living in such an era. Although conflicts of interest have been a fixture in the economic and political landscape almost from the outset of capitalism, the negative consequences of conflicts of interest seem to have worsened considerably in recent history. The most notorious of these consequences have been those involving the accounting industry. The accounting industry and the audit function it serves act as the primary safeguard for investors against malfeasance by corporate managers, but this function seems to have broken down in recent decades, contributing to a long string of scandals at major American corporations, including Enron, WorldCom, Global Crossing, Adelphia, and many others. But the conflicts of interest that have rocked our society in recent times are not restricted to auditors. As documented in many

1

of the chapters of this book, they also permeate other areas of business, medicine, law, and even academic research.

When conflicts of interest come into the public eye as a result of scandals, there typically are efforts at policy reform that in turn lead to debates between professionals and regulators over what form such reforms should take. Academics often play a role in such debates. Thus, several academics testified at the SEC hearings on auditor independence held in 2000, prior to the spate of accounting scandals, but that, unfortunately, failed to produce substantive reform. Ideally, academic input should be an essential ingredient of policy reforms. To remedy the problems caused by conflicts of interest – and enact effective policies to deal with them – an understanding of how conflicts of interest operate at the individual level is required. How does an auditor, whose profession claims independence as its cornerstone, end up complicit in management fraud by signing off on obviously cooked books? How do physicians, who are committed to serving the interests of their patients, end up routinely taking gifts from pharmaceutical companies, then prescribing those companies' unnecessarily expensive and often inferior drugs to their patients? How do academics end up selling their integrity for the fees they receive as expert witnesses?

Academics, however, have not had much influence in these debates. Economists traditionally have had the greatest influence in public policy, but economists have played a very limited role in discussions of policies dealing with conflicts of interest, perhaps because the widespread assumption that people act out of self-interest denies that professional responsibilities would hold any sway over professionals to begin with, outside of reputational concerns. Economic literatures on problems of agency (Jensen & Meckling, 1976) and auditor independence (Antle, 1984), for example, assume that economic actors are motivated exclusively by money and that they will always select the course of action with the highest expected value. Psychologists have better theoretical frameworks for dealing with situations, like conflicts of interest, which involve conflicting motives such as financial gain and ethical duty. But psychologists traditionally have had much less impact on public policies outside of those dealing directly with psychological issues such as reimbursement for psychotherapy. Our main purpose in organizing the conference from which this volume emerged, therefore, was to bring together economists, psychologists, and other academics dealing directly with a variety of professions in which conflicts of interest have led to problems to promote the development of new theoretical perspectives and new approaches to policy.

Currently, policies dealing with conflicts of interest are largely based on misguided intuitions about underlying psychological processes. For example, as Chugh, Bazerman, and Banaji point out, part of the reason that conflicts of interest have been allowed to become so pervasive is that most people think of succumbing to a conflict of interest as a matter of corruption, when in fact it is much more likely to result from processes that are unconscious and unintentional. Thus, many professionals deny – and almost certainly do not believe – that they could possibly be swayed by inappropriate influence. About the time we were putting the finishing touches on this book, for example, U.S. Supreme Court Justice Antonin Scalia had been accused of having a conflict of interest with respect to a case before the Court. Scalia, a longtime friend of Vice President Richard Cheney, had recently flown with Cheney on Air Force Two to participate in a duck-hunting excursion together. In a public statement in which he defiantly refused to remove himself from the case, Scalia insisted that his judgment would not be influenced by their friendship or by the fact that the vice president had given him a ride down to Louisana: "If it is reasonable to think that a Supreme Court Justice can be bought so cheap, the nation is in deeper trouble that I had imagined" (Scalia, 2004). Chugh et al. present evidence suggesting that the nation is indeed in deep trouble – conflicts of interest can bias professional judgment in subtle ways of which those professionals are often unaware. Even if outright and intentional corruption is rare, unconscious and unintentional bias could be common.

Learning what the research says on any given issue is often complicated by the fact that the knowledge is scattered across a number of different sources and is not easily synthesized. This is especially true of conflicts of interest, which tend to be studied, if at all, by specialists in the field in which they occur. Conflicts of interest are rarely taken as a topic of study deserving of its own focus. The scattered nature of scientific knowledge prevents research findings from specific applied domains from being synthesized into general insights. And it makes it easier for people to pay selective attention to research evidence. This book, then, is intended to take a first step toward such a synthesis. In the ten chapters of this book, leading scholars in a wide variety of fields have reviewed the current states of their fields with respect to issues surrounding conflicts of interest.

The resulting volume is somewhat depressing. Some of the chapters detail the extent to which conflicts of interest have corrupted the practice of what have been historically regarded as respectable, even noble, professions. For example, Kassirer, based on his extensive knowledge of the medical profession and his experience as a journal editor in dealing with conflicts of interest, concludes that the field of medicine is so pervaded by conflicts of interest that its reputation as a caring profession is threatened. During the eight years that he was editor-in-chief of the *New England Journal of Medicine*, Kassirer maintained a strict policy in which reviews and editorials could not be written by anyone with ties to drug companies whose products were being evaluated in the paper. However, it became so difficult to find writers and reviewers who were without conflicts – who were *not* receiving financial support from drug companies – that Kassirer's policy was eliminated by his successor at the *Journal*.

Nelson explores the diverse conflict of interest facing auditors. As in other professions, the charge that auditors have allowed themselves to become corrupted by conflicts of interest is a highly controversial one. Nelson tracks the evidence on this debate and concludes that the preponderance of evidence does support the conclusion that the judgment of auditors is likely to be compromised by conflicts of interest. Nelson's chapter also points out that auditors' conflicts of interest are a direct product of a conflict inherent in modern corporations: the conflict between a firm's owners (the stockholders) and its management. For example, stock options give upper management a powerful incentive to boost short-term stock prices at the expense of long-term viability of the firm. Auditors, who are charged with independently reviewing a firm's financial reports, ideally should uncover accounting practices that provide a false image of the firm's long-term prospects. But accounting firms have strong incentives to not render a negative option on the managers that hire them and pay their accounting fees as well as, in many cases, large consulting fees.

As noted, conflicts of interest have permeated fields beyond medicine and accounting, into law, real estate, investment banking, and even academic research. MacCoun highlights high political stakes at play in one specific area of research – public policy research – and notes the numerous conflicts that academics face, not only between academic honesty and pecuniary gain but also between, for example, the pursuit of truth and the promotion of personal political values. MacCoun argues that it is unrealistic to imagine that we could have (or ever did have) a purely inquisitorial system in which public policy researchers pursued the truth without regard to their own private interests or political agendas. And empirical tests suggest that traditional safeguards – peer review and replication – perform rather poorly, especially when research communities share political biases. An alternative approach is to move toward a more explicit adversarial system of research, but MacCoun suggests that disanalogies between policy conflicts and legal trials argue against such a system.

As MacCoun's chapter highlights, there are few clear or inexpensive solutions to conflicts of interest, a theme that is echoed in many of the book's other chapters. For example, one of the most popular responses to conflicts of interest historically has been disclosure. Disclosure is popular because, unlike such costly solutions such as divestiture or recusal, it requires minimal disruption of the status quo (Davis, 2001). The assumption underlying disclosure is that people will be able to use disclosure to help them make better decisions. For example, knowing that my real estate agent only gets paid when I buy a house should help me determine the degree to which she is glossing over the house's problems when she encourages me to buy it. Knowing that my doctor gets paid more when she performs a diagnostic test should help me decide whether to follow her recommendation. But the chapter by Cain, Moore, and Loewenstein discusses psychological evidence suggesting that disclosure may be not be able to provide these promised benefits. Worse yet, as Cain et al. suggest, experts may sometimes be more comfortable indulging their private interests and giving more biased advice when they have disclosed them. The surprising upshot is that sometimes consumers may be left worse off for having been warned about a conflict of interest.

Another popular response to conflicts of interest has been to provide incentives for desirable behavior by establishing penalties that outweigh the benefits of malfeasance. The most common approach in this vein has been to legislate stiff penalties for indulging in fraud or corruption. This is generally the approach taken by the Sarbanes-Oxley Act of 2002, passed in response to accounting scandals. But threats of legal sanction are rarely effective at counterbalancing professionals' strong rewards for indulging in self-interested behavior. One of the problems associated with such threats of punishment is that it is often difficult, if not impossible, to prove bias. As such, the probability of being punished is small. Given this small probability, it is usually impractical to increase the size of the penalty so that its expected value outweighs the rewards of self-enrichment, as Issacharoff explains in his chapter.

Issacharoff offers a general framework for understanding policy responses to the conflicts of interest that occur in law, most notably in the relationship between attorneys, who are enjoined to act on behalf of their clients but who often face conflicting incentives. He distinguishes between three broad categories of legal responses to conflicts of interest, which he terms "substantive regulation," "liability rules," and "procedural regulations." Substantive regulation involves prohibitions on certain well-specified behaviors – for example, the rule that client funds cannot be invested in attorneys' home, business, or other private undertakings. Liability rules attempt to deter misbehavior by introducing sanctions for breach of fiduciary trust. Finally, procedural regulations involve prohibitions not on substantive outcomes, but on participation in decision making by conflicted agents – for example, a prohibition on government officials negotiating contracts with firms in which they have or have had a financial involvement. Issacharoff concludes that procedural regulations are the single most effective strategy for dealing with conflicts of interests. Substantive regulation is difficult to apply and liability regimes suffer from a dependence on the proper ability of agents to internalize the cost calculus, which cannot be taken for granted. Procedural regulation cuts straight to the heart of the matter by attempting to remove conflicts of interest altogether.

What Issacharoff calls procedural regulation is likely to be the most effective solution to conflicts of interest precisely because procedural regulation changes decision-making or fee procedures to eliminate conflicts of interest. However, this sort of regulation is likely to be politically controversial, difficult to implement, and expensive. Andrew Stark's chapter reminds us of the many varieties of "internal" conflicts of interest that are so inextricably bound to professional roles that eliminating them would be prodigiously costly. For example, in the academic peer-review process, the people who are most likely to be reviewing one's work are those whose own work is most relevant. Their expertise in the area makes them most qualified to review it but also makes it likely that they will have a personal interest in promoting or derogating the research because of its implications for their own work. In Stark's words, "such biases, rivalries or axes-to-grind may (in and of themselves) be functionally internal for the biomedical scientist in his professional role as a researcher." Although one can imagine rules that would minimize these internal conflicts of interest, they are far from costless. For example, academic peer review could be conducted exclusively by people whose own research is unrelated to that being reviewed. Medical patients could see to it that they always receive their diagnoses and treatments from different physicians. As big as these changes would be, they also are not immune from the possibility that quid pro quo arrangements creep back into the process, threatening the independence of outside opinions. Indeed, such favor exchange often threatens the independence of corporate boards of directors from management.

The chapters by Kassirer, Stark, and Nelson suggest that conflicts of interest are both more serious and widespread than is widely recognized. The chapters by MacCoun and Cain et al. suggest that policies for dealing with them are far from straightforward. However, the situation is not entirely devoid of cause for hope. Tyler, for instance, points out that people do not always act in ways that are consistent with their own narrow self-interest. In fact, people regularly comply with ethical precepts even when doing so incurs real costs (or forgone opportunities for gain). This compliance sometimes comes in the service of some larger entity or organization. Often, that entity is the profession or the industry in which the individual works. For instance, it may be in the interest of a particular politician or a particular corporation to engage in negative advertising in order to criticize and attack its rivals. However, the more politicians or corporations use negative advertising strategies, the more the entire profession or industry falls in public esteem. The truth is that industries whose members choose to cooperate with each other and thereby promote the welfare and success of the entire industry are more likely to prosper collectively; but the benefits of collective cooperation do not eliminate the incentives for individuals to make noncooperative choices. Although cooperation may be undesirable when it comes to price-setting, it is certainly desirable when it comes to the upholding of professional codes of conduct and resistance to the corrupting influences of conflicts of interest. Tyler presents evidence suggesting some of the ways in which organizations can reinforce such cooperation.

Frank's chapter concurs with Tyler's perspective. Indeed, he suggests that absolute (nonconsequentialist) moral principles are likely to be a better guide for organizational practice and for public policy than are utilitarian goals of producing the greatest good. The reason, Frank argues, is that utilitarian prescriptions depend on identifying and predicting "good" outcomes. Because those judging the value of these outcomes are likely to be biased by their own conflicts of interest, a disinterested prediction of policy outcomes will be exceedingly difficult to obtain. In other words, although it might be desirable (as Rawls, 1971, has argued) for those making public policy to not have any personal stake in the outcome, Frank points out that it is almost never practically feasible. Perhaps, as Frank suggests, better results are likely if we adopt codes of conduct that are less prone to biased interpretation.

Perhaps the last defense against conflicts of interest, therefore, is professionals' personal concern for their clients, customers, and constituents.

Even when legal regulations are weak or unenforceable, as Tyler discusses, people will comply with norms of professional conduct simply because it is the right thing to do. For example, people observe norms of fairness, even in one-shot encounters with anonymous others (Güth, 1995; Güth, Schmittberger, & Schwarze, 1982; Kahneman, Knetsch, & Thaler, 1986, 1987). They will behave altruistically – looking out for the interest of others whom they might exploit – because it is the right thing to do (Camerer & Thaler, 1995). But Dana reminds us that this altruistic behavior is unreliable. People will steer clear of situations that activate these preferences in them. For example, people will avoid walking past a beggar, in part because they anticipate the risk that they might feel compelled to give something. Furthermore, the same people who would not knowingly cause harm to others often will take action to intentionally remain ignorant of harm which they bring about. The implication of this stream of research for addressing conflicts of interest would seem to be that professionals should not be allowed to remain ignorant of the costs of their choices for others toward whom they have a fiduciary responsibility. For instance, physicians, who are routinely ignorant of the fees associated with the tests and treatments they prescribe, should be sent copies of the bills that their patients get. Dana argues that neither people nor firms should be judged less guilty of crimes committed on their behalf because they were willfully ignorant of those crimes. For example, although we would surely punish a pharmaceutical firm that deliberately fabricated data from drug trials, we also should punish a firm that outsources its drug trials, offers clear incentives for favorable results, and then turns a blind eye to questionable research practices. MacCoun's chapter brings this lesson home for researchers by recommending research practices that pit alternative hypotheses against each other. He argues that we need to promote research practices that encourage within-study hypothesis competition ("strong inference") and boundary seeking on effects ("condition seeking" and "destructive hypothesis testing"), as well as a greater reliance on meta-analysis rather than single studies.

In this brief introduction, we have only mentioned a few of the many conflicts of interest that permeate professional life in the United States. Justice Scalia's choice not to recuse himself from the case involving his friend is only the latest of a long series of recent events in which conflicts of interest have been enacted in part because of what appears to be an erroneous understanding of psychology. It is exactly this ignorance, pervasive among members of government, industry, and the general public, which has led to institutions and policies that deal ineffectively, and even sometimes counterproductively, with the problems caused by conflicts of interest. Our goal in creating this book was to see what insights the social and behavioral sciences could offer to the problem of conflicts of interest and to the design of policies intended to deal with the problems that they cause. We hope that the diverse insights represented by the different chapters will not only stimulate further investigation but also help to spur the development of more effective policies for dealing with what has become a pervasive problem facing our society.

References

Antle, R. (1984). Auditor independence. *Journal of Accounting Research*, 22(1), 1–20.

Camerer, C. F., & Thaler, R. H. (1995). Ultimatums, dictators, and manners. *Journal of Economic Perspectives*, 9(2), 209–219.

Davis, M. (2001). Introduction. In M. Davis & A. Stark (Eds.), *Conflict of interest in the professions*, (pp. 3–19). Oxford: Oxford University Press.

Güth, W. (1995). On ultimatum bargaining experiments – A personal view. *Journal of Economic Behavior and Organization*, 27, 329–344.

Güth, W., Schmittberger, R., & Schwarze, B. (1982). An experimental analysis of ultimatum bargaining. *Journal of Economic Behavior and Organization*, 3, 367–388.

Jensen, M. C., & Meckling, W. H. (1976). Theory of the firm: Managerial behavior, agency costs, and ownership structure. *Journal of Financial Economics*, 3, 305–360.

Kahneman, D., Knetsch, J. L., & Thaler, R. H. (1986). Fairness as a constraint on profit seeking: Entitlements and the market. *American Economic Review*, 76(4), 728–741.

Kahneman, D., Knetsch, J. L., & Thaler, R. H. (1987). Fairness and the assumptions of Economics. In R. M. Hogarth & M. W. Reder (Eds.), *Rational choice: The contract between economics and psychology*, (pp. 101–116). Chicago: University of Chicago Press.

Rawls, J. (1971). *A theory of justice*. Cambridge, MA: Belknap.

Scalia, A. (2004). Richard B. Cheney, Vice President of the United States, et al. v. United District Court for the District of Columbia et al., on petition for writ of certiorari to the United States Court of Appeals for the District of Columbia Circuit (Vol. 03–475): Supreme Court of the United States. Downloaded September 3, 2004 from: http://www.supremecourtus.gov/opinions/03pdf/03-475.pdf.

PART ONE

BUSINESS

ONE

Managing Conflicts of Interest within Organizations

Does Activating Social Values Change the Impact of Self-Interest on Behavior?

Tom R. Tyler

New York University School of Law

ABSTRACT

Many organizational conflicts involve tensions between a person's motivation to act in their own self-interest and the efforts to authorities, rules, and institutions to bring people's conduct into line with social values involving justice and morality. This chapter explores the manner in which people in organizational settings manage personal conflicts between their self-interest and their views about what is just or moral. Past explorations of people's behavior in mixed-motive situations presents behavior as developing from a balancing of self-interested and moral/justice-based motivations. In contrast, the approach used here – the social value activation model – focuses on the consequences of activating social values. The results of several studies suggest that self-interested and ethical motivations interact, that is, once people's ethical motivations are activated they subsequently give less weight to calculations of personal self-interest when making behavioral decisions. Implications for the management of conflicts of interest in organizations are explored.

When people make decisions within organizations, they are often faced with conflicting motivations. One motivation is to act in ways that benefit themselves and/or the groups to which they belong in the immediate situation – the motive of personal or group self-interest. This motivation is often partially or even completely at odds with the motivation to make decisions in ways that are consistent with their justice-based or moral

Paper prepared for presentation at the conference on conflicts of interest (Daylian Cain, Don Moore, George Loewenstein, and Max Bazerman, organizers). Pittsburgh: Tepper School of Business. Carnegie Mellon University.

values. Hence, people have to trade off between their concerns about their self-interest and their desire to act based on their judgments about what is just and/or morally right.

If nothing else, recent corporate scandals make it clear that the people in groups and organizations often face such conflicts of interest. These scandals further demonstrate that how people resolve those conflicts has important implications for the viability of the organizations to which they belong. When people act solely or largely based on their self-interest, they can act in ways that hurt their group or organization, damaging its effectiveness, efficiency, and viability.

The reality of conflicts of interest is hardly news to either psychologists or economists. Early work on mixed motive games such as the prisoner's dilemma game and the ultimatum game is a central aspect of economics (Poundstone, 1992). Similarly, work on the dilemma of the commons is a core aspects of the social dilemma literature in psychology (Kopelman, Weber, & Messick, 2002). Both approaches share a common concern with understanding how people resolve mixed motive dilemmas – that is, conflicts between immediate self-interest and the interests of groups or organizations, reflected in their ethical or moral codes – when making decisions with groups and organizations. In particular, these literatures explore the degree to which people cooperate with others when they have mixed motivations – some cooperative, some self-interested.

One way that such cooperation is expressed is via adherence to group-based principles of justice and morality – that is, to social values. For the purposes of this chapter, I will not distinguish among the different types of social norms or values that might shape actions. I will treat judgments about distributive justice – believing that an outcome is fair – and morality – thinking that something is morally right – as reflections of a person's social values.

My concern is with the manner in which people resolve conflicts of interest in organization situations. I will focus on one particular issue – people's decisions about the degree to which they will cooperate with others in mixed motive situations in which their immediate self-interest differs from what is just, moral, or ethical. I will examine two types of conflict – conflicts between justice and self-interest and conflicts between morality and self-interest.

In both cases, the focus on concern will be on people's willingness to defer to the decisions of organizational authorities and to rules that define appropriate conduct in an organization. Gaining deference to rules and third-party decisions is the traditional area of regulation – the bringing of the conduct of people within organizations into line with guidelines about what is reasonable and appropriate. Such guidelines may develop when third-party authorities (police officers, judges, managers) make decisions about how to resolve conflicts of interest or how to best serve the interests of the organization they represent. On the more general level, rules provide guidelines for behavior that best serves the interests of the organization.

Regulation develops from the recognition that adherence to decisions and/or to rules often conflicts with acting in one's own self-interest, producing a conflict of interest within the individual. On the one hand, people want to reject unfavorable decisions and they want to violate laws that prohibit conduct that they think is in their self-interest. On the other hand, they have moral- and justice-based social values that indicate that conduct that motivates them to engage in ethical conduct that serves broader organizational purposes.

The issue of justice arises when people are trying to decide whether or not to accept a decision that is or is not favorable to them. They may make that decision based on their own self-interest, in which case they will accept favorable decisions and reject unfavorable decisions. This motivation may conflict with their justice-based judgments, which lead them to accept decisions based on their fairness (i.e., in response to distributive justice judgments). Organizational studies make clear that authorities benefit and the interests of the organization are served when people are motivated to act on principles of fairness. Authorities seldom can provide everyone with everything they want or feel that they need, so the effectiveness of authorities depends on their ability to secure acceptance through the fairness of their decisions.

The issue of morality arises when people are determining whether and to what extent to follow rules in groups and organizations. These rules may be formal laws or the more informal rules of a work organization. In either case, such rules often exist to limit people's freedom to act in ways that maximize their short-term self-interest. Hence, people must decide whether to follow their self-interest or to bring it into line with moral values about what is appropriate and ethical in a given situation. This is particularly crucial in situations in which morality exists to discourage personally profitable behaviors – situations ranging from robbing a bank to stealing office supplies and downloading music from the Internet. For the law to be effective, people need to defer to legal rules (Tyler, 1990). Similarly, for work organizations to be effective, people need to defer to organizational policies and rules (Tyler & Blader, 2000). Moral rules generally serve the function of bringing people's conduct into line with organizational rules, because many of the behaviors that are against those rules also are viewed by most people as contrary to their own moral values.

BALANCING BETWEEN SELF-INTEREST AND SOCIAL VALUES

The model traditionally used to explore how people deal with conflicts between self-interest and social values assumes that people balance their concerns about self-interest and their judgments about what actions are consistent with their social values. The issue is how much weight they put on each factor during this balancing process.

In the case of decision acceptance, people balance between the favorability of an outcome and its fairness. In this analysis, I will focus on the distributive fairness of the decision (i.e., does the person feel that the outcome reflects what is deserved, i.e., that it is "fair"?). For example, Tyler and Huo (2002) examined the role of these two factors in shaping decision acceptance when people have personal experiences with police officers or judges. They found that both factors matter. Together, the factors explain 34 percent of the variance in decision acceptance; with both distributive justice ($r = 0.40$, $p < .001$; $\beta = 0.26$, $p < .001$) and outcome valence ($r = 0.45$, $p < .001$; $\beta = 0.45$, $p < .001$) explaining significant independent aspects of decision acceptance. This finding is consistent with the argument that people balance between the favorability of a decision and judgments about its fairness when deciding whether or not to accept it, and they give approximately equal weight to both factors.

In the case of general rule-following behavior, people similarly balance their judgments about their self-interest against their principles of morality. In other words, we would expect people to be especially unlikely to do things that they view as neither rewarding nor ethically appropriate. Tyler (1990) explored this balancing in the context of laws, using the risk of being caught and punished as the outcome favorability factor and a judgment of the congruence between the person's moral values and the law as the ethical factor. The analysis found that both judgments together explained 21 percent of the variance in compliance with the law. Again, both factors were independently important influences on compliance – morality ($r = 0.46$, $p < .001$; $\beta = 0.43$, $p < .001$) and risk ($r = 0.23$, $p < .001$; $\beta = 0.08$, $p < .01$). As with decision acceptance, people balance personal self-interest in the form of their estimates of the likelihood that they will be caught and punished for engaging in wrongdoing and their moral judgments about the degree to which the behaviors that are against the law are also immoral (i.e., the congruence of the law with their own sense of right and wrong) when making decisions about whether to obey the law (MacCoun, 1993).

Tyler and Blader (2000) explored the role of morality and risk within work organizations. They used estimates of the likelihood of being caught and punished for wrongdoing as the risk judgment and indexed morality using an overall judgment of the degree to which the outcomes in the organization were distributively fair (i.e., the frequency with which people received what they deserved). Again, they found that both factors matter in an overall equation (whose total adjusted $r^2 = 11\%$); with an influence for morality ($r = 0.21, p < .001; \beta = 0.19, p < .001$) and for risk ($r = 0.28, p < .001; \beta = 0.27, p < .001$).

These findings suggest that one way to think about how people manage conflicts of interest is to view people as balancing between personal self-interest and their justice-based and/or moral values. People may compromise between these two factors – placing weight on both and arriving at some balanced motivation to cooperate. Based on these findings, it can be argued that one way to regulate behavior is to shape self-interest by varying the favorability of decisions and the risks of rule breaking. In the case of decisions, people will be more willing to accept decisions if those decisions are more personally favorable. In the case of rule following, these findings suggest that as the threat of sanctions becomes stronger (i.e., risk estimates go up), people are more likely to follow rules. These findings are consistent with the general finding in the sanction-based deterrence literature that increased sanctions are associated with reduced levels of rule-breaking behavior (MacCoun, 1993).

By contrast, this model also suggests why deterrence strategies may be problematic as a social control mechanism. In corporate scandals, for example, people often stand to gain a great deal in situations in which the risk of loss is minor or even nonexistent. Hence, even the modest positive impact of risk can be counteracted by opportunities for great gain, or at least opportunities for modest gain at low risk.

In addition to this sanctioning influence, the balancing model suggests that moral values/justice concerns also shape decision acceptance and rule following. So, we can also: (1) encourage decision acceptance by making decisions that people will view as fair and (2) bring people's behavior into line with rules by activating their social values. These studies are consistent with the literature suggesting that moral values and justice judgments have a distinct influence on behavior (Tyler, Boeckmann, Smith, & Huo, 1997).

Again, the limits of moral judgments as a social control mechanism also become clear when the balancing model is considered. If the risk of sanctioning is low, or the valence of an outcome very positive, then people are motivated to engage in actions even when they view them as immoral or unjust. The balancing approach implies that morality and justice may minimize the motivation to engage in rule breaking, but they would not stop it.

THE SOCIAL VALUE ACTIVATION MODEL – AN INTERACTIVE MODEL

I want to propose and test an alternative model for understanding the relationship between outcomes, social value judgments, and cooperative behavior. That model is the *social value activation model*. It argues that people do not balance between outcomes and social value judgments. Rather, they use social value judgments as a filter through which to shape their actions. If actions do not pass a test of justice or morality, then people are generally less inclined to take them, even when they are personally beneficial and produce favorable and desirable outcomes. This model predicts an interaction between outcomes and justice/morality, with outcome favorability judgments having less influence on people's actions if those actions are not viewed as being moral.

There are two aspects of this argument. First, consider the issue of decision acceptance. If people view a decision as fair, that activates a justice framework. People respond by high levels of acceptance and by paying less attention to gain or loss. If a justice frame is not activated, people decide whether to accept a decision based primarily on self-interest.

Second, consider the issue of rule following. Rules prohibit engaging in personally rewarding actions ranging from robbing banks to stealing software. Hence, the question is the extent to which people will abandon their pursuit of self-interest and obey the rules. The argument here is that, if people think the action is morally wrong, a moral frame is activated, and they are generally more likely to obey the rule and not engage in the action. If people think the action is morally acceptable, self-interest dictates whether people follow the rule. So, people decide not to commit murder by considering whether it is a moral act, and do not then consider the likelihood of being caught and punished for committing murder.

The balancing model does not consider the possibility of interactions between self-interest and morality/justice. The social value activation model, in contrast, is an interactive model because it argues that the importance of one factor – outcome valence – in shaping behavioral choices changes depending on the level of the other – morality/justice. The social value activation model argues that people first evaluate actions against a criterion or morality and justice. If they think that an action is morally appropriate or inappropriate, people act based on that moral judgment, and are much more likely to take the action if it is viewed as morally appropriate. Once an action has been assessed morally, people then act without considering, or at least after giving less weight to, the costs or benefits of the action. Hence, it predicts that people's behavior is most strongly shaped by cost/benefit assessments when their actions are outside the range of moral values or justice judgments. People may primarily engage in cost/benefit analyses when moral or justice-based criteria are not activated.

Consider the example of robbing a bank. According to the social value activation model, people do not decide whether to rob a bank by balancing the amount of money to be gained and the risk of punishment against the moral rightness or wrongness of the action. Instead, people decide not to rob a bank because they think it is wrong, and do not balance this judgment against how much money is in the bank and/or the risk of being caught and punished for committing robbery.

Similarly, people do not decide whether to accept a decision based on a simple balancing of self-interest and fairness. If people think a decision is fair, they accept it, without considering how much they gain or lose from the decision. If a decision is not fair, then people accept it if it is in their self-interest and reject it if it is not. In other words, when moral values are not activated, people go with their self-interest. To the extent that people act in this way, morality and justice moderate the influence of self-interest on behavior. Self-interest calculations are of little or no importance when people view an action as moral or justice – people simply comply. But, self-interest calculations are important in the absence of activated justice-based standards.

Why is this model potentially important? If it is true, it suggests that an especially effective way to motivate desirable behavior when people are being asked to do something not in their self-interest is to focus on activating people's justice-based and moral values. If people view something as just or moral, they may simply decide to do it, without considering the outcomes involved. If so, then people are less likely to be tempted by those outcomes.

Consider again the example of robbing a bank. Most people do not rob banks because they think it is wrong to rob banks. I would argue that you could put more money in banks and most people would still not

rob them. Similarly, you could take the guns away from bank guards, or
remove guards entirely, and most people would still not rob banks. Why?
Because most people filter their actions, deciding not to rob a bank for
moral reasons, and not giving "rational" calculative attention to the gains
and losses of committing such a robbery.

Of course, this argument should not be overstated. There is considerable evidence that self-interested calculations play a role in behavior.
Hence, whereas the social value activation model argues that the role of
self-interested calculations is diminished when social values are activated,
it may not be eliminated entirely. There may be a combination of enough
money in the bank, and low enough risk, that even normally law-abiding
people will commit a robbery.

EMPIRICAL EXAMINATION

Justice and Decision Acceptance

The argument in the case of decision acceptance is that people evaluate
a decision against a criterion of distributive justice – the fairness of the
outcomes involved in the decision. If people view the decision as fair, they
are then motivated to accept it. Furthermore, at that point issues of gain
or loss are given little or no weight. In other words, moral judgments act
as a threshold assessment that provides an initial evaluation that leads to
action. Outcome valence becomes important when people do not see the
issue involved as one of justice. If an action is not viewed as just, people
will still accept it if it is in their self-interest. But they will not accept it if
it is not in their self-interest.

This argument is tested using four data sets. The first is from a sample
of interviews drawn from residents of Oakland and Los Angeles. Each is
asked about a recent experience with the police and/or courts. The sample distinguishes between two types of contact: nonvoluntary (n = 687)
and voluntary (n = 969), and each will be separately considered here.
The details of this sample are outlined in Tyler and Huo (2002). The third
dataset involves interviews with 305 employees at a public sector institution in California. Each is asked about a recent experience with their
supervisor. Details of the study are provided in Huo, Smith, Tyler, and
Lind (1996). A final sample of employees was obtained from a random
sample of employees in Chicago (n = 409) interviewed over the telephone.

In each study, respondents are asked if the decision made in their
recent experience with an authority was favorable or unfavorable, and

Table 1.1. *Outcome valence, distributive justice, and decision acceptance*

	Legal authorities				Experiences with supervisors in work settings			
	Nonvoluntary experience		Voluntary experience		California		Chicago	
	d.f.	MS	d.f.	MS	d.f.	MS	d.f.	MS
Outcome favorability	1	31.24***	1	110.98***	1	3.41*	1	20.58***
Distributive justice	1	7.76**	1	54.25***	1	41.68***	1	45.75***
OF*DJ	1	5.09*	1	1.79^	1	6.04*	1	5.52*
Error	639		925		241		384	

^p < .10; *p < .05; **p < .01; ***p < .001.
Note: The dependent variable is the willing acceptance of third-party decisions.

distributively fair or distributively unfair. They were then asked how willing they were to accept the decision. The social value activation model argues that people will be influenced primarily by gain/loss considerations when there was not a justice-based reason for accepting the decision.

Table 1.1 tests the argument that outcome favorability and outcome fairness interact in their impact on decision acceptance. As we would expect, there are two main effects on acceptance. People were always more willing to accept decisions that were favorable. Separately, they were always willing to accept decisions that they viewed as distributively fair. However, beyond these main effects, interactions were always found, supporting the argument that moderation was occurring. In other words, self-interest and outcome fairness are not simply being balanced but are combining interactively.

To explore the nature of the moderation effect, Figures 1.1 and 1.2 show the average level of decision acceptance at high and low levels of outcome favorability and high and low levels of distributive fairness – Figure 1.1 for law and Figure 1.2 for work. The results that are shown in the two figures support the social value activation argument. People were always more strongly influenced by gain and loss when they did not view the decision as fair. When people viewed a decision as distributively fair, there were two effects: (1) acceptance went up and (2) gain/loss issues had a lower level of impact on acceptance.

When the decision was fair, acceptance was high irrespective of whether or not the decision was favorable. People did not strongly

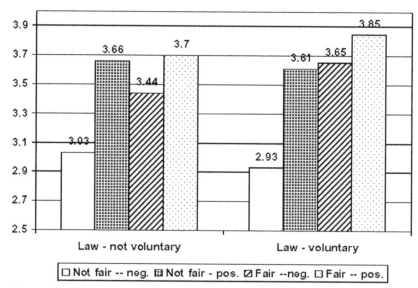

Figure 1.1. Outcome favorability, outcome fairness, and willingness to accept decisions made by police officers and judges (H = willing to accept)

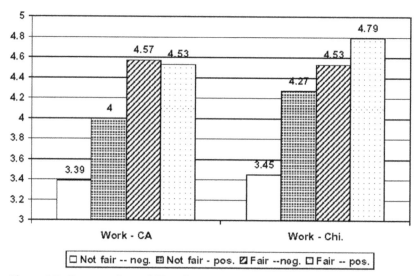

Figure 1.2. Outcome favorability, distributive fairness, and willingness to accept decisions by supervisors (H = accept the decision)

consider gain/loss when they felt that the decision was fair. They just accepted the decision. However, when the decision was not fair, acceptance was strongly linked to favorability. A favorable decision was accepted, but an unfavorable decision was not accepted.

MORALITY AND RULE-FOLLOWING BEHAVIOR

If social value activation occurs, we also would predict an interaction between moral judgments, risk judgments, and rule-following behavior. In other words, we would predict that people would be more strongly influenced by the risk of being caught and punished for wrongdoing when deciding whether to break rules when they think that moral issues are not related to the conduct involved. If the conduct is viewed as immoral, then people are expected to not engage in it, and to decide to do so putting little or no weight on a cost/benefit decision.

Three data sets are used to examine this argument. The first is based on interviews with a random sample of the residents of Chicago (n = 1, 575) interviewed over the telephone (see Tyler, 1990, for details). This study explores the antecedents of compliance with the law. A second data set is based on interviews with a random sample of the residents of New York City (n = 1,653). This study examines the antecedents of the willingness to comply with the police. Finally, the third data set is based on questionnaires completed by a group of employees of various companies in New York City (n = 404). The concern of this final study is with the antecedents of rule following in work organizations.

Each study considers two potential antecedents of cooperation: risk assessments and moral judgments. In the case of the two studies focused on law, people evaluated the likelihood that they would be caught and punished for wrongdoing. Employees evaluated the likelihood that they would be caught and punished for breaking organizational rules. In the studies of law, people also evaluated the moral congruence of the law with their own moral values, whereas employees evaluated the general fairness of the distribution of resources in their organization.

The first question is whether there is evidence of moderation in the impact of risk and morality on cooperation. Table 1.2 examines the possibility of an interaction in the datasets outlined. The results indicate that risk and morality do interact in their impact on cooperation. The nature of that interaction is shown in Figure 1.3.

Again, the pattern of the data supported the argument that people were primarily influenced by issues of risk when they are in a situation in which

Table 1.2. *Morality and rule following*

	Law – Compliance (Chicago)		Law – Compliance (New York)		Work – Compliance (New York)	
	d.f.	MS	d.f.	MS	d.f.	MS
Risk of being caught and punished for wrongdoing	1	2.05***	1	13.64***	1	7.58***
Morality of the action	1	49.82***	1	27.89***	1	7.38***
Risk*morality	1	1.37**	1	1.71*	1	1.56*
Error	1,547		1,649		397	

$\hat{}p < .10$; $*p < .05$; $**p < .01$; $***p < .001$.

Note: The dependent variable is the level of compliance with rules.

moral issues were not salient. When people thought that compliance was the morally appropriate thing to do, (1) compliance went up and (2) risk assessments had little or no influence on cooperation decisions. When people did not view morality as relevant to cooperation, then cooperation was lower and was more strongly linked to whether or not there were risks associated with engaging in the actions.

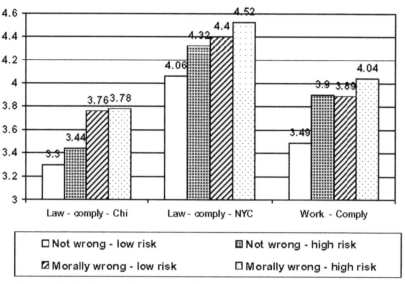

Figure 1.3. Risk, morality, and rule-following behavior (H = follow rules)

OVERALL FINDINGS

The findings outlined have two implications: first, when a decision or rule was consistent with social values, acceptance was higher; second, when a decision or rule was consistent with social values, its favorability became a less important basis on which to decide whether or not to accept it. In other words, the findings outlined suggest that there was a partial social value threshold.

The pattern with decision acceptance and rule following was the same. When morality was activated, people generally followed rules and accepted decisions. When morality was *not* activated, people were more strongly influenced by self-interest. When morality was activated, self-interest became of lesser importance. This form of interaction was found in all of the analyses performed in this chapter.

COMPARING THE SOCIAL VALUE ACTIVATION ARGUMENT TO AN OUTCOME VALENCE ARGUMENT

The findings supported a social value activation model. However, one issue that must be addressed is whether it is most consistent with the data to talk about social value activation or about outcome activation. Would it make sense to say that people only cared about moral issues when deciding whether to accept a negative decision? In other words, if people received a favorable outcome, did they simply accept it without considering whether it was or was not moral? Similarly, when an action had low risk, did people simply do it? These models can be called outcome activation models. A favorable outcome might simply lead to acceptance, a low risk to engaging in desired behavior. In this reversal of our thinking, we would expect that people consider moral issues when deciding whether to accept an unfavorable decision and whether to act in the face of a high risk of detection and punishment.

To address this question, difference scores were computed. First, one index assessed how much impact outcome valence/risk has when social values are activated. The social value activation argument is that valence/risk will have the most influence when social values are absent, because when social values are present people do not consider costs, or at least give them a lower weight. Hence, it predicts that there will be very little influence of cost when morality or justice has been activated.

Second, an index assessed how much impact the presence/absence of morality had under positive outcome conditions. If an outcome is

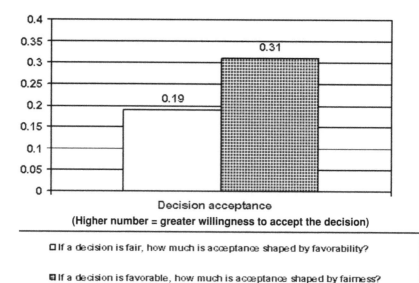

Figure 1.4. Is social value mediation the right way to think about these findings?

favorable, or the risk of being sanctioned low, we would predict that people would simply engage in the action. So, for example, people would simply accept a favorable decision. Here we expect that levels of acceptance should be the same when that favorable decision is fair and when it is unfair.

To test the arguments outlined we compared behavior in two conditions: the influence of risk when morality is activated and the influence of morality when outcome favorability/low risk is activated. The results are shown in Figure 1.4 for decision acceptance and Figure 1.5 for rule following. If the social value activation model is correct, we would predict that people should not consider outcomes when morality has been activated. The mean difference between favorable and unfavorable outcomes (and high/low risk) is 0.15 across the two figures. So people give some attention to outcomes when morality is activated, but the degree of attention is small.

We can compare this difference to that predicted by the outcome activation perspective. That model says that if the decision is favorable, or the risk of being punished for taking an action you want to take small, then behavior should flow from that positive outcome assessment. Whether you take action should not be shaped by moral issues or justice concerns. However, if we look at the mean level of behavior at high and low

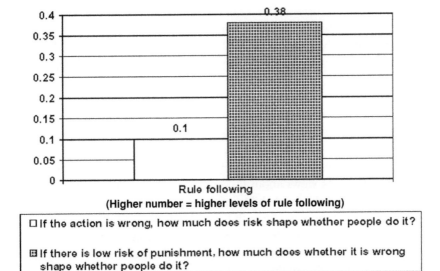

Figure 1.5. Is moral mediation the right way to think about these findings?

levels of justice/morality when the outcome is favorable, the difference is 0.35.

In other words, people give more than twice as much attention to morality/justice when they are deciding whether to do something that has a good outcome as they give to what they might gain or lose once they know that an action is unjust or immoral. This suggests that the social value activation model is a better general description of people's motivation than a model that argues that outcomes activate action. It does not suggest that social value activation eliminates the influence of self-interest, only that it minimizes that influence. But it is more consistent with the data to argue that the activation of social values minimizes self-interest concerns than it is to say that once people receive a favorable outcome, they do not consider if it is moral before they accept it.

POLICY IMPACT

These findings suggest that it is important to focus on how to activate people's social values. We could potentially increase rule following either by altering outcome valence or by activating social values, and the findings outlined suggest that both approaches have an influence on behavior. However, they further suggest that activating social values may be an especially promising way to manage conflicts of interest, because the activation of social values both raises the level of rule following and minimizes the influence of self-interest on behavior.

What will activate moral values? This is a topic that Steve Blader and I address in several studies of employees (Tyler & Blader, 2000, 2004). These findings examine the relationships between the policies and practices of a work organization, and the degree to which employees believe that the organization acts in ways consistent with their social values.

The particular aspect of policies and practices suggested by our past research to be connected to the activation of social values is procedural justice. We can test the influence of procedural justice here by examining whether it shapes views about the fairness of decisions separately from judgments about the favorability of those decisions. It has already been shown that both outcome favorability and outcome fairness influence decision acceptance, both directly and through an interaction. However, what shapes judgments about the fairness of decisions, and thereby activates the social value of distributive justice?

The role of procedural justice can be tested by using procedural justice and outcome favorability as factors shaping judgments of distributive justice. Procedural justice was assessed both as an overall judgment (How fair are the procedures?) and in terms of the fairness of two key components of procedural justice (Tyler & Blader, 2000): the quality of decision making and the quality of interpersonal treatment.

The results of this analysis are shown in Table 1.3 for the four studies involving personal experiences. They suggest that people in both legal and work settings were more likely to view decisions as fair if: (1) they were favorable and (2) they were fairly arrived at. In terms of the activation of social motivations, these findings suggest that procedural justice is one mechanism that can activate social values. It seems to have an especially strong influence in work settings, where the influence of overall procedural fairness judgments is strongest. However, even in legal settings, procedural justice judgments were stronger than outcome favorability judgments in their influence on distributive justice.

In both settings, the overall procedural justice evaluations were stronger influences on distributive justice than were the assessments of the components of procedural justice. This was the case because the two aspects of procedural justice were intercorrelated, diminishing the unique contribution of each component. However, in all four studies, both of the components made a statistically significant unique contribution to judgments about distribution justice. It is particularly striking that how a person was treated shaped whether they thought that the outcome was fair.

Table 1.3. *What activates social values? The influence of procedural justice on the extent outcomes of decisions are viewed as fair?*

	Legal authority				Managers			
	Not voluntary		Voluntary		California		Chicago	
Beta weights								
Fairness of organizational procedures								
Overall fairness	.26***	—	.28***	—	.65***	—	.52***	—
Components								
Decision making	—	.13*	—	.10*	—	.25***	—	.12*
Interpersonal treatment	—	.15*	—	.22***	—	.25***	—	.36***
Outcomes								
Favorability of decision	.12*	.13**	.22**	.20***	.28**	.45***	.33***	.36***
Adjusted R.-squared	11%	11%	18%	20%	77%	70%	53%	49%

^p < .10; *p < .05; **p < .01; ***p < .001.

The same analysis also can be conducted on two of the studies that explore the general characteristics of organizations (in the third study, general level measures of procedural justice were not collected). In this case, the argument is that when an organization acts in procedurally just ways, it leads its members to believe that its policies and practices are consistent with their own moral values. This argument is tested by exploring the influence of procedural justice on judgments about the morality of organizational policies.

The results of the analysis are shown in Table 1.4. They indicate that procedural justice judgments played a role in activating social values. If people experienced an organization as acting via fair procedures, they viewed it as having policies that were more strongly consistent with their own moral values. Again, it is interesting that both the quality of decision making and quality of interpersonal treatment shaped the activation of moral values. So, when people were treated politely and with respect, they viewed the organization as following more strongly moral policies.

DISCUSSION

This chapter explores how to best think about managing the conflicts of interest occurring within organizational settings. The data provide support for a social value activation model. This model argues that self-interest may not become an important issue in shaping behavior if people's moral values or justice judgments can be activated within a particular setting. Once people's justice judgments and/or their moral values have been activated, self-interested calculations are preempted and minimized in their importance in shaping behavior. The decision about how to behave becomes framed as a justice-based or moral decision, and self-interested concerns diminish in importance.

The social value activation model is important because of the two effects that are observed in the studies outlined. First, when people's social values are activated, their deference to rules and authorities increases. The findings consistently suggest that people act on their social values, with decision acceptance and rule following higher when moral values have been activated.

Second, when social values are activated, the role of self-interest in decision making decreases. This latter finding is particularly relevant to issues of organizational governance, as it is the ability of self-interest to overwhelm morality that leads to the difficulties with the balancing model.

Table 1.4. *What activates social values?: The influence of procedural justice on the extent policies are viewed as moral?*

	NY employees		NY residents and the police	
Beta weights				
Fairness of police procedures				
Overall fairness	.52***	—	.31***	—
Components				
Decision making	—	.17***	—	.25***
Interpersonal treatment	—	.38***	—	.21***
Outcomes				
Sanctions for rule breaking	.06	.04	.08***	.05*
Adjusted R.-squared	27%	28%	10%	19%

Note: The first law study, conducted in Chicago, was not included because system level judgments about fairness were not assessed.

The results presented consistently show that the activation of social values works against this possibility by lowering the role of self-interested calculations in shaping decisions.

Although the social value activation model is supported by the studies considered, it is equally important to note that the activation of social values does not eliminate the influence of self-interest on behavior. Hence, at extreme levels, people may still act out of self-interest even when social values are salient. The findings suggest that social value activation is a generally promising strategy for managing conflicts of interest, but self-interest still shapes behavior.

In addition, it is important to pay attention to the concerns raised by Dawes. He argues, first, that self-interest is expressed in the way that people define what is just or moral (see Messick & Sentis, 1985). So, for example, those high in ability say it is fair to pay by performance, those low in ability via equality. To the degree that people act based on principles of justice or morality, but define their meaning in self-interested terms, the power of the social value activation model is diminished. I agree with this point but would suggest that people do not simply define justice with reference to self-interest. They also are influenced by broader social values that define distributive fairness and morality in ways that are distinct from personal self-interest. So, the glass is half-empty but also half-full. To the degree that justice is distinct from self-interest, a social value activation model has traction.

Considering Dawes's comments on a more pragmatic level, however, the regression equations shown in the various tables and figures in this chapter take account of this concern in that they indicate the influence of one factor that is distinct from the other. If, as Dawes suggests, self-interest defines justice, then if we put indices of self-interest and justice in a single equation, neither will emerge as a significant influence. Hence, the findings outlined support the argument that justice and morality have influences that are distinct from the influences of self-interested judgments of risk and/or gain.

Dawes also makes a second important point when he suggests that there may be domains within which justice matters but other domains in which it does not. Again, this is an important point, and one supported by the finding that there are situational variations in both the importance and the meaning of justice (Barrett-Howard & Tyler, 1986; Tyler, Boeckmann, Smith, & Huo, 1997). The queston becomes that of identifying the domains of importance given our organizational concerns. I would argue that the studies outlined, which explored organizational settings, reflect the domain within which issues of conflict of interest are likely to be important to corporate governance concerns.

Furthermore, the range of justice effects is striking. Recent studies suggest that issues of justice are important in less social settings, including in bilateral negotiations (Hollander-Blumoff & Tyler, 2004); in market transactions (Sondak & Tyler, 2004); and even when people are seeking expert investment advice (Tyler, 2004). Hence, even in situations that are less social in character than those considered here, issues of justice continue to shape people's thoughts and actions.

The argument that people have trouble balancing self-interest and social values is similar to the suggestion that people have trouble accepting compensation for immoral actions because they view trading money for moral wrongs as a "taboo tradeoff." The taboo tradeoff argument suggests that people view money and moral values as associated with distinct spheres of life (Fiske & Tetlock, 1997). For this reason, both trying to compensate for a moral wrong with money (giving cash to compensate for raping someone) and trying to use money to gain something that ought not be for sale (i.e., buying a baby) is upsetting and provokes outrage. In other words, "there is a strong taboo against using market pricing with regard to entities that people regard as intrinsically belonging to the domain of communal sharing." Communal sharing refers to the norms and values that hold the group together. This line of thinking is consistent with the argument being advanced here – that people think that something that is wrong should not be done, and they do not think of money and social values as being in a tradeoff or balancing relationship.

These findings suggest the importance of a regulatory strategy that emphasizes the activation of moral values and justice concerns. If activated, these values moderate the influence of self-interest on rule following. Hence, people do not simply balance self-interest and morality/justice. If morality and justice are salient, self-interested considerations become of less importance.

More broadly, this argument suggests that a root of ethical problems in corporations lies in the failure to: (1) develop a justice-based or moral framework for viewing actions within the company, and (2) the failure to activate justice/moral values. Either or both of these can form the basis for a strategy for managing conflicts of interest.

In the case of creating a framework, many actions such as "stealing" office supplies or using computer software that one does not own are shrouded in ambiguity in the public mind. Are these actions really wrong?

To more effectively activate moral values, we need to more clearly activate a framework that labels actions morally wrong.

It also is often the case that moral values and justice concerns are not activated. Consider the ubiquitous warnings prior to every film watched at home: "If you illegally copy this film, you face severe penalties." This warning seeks to motivate action by activating a risk frame. Why not try to activate a morality or justice frame? Why not appeal to a sense of fairness to the producers or to the morality of stealing? If we believed that people had a moral frame for viewing actions, then we would be led to the strategy of trying to activate their moral values rather than their risk assessments.

The idea of social value activation fits closely with the idea of professional obligations and responsibilities. Across a wide variety of settings, ranging from auditing, law, and medicine to education, people learn norms and values that define professional roles. For example, doctors learn to put patient welfare above self-interest, auditors to put honesty above the desires of particular clients. The social value activation model argues that we need to focus on how to activate these feelings of obligation and responsibility. In part, such feelings are reflected in reactions to judgments about what is moral or immoral. However, it also is important to note that obligation and responsibility – often labeled legitimacy – can be viewed as distinct from morality. Although legitimacy is not directly addressed here, findings in the legitimacy literature are similar to those reported here. Legitimacy shapes decision acceptance and rule following, and a key antecedent of feeling obligations is the judgment that organizational procedures are just (Tyler, 1990; Tyler & Blader, 2004). Hence, we could conceptualize the issue as one of activating the social value of professional obligation and responsibility, and, if we did, we would report a similar set of findings to those outlined about the activation of the social values of morality and outcome fairness.

References

Barrett-Howard, E., & Tyler, T. R. (1986). Procedural justice as a criterion on allocation decisions. *Journal of Personality and Social Psychology*, *50*, 296–304.

Fiske, A. P., & Tetlock, P. E. (1997). Taboo trade-offs: Reactions to transactions that transgress the spheres of justice. *Political Psychology*, *18*, 255–297, p. 278.

Frey, B. S. (1997). *Not just for the money*. Cheltenham, England: Edward Elgar.

Hollander-Blumoff, R., & Tyler, T. R. (2004). *Fairness issues in bilateral negotiation*. Unpublished manuscript, New York University.

Huo, Y. J., Smith, H. J., Tyler, T. R., Lind, E. A. (1996). Superordinate identification, subgroup identification, and justice concerns: Is spearatism the problem; is assimilation the answer? *Psychological Science*, Vol. 7(1) (Jan 1996): 40–45.

Kopelman, S., Weber, J. M., & Messick, D. M. (2002). Factors influencing cooperation in commons dilemmas: A review of experimental psychological research. In E. Ostrom, T. Dietz, N. Dolsak, P. C. Stern, S. Stonich, & E. U. Weber (Eds.), *The drama of the commons*. Washington, DC: National Academy Press, (pp. 113–156).

MacCoun, R. (1993). Drugs and the law. *Psychological Bulletin, 113*, 497–512.

Messick, D. M., & Sentis, K. P. (1985). Estimating social and nonsocial utility functions from ordinal data. *European Journal of Social Psychology, 15*, 389–399.

Poundstone, W. (1992). *Prisoner's dilemma*. New York: Doubleday.

Sondak, H., & Tyler, T. R. (2004). *A relational perspective on the desirability of markets*. Unpublished manuscript, University of Utah.

Tyler, T. R. (1990). *Why people obey the law*. New Haven, CT: Yale University Press.

Tyler, T. R. (2004). *Process utility and help seeking: What do people want from experts?* Unpublished manuscript, New York University.

Tyler, T. R., & Blader, S. L. (2000). *Cooperation in groups*. Philadelphia: Psychology Press.

Tyler, T. R., & Blader, S. L. (2004). *Can businesses effectively regulate employee conduct? The antecedents of rule following in work settings*. Unpublished manuscript, New York University.

Tyler, T. R., Boeckmann, R. J., Smith, H. J., & Huo, Y. J. (1997). *Social justice in a diverse society*. Boulder, CO: Westview.

Tyler, T. R., & Huo, Y. J. (2002). *Trust in the law*. New York: Russell Sage.

TWO

Commentary

On Tyler's "Managing Conflicts of Interest within Organizations"

Robyn Dawes

Carnegie Mellon University

I want to frame what I have to say about Tyler's excellent and provocative chapter by contrasting its results to my previous favorite and provocative work examining the relationship between egoistic preference and norms of fairness. That work is of Eddie Van Avermaet in his 1974 dissertation at the University of California in Santa Barbara (as summarized by Messick & Sentis, 1983).

Van Avermaet's work was experimental, and it was based on a mild deception. Subjects entered the laboratory in pairs and were asked to fill out a number of questionnaires. "When the subject finished the questionnaires, the experimenter entered the room and said in a rather irritated way that the other person had to leave immediately. He explained that he could pay each pair of subjects $7.00 for their help and they had wanted the two subjects to jointly decide how to divide the money. Now that the other had left, the experimenter could not do that and, moreover, the experimenter said he himself had an appointment in a very few minutes. After reviewing the amount of time and the number of tests that the subject and the other person had done, the experimenter suggested that the subject take the entire $7.00 along with a stamped envelope addressed to the other subject, take what the subject considered to be his or her share of the $7.00, put the remainder into the envelope, and mail it to the other subject. The envelope contained six one-dollar bills, three quarters, two dimes, and a nickel" (p. 77).

There was, of course, no real other subject that was called away, and the experimenter, of course, had no appointment. Some more bogus information followed. Subjects themselves knew whether they had filled out six or three questionnaires, and whether they had spent ninety minutes or forty-five. This personal information was crossed with the bogus information that the other subject had filled out either six of three questionnaires, and had spent either forty-five minutes or ninety minutes doing so.

Time worked	Quantity of Work (subject, other)		
(subject, other)	6,3	3,3	3,6
90,45	4.68	3.94	3.78
90,90	4.38	Data not collected	3.50
45,90	4.18	3.54	3.33

Messck & Sentis (1983), Table 4.2.

What were the results? I am presenting them in their entirety from Table 4.2 from Messick and Sentis. First, only one subject failed to send back money (and given the state of the U.S. mail – even in California – that subject may have actually sent something). Second, judging from the averages of the amounts mailed, very few subjects send less than a third of the $7.00. But what happened as a result of the manipulations? If the actual subject *either* accomplished more *or* spent more time, the subject sent back somewhere between a third and a half – approaching one-half, which is what the actual subjects sent when they were on the short side of both dimensions. (Remember that in Table 4.2, the entries refer to the amount *kept* of the $7.00, not to percentages, and not to amount sent.)

The data roughly correspond to the following principles: if a dimension can be discovered for defining fairness that favors the subject, the subject used it. If no such dimension can be found, the subject became a believer in equality; after all, the subject and the bogus other were similar in both being students and both volunteering for the same experiment.

As a result of being a department head of different departments in two universities for a total of twelve years, I found these results to be very compelling. Whenever I discussed raises with people, they immediately brought up dimensions of fairness on which the raise should be based; they and I agreed about the nature of these dimensions, but they somehow reached the conclusion that the major dimensions that should be considered (again, of fairness, not of self-interest) were those that favored them. Excellent researchers pointed out the overriding importance of research and reputation for the university; those who garnered a lot of money, even if based on the Defense Department's misunderstanding of the implications of what they did, talked about ability to bring in revenue (and after all, is not a university – like every other organization in a capitalist society – dependent on money?). Those who had excellent teaching ratings pointed out that the bottom line function of a university is to inform, and those who spent time on university governance and committees argued that there should be monetary compensation for doing onerous work, while research and teaching are a lot more fun. In addition, everyone believed that comparison salaries from "comparable others" should be a factor. In an interdisciplinary department involving people from computer scientists through economists to anthropologists, however, the anthropologists pointed out that the comparable others were their fellow department members, while the computer scientists and economists argued for national norms. Just as virtually no one in Van Avermaet's experiments kept all the money simply on the basis that "I'm me," none of my department members ever proposed that they receive a salary increase that is more than fair. It was just a question of deciding what dimension or dimensions should be used to define fairness.

Now, at face value, Tyler's work appears to contradict this experimental finding and my experience. I suggest that it does not. But both the Van Avermaet experiment and my experience are based on the idea that people recognize that there are *boundaries* defining fairness. Within those boundaries, people argued for specific points or areas that benefited themselves. These boundaries are defined in terms of what can be termed *minatory norms*. These are the norms that indicate what "thou shalt not" do. Neither experimental subjects nor my department members propose that compensation should be granted to favor them for which no fairness dimension can be found. That would be simply "out of bounds." They would not propose doing it.

In addition, there is a general agreement about such boundaries and about minatory principles in general. Thou shalt not – do a whole slew of things according to the Ten Commandments. These commandments do not tell you exactly how you should love your neighbor, how you should honor your parents, or how you should worship your god. Nevertheless, Christians tend to agree about what is unethical and immoral, at least in terms of violating the commandments. Another example can be found in attitudes toward the death penalty. Both people who are opposed to or in favor of it agree that it should *not* be implemented when someone in fact did not commit a crime for which he or she has been condemned. (Well, there is one crazy Supreme Court ruling once....)

What I am suggesting is that the power that Tyler finds for the norms as almost lexicographic in determining choices – and the fact he finds egoistic preferences very important only in the absence of norms – is that most of the norms being considered are minatory ones; these, as opposed to the hortatory ones of "thou shalt," yield both consensus and clout. We do not, for example, balance self-interest and morality when we view trading money for moral wrongs. That is a "taboo tradeoff," because the moral wrongs considered (ranging from robbing a bank to murder) yield minatory norms. I suspect (suspect!) that had he used examples that facilitate hortatory norms and moral values, the results would not have been that clear. Moreover, as illustrated by the Van Avermaet experiment, people *do* consider their preferences once they have behaved in a way they believe is consistent with minatory norms – which I claim is consistent with trying to maximize preferences within the boundaries provided by these norms.

Two other minor points. The figures provide pretty compelling evidence for Tyler's thesis, whereas the "coup de gras" is provided by the significance levels. But significance levels are partly a function of sample size. The other point is one that I find baffling, which is the identification of "what is appropriate and ethical in a given situation" with the norms of an organization. Let me quote from the president of what is probably the largest organization in Pittsburgh: the University of Pittsburgh Medical Center (UPMC, which now goes by a slightly augmented name). "As long as there is another hospital that is willing to cross the line, the one that isn't willing to cross the line runs the risk of losing business." In the context of the newspaper article in which this single statement appeared, it was quite clear that the meaning was exactly as unethical in its implication as it appears to be when taken in isolation. (I happened to be a patient in that hospital when I read this statement – being treated for a life-threatening condition of the type that happily just goes away if it does not kill you immediately. I contacted the president. "Did you really say that? Or were you misquoted?" My letter received no response.) Often, it is the organization itself that is urging its employees to behave in an unethical manner, so that behaving ethically involves violating rather than following organizational norms.

Experimental results reinforces the conclusion that often it is the group (ad hoc "organization") that leads to norm violation. Acting for the benefit of "us" – not "me" – enhances cooperation when that benefits the group but defection when the group is benefited by defection (see Dawes, 2001).

References

Dawes, R. M. (2001). The past and the future of social dilemma research. Keynote talk at the North International Conference on Social Dilemmas, Chicago, Illinois, June 29.

Messick, D. M., & Sentis, K. (1983). Fairness, preference, and fairness bias. In Messick, D. M. & Cook, K. S. (Eds.), *Equity theory: Psychological and sociological perspectives*. New York: Praeger.

Pittsburgh Post-Gazette. February 11, 1996, Page A-17.

Van Avermaet, E. (1974). *Equity: A theoretical and experimental analysis*. Unpublished doctoral dissertation, University of California, Santa Barbara.

THREE

A Review of Experimental and Archival Conflicts-of-Interest Research in Auditing

Mark W. Nelson*

Cornell University

ABSTRACT

I review empirical (archival and experimental) accounting research that
has addressed the issue of conflicts of interest, focusing on the audit setting
that has received so much recent attention. I start with a brief discussion
of the audit function and auditors' incentives, viewing auditors as weighing
incentives that favor acceding to client demands against incentives that favor resisting client demands, and also as influenced by psychological and
social aspects of audit settings. Then, I discuss various different research
approaches to investigating conflicts of interest in this setting. The review is
not intended to be exhaustive. Rather, I highlight key strengths and weaknesses of each approach and illustrate each approach with a representative
study. I also discuss the main insights provided by each approach. I finish by
relating the insights provided by different approaches and suggesting some
directions for future research.

The general topic of conflicts of interest has been of particular recent concern in accounting and auditing. Large financial failures and accounting
scandals suggest potential conflicts that have reduced the effectiveness
of corporate governance, the reliability of financial statements, and ultimately investor confidence. Policy makers have responded with unusual
speed by passing numerous new regulations, culminating in passage of the
Sarbanes-Oxley Act in July 2002. Yet, many of these regulatory changes

* This paper was written for the NSF/CBI Conference on Conflicts of Interest. I am grateful
for financial support provided by Cornell's Johnson Graduate School of Management;
comments provided by Rob Bloomfield, Laureen Maines, Brian Mayhew, Don Moore,
Zoe-Vonna Palmrose, and an anonymous reviewer; and for research assistance provided
by Shana Clor-Proell.

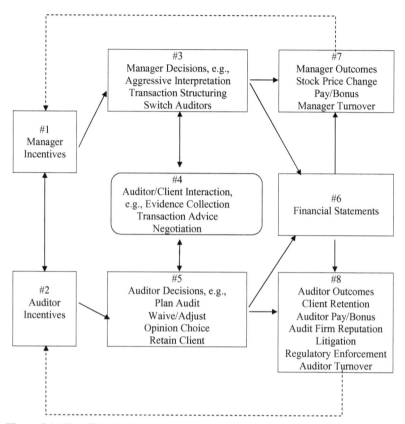

Figure 3.1. How Do Auditor and Manager Incentives Affect Audit Outcomes?

have occurred without much consideration of evidence provided by the extant experimental and archival empirical research literatures. Also, the empirical research literature itself is broad and somewhat fragmented methodologically, making it difficult for accounting and nonaccounting researchers to identify what has been learned and what questions remain.

This review discusses how empirical accounting research has addressed the issue of conflicts of interest, focusing on the audit setting that has received so much recent attention. I start with a brief discussion of the audit function, based on the relationships and activities depicted in Figure 3.1. In the main body of the chapter, I discuss various different experimental and archival approaches to investigating conflicts of interest in the audit setting. The review is not intended to be exhaustive. Rather, as shown in Table 3.1, I highlight key strengths and weaknesses of each empirical approach and illustrate each approach with a representative study. I also discuss the main insights provided by each approach. I finish by relating the insights provided by different approaches and suggesting some directions for future research.

As with research in any applied setting, it is important to understand the key institutional features and necessary decision processes that underlie performance in auditing. Therefore, I start by describing the external audit process, and then go on to describe the incentive arrangements that can lead to conflicts of interest in the audit setting.[1]

The External Audit Process

The Securities Exchange Acts of 1933 and 1934 require that publicly traded companies hire an independent certified public accountant to provide an audit opinion as to the accuracy of their annual financial statements. However, audit opinions were sought prior to 1933, and often are sought today when regulations do not require them, because creditors, private investors, contract counterparties, and other stakeholders recognize that managers could have multiple incentives to bias financial information (see boxes #1, #3, and #7 in Figure 3.1), and therefore require assurance that reported information is accurate. For example, a credible audit opinion attesting to the accuracy of a company's financial statements might allow the company to obtain a higher price for their securities, borrow at a lower interest rate, avoid advance payments to suppliers, and so on (Kinney, 2000). This need for reduction of "information risk" underlies the economic demand for auditing.

To provide a credible audit opinion, auditors must complete a complex process of planning, information gathering, and evaluation that conforms to applicable auditing rules (see boxes #4 and #5 in Figure 3.1).[2] Auditors

---

[1] More complete descriptions of the auditing process, setting and incentives can be found in Kinney (2000), Johnstone, Sutton, and Warfield (2001), and Arens, Elder, and Beasley (2002).

[2] Historically, these rules were called "generally accepted auditing standards," or GAAS, which were set by the Auditing Standards Board (ASB), affiliated with the American Institute of Certified Public Accountants (AICPA). Recent regulatory changes have put audit standard setting under the control of the Public Company Accounting Oversight Board (PCAOB), a private-sector regulatory authority created by the Sarbanes-Oxley Act of 2002 and operating under the authority of the Securities Exchange Commission (SEC) to oversee the auditing of public companies.

Table 3.1. *Research Approaches: Example Studies, General Findings, Strengths and Weaknesses*

Approach	Description	Recent Study	General Results	Strengths	Weaknesses
Archival: Abnormal Accruals	Relates audit and non-audit fees to bias in financial reports	Frankel, Johnson and K. Nelson (2002)	Mixed results, depending on how independent and dependent variables measured	Real-world incentives and financial reports	Results appear sensitive to choice of measures; Auditor decisions inferred from financial reports rather than examined directly; Archival data so difficult to infer process or causality
Archival: Restatements	Compares audit and non-audit fees between firms that were v. were not forced to restate financial statements to correct aggressive reporting	Kinney, Palmrose, and Scholz (2003)	Little evidence that higher non-audit fees increase likelihood of aggressive reporting	Real-world incentives and financial reports; Less-noisy identification of aggressive reporting firms	Real-world incentives and financial reports rather than examined directly; Archival data so difficult to infer process or causality
Archival: Audit Opinions	Relate audit fees or bias in financial reports to audit opinions	DeFond, Raghunandan, and Subramanyam (2002)	Results indicate either no effect or that audit opinions tend to go against client pressure when clients are high-risk	Real-world incentives and decisions; Focus more directly on an auditor decision (opinion)	Results appear sensitive to choice of measures; Archival data so difficult to infer process or causality; Limited variance in dependent variable because most effects occur earlier in the audit process

Table 3.1 (continued)

Approach	Description	Recent Study	General Results	Strengths	Weaknesses
Archival: Audit Adjustments	Relates client size, adjustment materiality, and other factors to auditors' decisions about whether to require clients to make audit adjustments	Wright and Wright (1997)	Adjustments increase conservatism of financial statements. Auditors are more likely to require adjustment of amounts that are more material or subjective, and when clients are small.	Real-world incentives and decisions; Focus more directly on an auditor decision (audit adjustment)	Results sensitive to choice of measures; Limited archival proxies for many incentives; Archival data so difficult to infer process or causality
Surveys of Aggressive Accounting	Relates latitude in rules, adjustment materiality, client size, and other factors to auditors' decisions about whether to adjust aggressive reporting	Nelson, Elliott, and Tarpley (2002)	Same as archival audit adjustments studies, but much description of specific incentives and transactions. Also, auditors sometimes help clients structure transactions to circumvent specific accounting rules.	Much specific data about real-world incentives and decisions; Focus more directly on an auditor decision	Measured rather than manipulated variables so difficult to infer process or causality; Survey approach vulnerable to response biases

(continued)

Table 3.1 (*continued*)

Approach	Description	Recent Study	General Results	Strengths	Weaknesses
Experiments with Non-Interacting Auditors: Effects of Incentives	Examine effect of incentive manipulations on experienced auditors' decisions about high-fidelity cases	Hackenbrack and Nelson (1996)	When latitude exists, auditors' judgments are affected by their incentives	Strong causal inferences enabled by experimental manipulations; Using experienced auditors enhances external validity	Some necessary abstraction reduces generality of descriptive results; Focus on decision rather than process. Lack of interaction reduces ability to examine process of auditor/client interaction
Experiments with Non-Interacting Auditors: Psych. processes	Examine effect of incentive manipulations on evidence evaluation and/or weighting as well as decisions	Beeler and Hunton (2003)	Incentives affect not only final decisions, but also such unconscious processes as cue measurement and cue weighting	Same as "effect of incentives" experiments; Also, provide insight into process	Same as "effect of incentives" experiments; Also, elicitation of process variables may affect processing
Experiments with Non-Interacting Auditors: Constraining effect of incentives	Examine effect of interventions like new regulations for reducing the amount of aggressiveness that auditors allow in financial reports	Libby and Kinney (2000)	Interventions often unsuccessful, with incentives typically still affecting auditor decisions	Same as "effect of incentives" experiments; Also, provide a way to assess effectiveness of enacted or planned interventions	Same as "effect of incentives" experiments

Table 3.1 (concluded)

Approach	Description	Recent Study	General Results	Strengths	Weaknesses
Experiments with Interacting Auditors	Examine effect of alternative negotiating preparations on outcomes of case negotiations between experienced auditors and confederate playing role of client management	Trotman, Wright, and Wright (2002)	More conservative outcomes anticipated or obtained when there is less latitude, stronger audit committee support, or better preparation by auditor in terms of understanding client motivations and position	Same as non-interacting experiments; Examine more directly interaction between auditors and managers	Some necessary abstraction reduces generality of descriptive results; Actual auditor/client negotiating dyads very difficult to access, so compromise in various ways (e.g., elicit anticipated outcomes from auditors; use confederates) which may affect results
Experiments with Interacting Students	Create abstract economies in which students play role of auditors, managers, and shareholders and manipulate incentives, information, and market characteristics	Mayhew, Schatzberg, and Sevcik (2001)	Results similar to those of high-context experiments with non-interacting auditors, with auditors more likely to allow aggressive reporting when latitude exists and incentives favor it	Experimental control allows strong inferences about effect of information and incentives; Can examine interaction more easily than with experienced participants	Much abstraction, so must generalize with care

first have to decide whether to do an audit, as there are circumstances in which a company's financial records are so incomplete, its activities so risky, or its management so unreliable that the auditor does not believe a defensible opinion can be provided. Given that an audit is to be conducted, auditors must gain an understanding of their client's accounting systems and the internal controls that are designed to ensure accuracy of transaction processing, test those systems and controls for proper performance, and test the output of those systems and the company's financial statements and other disclosures for correspondence to generally accepted accounting principles (GAAP). If the auditor discovers material inaccuracies (with "materiality" defined as potentially affecting the decisions of a user of the financial statements), the auditor's client must correct the inaccuracies or the auditor should issue a modified opinion that communicates that the financial statements are not free of material misstatement. Thus, an unqualified or "clean" audit opinion does not indicate that the client is healthy or a good investment but, rather, only that the auditor believes their client has fairly reported its financial condition and performance.

Auditors also provide many types of nonaudit services. Some nonaudit services are similar to audit services in that they require that auditors provide some sort of independent attestation about the accuracy of some representation or the functioning of some process (for these services, auditors attest to something other than correspondence of financial statements to GAAP). Other nonaudit services do not involve attestation but rather involve some other form of consulting (e.g., information system design, tax advice, bookkeeping).

Independence and Incentives

The value of an audit opinion depends on the objectivity and expertise of the auditor. Thus, freedom from conflicts of interests, typically labeled "independence" in the auditing profession, is a fundamental concern.

> Independence in auditing means taking an unbiased viewpoint in performing audit tests, evaluating the results, and issuing the audit report. If the auditor is an advocate for the client, a banker, or anyone else, the auditor cannot be considered independent. Independence is regarded as the auditor's most critical characteristic. The reason that many diverse users are willing to rely on the CPA's reports as to the fairness of financial statements is their expectation of an unbiased viewpoint. (Arens et al. 2002)

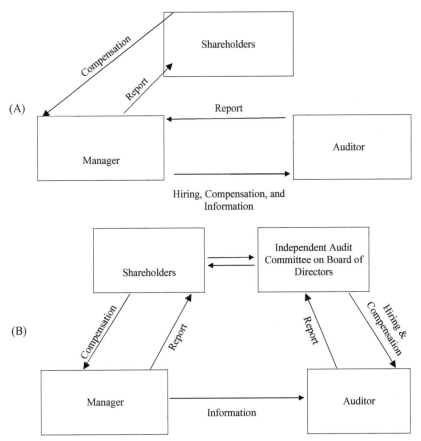

Figure 3.2. Panel A Relationships When Auditor Hired by Manager. Panel B Relationships When Auditor Hired by Board of Directors.

Regulations promulgated by Congress (e.g., the Sarbanes-Oxley Act of 2002), the Securities and Exchange Commission (SEC), the Public Companies Accounting Oversight Board (PCAOB), the American Institute of Certified Public Accountants (AICPA), and various stock exchanges specify conditions designed to promote both "independence in fact" (i.e., actual objectivity) and "independence of appearance" (because audit opinions are devalued if auditors who are objective are not perceived as such) by avoiding potential conflicts of interests. Many of these regulations address how auditors are hired and compensated. For example, consider the two arrangements shown in panels A and B of Figure 3.2.

Panel A indicates an arrangement in which managers hire and compensate auditors, in addition to providing auditors with much of the information necessary to conduct an audit, and auditors report back to managers. In this arrangement, managers report to and are compensated by shareholders (via the board of directors). A potential lack of independence in this arrangement is indicated by auditors being hired and compensated directly by management, and reporting back to management.

Panel B indicates the arrangement that is required for public companies today. Rather than being hired by management, auditors are hired by shareholders (via an audit committee that is comprised of nonmanagement members of the board of directors). This arrangement is more independent, as auditors receive only information from managers, and are hired and compensated by the board that also hires and compensates managers. Of course, to the extent the audit committee is not truly independent of management, panel B collapses to panel A. Also, even under the panel B relationship, various aspects continue to raise concerns about audit independence, because auditors still face a variety of conflicting incentives (see boxes #2 and #8 in Figure 3.1).

On the one hand, incentives to thwart aggressive reporting are provided by the threat of litigation; actions by the PCAOB, SEC, and other regulatory bodies; reputation loss that reduces the audit firm's ability to attract clients and maintain higher fees for audit services; professional censure by governing bodies such as the American Institute of Certified Public Accountants (AICPA); loss of position; and potential loss of partnership capital and retirement payouts. The recent demise of Arthur Andersen and previous demise of Laventhol & Horwath underscore that these incentives are very real.

On the other hand, offsetting incentives to allow aggressive reporting are provided by auditors' long-run need to attract and retain clients, as well as their potential interest in obtaining future employment with clients. Audit and nonaudit fees can affect auditor compensation either directly (via fee-linked bonuses and "partnership shares") or indirectly (via professional advancement and retention), and disagreements with clients can jeopardize client relationships and result in loss of fees. This concern may be increased if the audit firm "low-balled" initial audit fees (i.e., reduced fees in early years of an engagement to compete successfully for clients) as profitability is tied even more strongly to preserving a long-term relationship. Also, because many auditors eventually leave public accounting to join the financial management of their former clients, they may be reluctant to damage relations with management.

In addition to the extrinsic incentives listed earlier, auditors form numerous relationships and face various social pressures that likewise may influence their decision making. On the one hand, auditors interact frequently with their clients, and as a result face immediate social pressures toward compliance with client wishes that may seem more compelling than future, probabilistic disincentives (Bazerman, Morgan, & Loewenstein, 1997). On the other hand, auditors also are part of audit teams and audit firm cultures that have a professional identity and focus in part on audit quality (King, 2002), and audit judgments are subjected to an elaborate process of hierarchical review that is designed to reveal and correct individual errors and biases (Libby & Trotman, 1993; Solomon, Rich, & Trotman, 1997). Unless indicated otherwise, I will include these sorts of pressures in the broader class of incentives that auditors face, recognizing that, although not extrinsic, these pressures can influence auditors' judgment in ways similar to extrinsic incentives.

Given the existence of these many powerful but conflicting incentives, it is perhaps not surprising that the auditing research literature has not tended to view auditors as completely objective decision makers but, rather, as being influenced by the balance of incentives that they face in a particular context.[3] As described in the next section, a variety of empirical research approaches have been used to examine whether and how the balance of these incentives affect auditor judgment.

Empirical Approaches for Examining Effects of Auditing Conflicts of Interests

Table 3.1 lists various empirical research approaches that have been used to examine whether and how auditors' incentives affect their judgments, and also lists important attributes that can be used to distinguish research approaches and the contributions that approaches can make. Research approaches differ in their strengths and weaknesses, and also in the specific linkages of Figure 3.1 that they examine. I begin with archival approaches, and then discuss experimental approaches.

Archival Approaches

Archival approaches analyze data about previous auditor decisions to infer the effect of potential conflicts of interest. These studies constitute

---

[3] There is a theoretical literature which develops economic models of how investors, auditors, managers, and others interact under various assumptions about incentives, roles, and so on. This review focuses on empirical research, and so does not examine this theoretical literature. For examples of influential theoretical studies of auditing conflicts of interest, see Goldman and Barlev (1974), Nichols and Price (1976), DeAngelo (1981), Antle (1982, 1984), Fellingham and Newman (1985), Magee and Tseng (1990), Antle and Nalebuff (1991), Teoh (1992), and Bloomfield (1995).

a large part of the conflict-of-interest literature in auditing. I subdivide this literature primarily according to dependent variable: specifically, abnormal accruals, earnings restatements, audit outcomes, and audit adjustments (obtained both from audit work papers and from surveys). I start the discussion with studies that focus on the financial-statement end products of the audit process, and then address studies that focus on decisions made earlier in the audit process.

Abnormal Accruals

A large archival accounting literature examines the circumstances in which earnings appear to be biased, typically focusing on judgmental, noncash revenues and expenses (often called "accruals"; see, e.g., Jones, 1991) for which managers have latitude in determining which numbers to report. These studies typically (1) identify *ex ante* a proxy for a circumstance in which the researcher hypothesizes there to be an incentive for managers to bias reports; (2) compute "expected total accruals" based on prior relations between accruals and other accounting numbers; and (3) compute "abnormal (or "discretionary") accruals" by comparing actual to expected accruals. If abnormal accruals are of the sign implied by the incentive proxy, the study concludes that financial reports were biased to favor managers' incentives. Because these studies are always based on data from audited financial statements, they are viewed as indicating managerial bias that auditors did not prevent, either because auditors did not detect the managerial bias (i.e., imperfect auditing) or because auditors were not independent and allowed detected bias to remain in the financial statements (i.e., biased auditing).

Recently this approach has been extended to examine audit independence more directly by focusing on auditor incentives rather than manager incentives. Primarily, studies have focused on auditor incentives arising from fees for audit and nonaudit services. For example, Frankel, Johnson, and K. Nelson (2002) provide evidence of a positive relation between the absolute value of a company's abnormal accruals and the ratio of nonaudit to total (audit plus nonaudit) fees, and interpret that relation as evidence that auditors are more likely to allow clients to report aggressively when the clients pay relatively large nonaudit fees to auditors. However, the results of this study appear vulnerable to specific design choices with respect to both the independent variable (e.g., using fee ratio rather than total fees to proxy for incentives) and dependent variable (e.g., estimates of abnormal accruals are influenced by the particular accruals expectations model employed), with studies using methodological refinements typically finding little relation between nonaudit fees and unexpected accruals (e.g., Antle, Gordon, Narayanamoorthy, & Zhou, 2002; Ashbaugh, LaFond, & Mayhew, 2003; Chung & Kallapur, 2003). One notable exception is provided by Larcker and Richardson (2003), who find a relation between nonaudit fees and accruals for a sub-group of firms (approximately 20 percent of their sample) who have characteristics that imply weak corporate governance.

Abnormal accruals studies have the advantage of using real-world data in which auditors face the balance of incentives that they encounter in practice, and the focus on total accruals allows them to capture many transactions where relatively subtle biases may have occurred. However, referring to Figure 3.1, these studies omit the audit-process elements denoted by #4 and #5, instead focusing on correlations between #2 and #6. As a consequence, even if measurement problems associated with #2 and #6 can be alleviated, these studies provide only indirect evidence about auditor decisions, and struggle to infer causality from significant correlations between #2 and #6 (Kinney & Libby, 2002).

Earnings Restatements
Rather than struggling with noisy estimates of abnormal accruals as their dependent measure, Kinney, Palmrose and Scholz (2003) examine audit and nonaudit fees for companies that were forced to restate prior year earnings to correct non-GAAP misstatements that were discovered subsequently. Comparing a sample of firms that had earnings restatements with a matched sample of firms that had no restatement, Kinney et al. find limited evidence that fees from various types of nonaudit services increase the chance that a company will eventually have to restate earnings. Indeed, Kinney et al. provide evidence that spending more on tax services actually decreases the chance that a company will have to restate earnings. In addition, Kinney et al. provide evidence that auditors do not supply material nonaudit services to the vast majority of restatement companies. Overall, their results suggest that incentives from nonaudit-service fees do not explain auditors allowing egregious aggressive reporting.

The advantage of the Kinney et al. approach is that they avoid the measurement problems associated with estimating abnormal accruals (i.e., they have a more precise measurement of #6 in Figure 3.1), and they also obtain confidential fee data that arguably allows better measurement of auditor incentives (#2 in Figure 3.1). However, they can only examine extreme forms of aggressive reporting with restatement data, and thus

cannot speak to less extreme circumstances. Also, as with abnormal accruals studies, this approach does not directly examine auditor decisions.

Audit Outcomes
Another archival literature examines whether incentives and/or bias
in financial statements are related to audit outcomes like audit opinions and auditor changes. For example, DeFond, Raghunandan, and
Subramanyam (2002) find no association between propensity to issue
"going concern opinions" (where an auditor indicates doubt about the
company's ability to survive in the near future) and either total fees or
ratio of nonaudit to total fees, and Butler, Leone, and Willenborg (2002)
find a negative association between propensity to issue "going concern
opinions" and abnormal accruals. In general, these studies have similar
strengths and weaknesses to the abnormal accruals studies discussed earlier. In addition, they have the strength of focusing more directly on an
important auditor decision (e.g., opinion choice, #5 in Figure 3.1), but
suffer the weakness of focusing on an auditor decision for which there
exists little variance (i.e., most audit opinions are unqualified), with most
opportunities for nonindependence presumably occurring when auditors
are making various important decisions earlier in the audit process.

Audit Adjustments
Another type of archival study examines an earlier decision in the audit process by analyzing the audit adjustments that auditors propose and
document in their workpapers after completing their audit tests. These
adjustments capture the potentially material inaccuracies that auditors
believe exist in the financial statements. If management refuses to implement these adjustments, auditors have to decide whether the resulting
inaccuracy is material enough to require them to modify their audit opinion, and a recently issued regulation Statement on Auditing Standards
(SAS 89) also requires auditors to provide the client's audit committee
with a list of all adjustments that were proposed but not implemented.

Kinney and Martin (1994) provide a meta-analysis of nine adjustment
data sets and demonstrate that auditors tend to require their clients to
make adjustments that reduce earnings and net assets. Although this evidence indicates that auditing increases the conservatism of financial statements, it does not indicate whether the resulting financial statements are
as conservative as they should be, and also does not indicate specific incentive factors that might affect auditors' decisions about whether to propose
adjustment and require that clients implement adjustments.

A good example of a more recent study is provided by Wright and Wright (1997), who examine specific factors that affect auditors' decisions about whether to require that clients make audit adjustments to correct identified misstatements. Their results suggest that auditors are less likely to require adjustments that are less material, subjectively defined, and that are associated with larger clients. One interpretation of these results is that auditors' adjustment decisions are influenced by their incentives to retain large clients, but these results also are consistent with other explanations (e.g., auditors believe that the better reporting systems of larger clients reduce the risk of further undetected misstatements).

More generally, archival adjusting-entry studies have the advantage of capturing auditors' real-world decisions at a key point in the audit process. However, these studies provide no information about the audit process prior to the adjustment decision, or about decisions made with respect to amounts that the auditor decided not to even propose as an adjustment. Also, they have the familiar difficulty of inferring causality from correlations between measured incentive proxies (i.e., #2 in Figure 3.1) and measured auditor decisions (i.e., #5 in Figure 3.1).

Survey of Aggressive Accounting
Rather than obtaining data about auditor adjustment decisions from audit workpapers, other studies use survey methods to examine auditors' decisions with respect to aggressive accounting. For example, Nelson, Elliott, and Tarpley (2002, 2003) analyze 515 instances of attempted earnings management reported by 253 very experienced auditors. Similar to Wright and Wright (1997), Nelson et al. find that auditors are relatively unlikely to require adjustment when attempts involve subjective accounting rules, consistent with them using latitude to justify the accounting positions their client prefers. Nelson et al. also provide evidence that auditors are less likely to require adjustment of attempts made by large clients, even when the resulting misstatements are material, increase income, and are not viewed as consistent with GAAP, providing evidence that auditors may be more likely to acquiesce to large clients even when doing so could increase their vulnerability to litigation. Gibbins, Salterio, and Webb (2001) and Beattie, Brandt, and Fearnley (1999) are other examples of this approach.

Survey studies have the advantage of addressing a larger set of transactions than would be possible from audit workpapers, as some types of aggressive accounting might never be proposed as audit adjustments (e.g., successful transaction structuring to obtain aggressive accounting

treatments). The survey methodology also allows collection of more specific data about the particular circumstances surrounding each auditor
decision – referring to Figure 3.1, survey researchers can more easily collect information about perceived relations between #1, #3, and #7; about
the relation between #2, #5, and #8; and about #4. However, surveys suffer the same statistical limitations as do other archival studies, given that
independent variables are measured rather than manipulated, and addi-
tionally suffer from potential response noise and biases endemic to the
survey method.

Summary: Archival Approaches
These various archival approaches (whether based on archived financial
statement data, hand-collected workpaper data, or survey data) have produced a number of important findings. In general, research approaches
that focus on end products of the audit process like audited financial statements and restatements tend to find much evidence that financial statements are biased in the direction of manager incentives but less evidence
that particular auditor incentives encouraged auditors to allow aggressive
reporting. These "null effects" results are often difficult to interpret, as
both "independence" and "low power" offer plausible interpretations for
lack of effects of various incentive factors. Research approaches that focus on earlier decisions in the audit process (e.g., auditors' decisions with
respect to proposed audit adjustments or identified aggressive accounting) provide somewhat more evidence that auditor incentives affect their
decisions. All of these studies enjoy the advantage of examining data
that are disciplined by real-world incentives, but all also struggle to make
strong causal inferences, to understand the process by which incentives
affect auditor decisions, and to construct powerful tests.

Experimental Approaches

Experimental approaches have complementary strengths and weaknesses
to archival approaches (Libby, Bloomfield, and Nelson 2002). Experiments allow strong causal inferences because of experimental manipulation (rather than measurement) and random assignment of subjects
to treatments. In terms of Figure 3.1, because manager incentives (#1)
and auditor incentives (#2) can be manipulated, their causal effect on
decisions (#3, #5) is much clearer. Also, experiments allow researchers
to elicit data that shed light on the decision processes by which incentives affect behavior. However, a disadvantage is that abstraction from

real-world incentive systems requires that relatively more care be taken when generalizing results to practice. I subdivide the experimental literature according to the participants and level of interaction involved, starting with auditors (noninteracting, interacting) and then nonauditors (typically students who interact).

Experiments Involving Noninteracting Auditors

EFFECTS OF INCENTIVES. Numerous experiments examine auditors' decisions with respect to case studies that are designed to mimic audit tasks and invoke particular real-world incentives. Typically, these cases are ones for which accounting rules provide some latitude. For example, Moore, Loewenstein, Tanlu, and Bazerman (2003, experiment 1) examine whether auditors' judgments with respect to proper accounting for five cases were influenced by the role the auditor served on an engagement. Half of the subjects were told they were the external auditor for the company; the other half were told that they were providing advice to an outside investor. Moore et al. found that auditors were less likely to approve of client accounting when they were advising an investor. Similar evidence is provided by Ponemon (1995) with respect to auditors serving as expert witnesses in litigation cases, with auditors' opinions about appropriate accounting affected by whether they were hired by the defendant or the plaintiff. However, it is important to note that interpretation of both of these studies is complicated by the fact that auditors in at least one treatment condition are not delivering an audit opinion as an independent outside auditor, so may not have viewed themselves as bound by the same level of independence requirement. For example, it could be the case that Moore et al.'s "independent" auditors appropriately allowed client-favored accounting treatments because those treatments fell within GAAP, whereas their "outside investor employed" auditors inappropriately favored overly conservative accounting.

Other studies provide stronger tests of independence by holding constant auditors' role as independent outside auditor but varying their incentives in other ways. For example, Hackenbrack and Nelson (1996) perform an experiment in which auditors' incentives are manipulated by varying client characteristics that influence threat of litigation. Holding constant the relevant audit evidence and underlying reporting issue (i.e., determining whether it is possible to provide a "reasonable estimate" of future bad debts), Hackenbrack and Nelson vary the relevant accounting standard such that concluding estimability supported aggressive reporting in one context and conservative reporting in the other. Their results indicate that incentives influenced auditors' view of estimability and their reporting decisions. Similarly, Farmer, Rittenberg, and Trompeter (1987) find that experienced auditors' reactions to a client's novel accounting approach are influenced by factors like potential for client loss and potential for litigation.

A related stream of literature examines whether the effects of incentives are intentional or instead result from unconscious and often predecisional distortion of information similar to that demonstrated in other settings (see, e.g., Kunda, 1990; Russo, Medvec, & Meloy, 1996; Russo, Meloy, & Medvec, 1998; Russo, Meloy, & Wilks, 2000). For example, Wilks (2002) provides evidence that auditors' evaluation of evidence and subsequent judgments about a client's ability to continue as a going concern are biased in the direction of their supervisor's early views. Most recently, Beeler and Hunton (2003) provide evidence that audit partners' evaluation of evidence and going concern judgments are affected by whether the audit firm "lowballed" the audit fee (i.e., accepted a low fee in the initial year of the engagement in order to attract the client, making it more important to retain the client in future years) and offered significant future opportunities for nonaudit fees.

In general, these studies suggest that incentives not only affect auditors' decisions consciously, as typically assumed by economists, but also unconsciously, via processes like information assessment and weighting. These studies have the advantage of providing insights into process, but the disadvantage that eliciting process variables may affect processing. It is therefore important that the decision results of these studies converge with those of studies that do not elicit process variables.

REDUCE AGGRESSIVENESS OF REPORTING. Another branch of this literature examines the effectiveness of various proposed or enacted changes designed to reduce the aggressiveness of financial reporting. One obvious way to reduce the aggressiveness of financial reporting is to adjust incentives to favor conservative reporting. Thus, studies demonstrating that incentives affect judgment, either consciously or unconsciously, also can be viewed as demonstrating the effectiveness of interventions designed to modify incentives. Although these studies are not well-suited to identifying the specific level of incentive necessary to produce a given level of conservative reporting in practice, they are well-suited to indicating that directional change in incentive results in directional change in conservatism.

Assuming that the balance of auditors' incentives favor aggressive reporting, another way to reduce aggressiveness of reporting is to reduce the latitude available to auditors when applying accounting and auditing rules. Numerous studies in accounting (e.g., Braun, 2001; Hronsky & Houghton, 2001; Libby & Kinney, 2000; Nelson & Kinney, 1997; Nelson, Smith, & Palmrose, 2003; Salterio & Koonce, 1997; Trompeter, 1994) indicate that latitude is an important condition for incentive effects to be observed. Latitude might exist not only in the relevant accounting rules but also in other evidence used to determine appropriate accounting. For example, Cuccia, Hackenbrack, and Nelson (1995) provide evidence that moving to a precise, quantitative tax rule will not constrain the aggressiveness of tax positions when the relevant precedents offer sufficient latitude to justify an aggressive reporting position. However, reducing latitude is likely to reduce aggressiveness of reports only when incentives favor aggressive reporting – latitude can increase the conservatism of reports when incentives encourage auditors to report conservatively (Nelson, 2003).

Even if the balance of incentives favors aggressive reporting, some latitude is often necessary, because there are often circumstances in accounting where rules cannot be written *ex ante* to cover every contingency. Therefore, the existence of some latitude can be viewed as a given, and the question is whether other aspects of the accounting setting besides incentives can be modified to discourage aggressive reporting.

Recent studies have examined the effectiveness of regulatory changes. For example, Libby and Kinney (2000) examine whether auditors believe the final outcome of an audit would be to require adjustment of small misstatements, varying whether the misstatements are qualitatively material to the client, whether misstatements are subjective or objective in nature, and whether auditors are operating under a recently passed rule (SAS 89) that requires them to communicate to the audit committee any unadjusted misstatements. Libby and Kinney provide evidence that the new reporting requirement only modifies auditor behavior in circumstances where misstatements are *not* material to the client.

As another example, Kadous, Kennedy, and Peecher (2003) examine the effectiveness of another recent rule (SAS 90) requiring auditors to assess the quality and appropriateness of a client's preferred accounting position, rather than just its acceptability. Kadous et al. vary whether auditors performed the quality assessment, and also the extent of pressure that auditors would expect their client to exert (by varying whether the client had already released preliminary financial statements that used their preferred position). Results indicated that auditors were somewhat more likely to accept the client's position when they performed the quality assessment, which Kadous et al. suggest is driven by auditors focusing on the characteristics of the clients' position that were suggestive of high quality.

In general, experimental studies of noninteracting auditor decision making demonstrate a consistent role of auditors' incentives, manipulating #2 in Figure 3.1 and identifying consistent effects on #5. These studies also provide a mechanism for testing new or potential regulatory interventions, and in general provide somewhat pessimistic views of the effectiveness of interventions that are designed to reduce reporting aggressiveness. In addition, the external validity of these experiments is enhanced via their use of practicing auditors who assume real-world incentives.

Experiments Involving Interacting Auditors
Recently, a few experimental studies have examined auditor/client interaction more directly, typically drawing on the extensive negotiation literature in psychology and organizational behavior (see, e.g., Gibbins and Salterio, 2002; Neale & Bazerman, 1991; Thompson, 2001). Because it is very difficult to obtain access to financial managers and audit partners for purposes of observing actual interaction, researchers have taken various creative steps to gather data.

For example, Ng and Tan (2003) elicit from auditors not only their beliefs about the eventual outcome of an accounting dispute with their client (similar to a belief about a negotiated outcome) but also their initial recommendation about appropriate accounting (similar to the amount that would be proposed to adjust the financial statements). Tan and Ng provide evidence that auditors are less likely to allow aggressive reporting if there exists either authoritative guidance for a conservative position or a strong audit committee on the board to support the auditor's position. Ng and Tan also provide evidence that auditors' "opening move" in the negotiation typically equals their "preferred outcome," probably because auditors believe they can only propose adjustments that are valid according to GAAP.

Trotman, Wright, and Wright (2002) solve the "access to subjects" problem in a different way, by having audit partners actually negotiate over an aggressive accounting position with a researcher confederate who plays the role of client management. Trotman et al.'s results indicate that auditors obtain the most conservative outcomes if they have taken the role of client management in a prior negotiation, that they obtain the next-most conservative outcome if they have passively considered the positions and incentives that client management would take in negotiations, and the least conservative if there is no specific consideration of client position. Interestingly, Trotman et al. focus on an information-based explanation for aggressive accounting, in which auditors improve their negotiating position by better understanding their clients' incentives. This perspective contrasts with the typical concern about auditor/client interaction, in which auditors are viewed as understanding their clients' incentives only too well and being influenced by those incentives to allow aggressive accounting.

In general, experimental examination of auditor/client negotiation is still in its infancy. These studies are promising, as they provide additional insight concerning the process by which auditors interact with clients about aggressive accounting (i.e., referring to Figure 3.1, these studies are focusing more on #4). Unfortunately, this literature faces the formidable obstacle of access to subjects, as sophisticated auditor/client dyads are very difficult to obtain and will perhaps become even less available with auditor concern about public opinion. As discussed later, one way to address this problem is to examine auditor/client interaction using less sophisticated subjects in more abstract settings.

Experiments Involving Interacting Nonauditors
A growing literature examines interactions in abstract settings where students are assigned roles that have characteristics similar to those of auditors, managers, and/or investors. For example, Mayhew, Schatzberg, and Sevcik (2001) create multiperiod experimental markets in which managers try to sell assets to investors, auditors collect information about the value of assets and make a report to the market, auditors are hired by managers, and auditor reputations develop over time. Mayhew et al. find that, when auditors know the value of their client's asset with certainty, they are more likely to protect their reputations by accurate reporting than when there is known uncertainty in asset values. Similar to other archival and experimental evidence regarding the importance of latitude, Mayhew et al. interpret this result as indicating that auditors in the uncertain-asset case believed they could bias reporting in favor of managers because investors could not be sure whether the auditor lacked independence, even though the end result in that setting was very low faith in the accuracy of the audit report.

Most interacting/nonauditor studies are based on the experimental economics paradigm. As mentioned previously, a large theoretical literature has produced economic models of auditor/client interactions, and the experimental economic literature extends and empirically tests these models (see, e.g., Bloomfield, 1996; Calegari, Schatzberg, & Sevcik, 1998; Dopuch & King, 1991; Dopuch & King, 1996; Dopuch, King, & Schatzberg, 1994; King, 1996; Mayhew, 2001; Schatzberg & Sevcik, 1994). A strength of this approach is experimental control, with even participants' roles labeled neutrally (e.g., managers, auditors, and investors are called sellers, verifiers, and buyers in Mayhew et al., 2001), so predictions can be based on the incentives and market features that are the focus of these studies. Also, similar to experiments with noninteracting auditors, this approach allows researchers to investigate the effectiveness of proposed interventions. For example, Dopuch, King, and Schwartz (2001) provide evidence that mandatory rotation decreases auditors' willingness to issue biased reports.

A few recent studies have begun using this basic approach to examine more social or intrinsic aspects of the setting. For example, Moore et al. (2003) examine settings where auditors attest to the accuracy of their client's valuation of some item that the client is offering for sale. In their experiment 2, Moore et al. provide evidence that auditors' public reports about the accuracy of their client's assessment of the value of an item are affected by incentive arrangements but not by their role as "buyer's auditor" or "seller's auditor," whereas auditors' private judgments are biased by role, even in the face of monetary incentives for accuracy. In their experiment 3, Moore et al. vary role by having "anonymous" auditors never meet their clients, "impersonal" auditors sit next to their clients but communicate with them only via paperwork, and "personal" auditors exchange personal information for a few minutes with their clients before working together, and again provide results that role does not influence auditors' public reports, but does influence auditors' private judgments. Moore et al. interpret these results as indicating an important role for "self-serving bias," by which auditors' relationships with their clients bias their judgments. However, it should be noted that, even in the abstract setting used by Moore et al., role did not affect the public "audit report" that serves as the primary product of the auditing process.

King (2002) provides evidence that group affiliation can provide a disincentive that discourages auditors from excessively trusting their clients. King manipulates whether managers can make "cheap talk" promises to auditors, and whether auditors are part of a cohesive group (e.g., a group in which auditors are introduced, wear nametags, select a team name, work together on a quiz, and reveal among themselves late in the experiment the auditor who has been most penalized for incorrectly trusting managers).

King's results indicate that group affiliation discourages reliance on cheap talk, such that auditors in the "cheap talk, group identification" condition are insignificantly different in skepticism from auditors in the "no cheap talk, no group identification" condition. King interprets these results as suggesting that nonextrinsic incentives provided by auditor professional affiliation can counteract bias introduced by client familiarity.

Summary: Experimental Approaches
Whether involving noninteracting auditors, interacting auditors, or interacting students, the experimental literature generally provides evidence of consistent (and persistent) effects of auditors' incentives on their reporting decisions. Studies provide evidence that latitude tends to exacerbate the effect of incentives on reporting decisions, and that these effects can occur relatively early in the decision process, as evidence is encountered and weighted, as well as more overtly when making decisions in light of incentives.

SUMMARY AND DIRECTIONS FOR FUTURE RESEARCH

This review highlights that multiple research approaches have been used to examine issues relevant to conflicts of interest in audit settings. Although there is some variance in results across studies, the following broad findings have been produced:

1. Archival studies provide much evidence that *managers'* incentives affect the aggressiveness of financial reports. This could result because of imperfect auditing (i.e., an audit function that is not capable of completely debiasing financial statements given the complexity of transactions, latitude in GAAP, and information asymmetry inherent in financial reporting) or because auditor incentives lead them to approve managers' aggressive reporting.
2. Archival studies provide less evidence that *auditors'* incentives affect financial reports, with little evidence supporting the assertion that variation in aggressive reporting is driven by variation in auditors' focus on nonaudit services.
3. Archival studies examining dependent variables that capture decisions that occur relatively earlier in the audit process (e.g., audit adjustment decisions) provide relatively more evidence of auditor incentive effects than do archival studies that examine outcomes of the audit process (e.g., abnormal accruals; audit opinions).

4. Experimental studies provide evidence that various incentives affect auditors' reporting decisions, particularly when there are large amounts of latitude available. These results hold regardless of whether studies use high-fidelity cases with experienced auditors or lower-fidelity cases with student subjects, and whether incentives are financial in nature (e.g., future fees from retaining a hypothetical client) or from actual dollar payoffs in laboratory experiments.

5. A few experimental studies provide evidence that social pressures can affect auditors' reporting decisions in a manner similar to the effects of countervailing incentives.

6. A few experimental studies also have moved beyond asking "when do incentives affect decisions?" to ask "*how* do incentives affect decisions?" Results indicate processes similar to those found in other contexts, with effects occurring as a result of conscious economic reasoning as well as through such psychological processes as evidence evaluation and weighting.

Overall, experimental studies provide more support than do archival studies for the proposition that potential conflicts of interest affect decisions in audit settings. There are a few explanations for this lack of correspondence.

First, experiments arguably use more powerful designs to investigate this question. From an independent-variable perspective, archival studies measure incentives with noise and often cannot operationalize the conditions that would provide a strong test (e.g., there is not an archival "no audit fee" condition to examine for purposes of determining the incentive effects of audit fees), whereas experiments can use strong manipulations. From a dependent-variable perspective, archival studies often use noisy measures such as abnormal accruals, or variables with little variance like audit opinion, whereas experiments can examine specific decisions. An important direction for future archival work will be further improvement of measures and designs (e.g., focusing on restatements as in Kinney et al., 2003; focusing on subsets of companies that have particular characteristics as do Larcker & Richardson, 2003).

Second, experimental contexts may exclude offsetting incentives or quality control processes that counteract the effects of whatever incentives are being manipulated in the experiment. Experimental replication and triangulation plays a crucial role here, as multiple experiments in multiple contexts and involving both more and less experienced auditors have produced similar findings. Still, an important direction for future experimental work is to better understand aspects of the audit process and auditor-client interaction that create or moderate incentives for aggressive reporting.

Future experimental research also could continue working to understand better the process by which incentives affect auditor decisions. The modal experimental study examines the effect of some extrinsic incentive on auditor decisions. Relatively few studies examine decision processes, or examine whether (and, if so, how) less-extrinsic pressures that arise from auditor–client interactions affect auditor decision making differently than do more extrinsic incentives.

Recent policy changes and current policy recommendations also offer fruitful directions for future research. For example, Bazerman, Loewenstein, and Moore (2002) critique various enacted and proposed reforms (e.g., audit fee disclosures, disallowing nonaudit and tax services, and requiring mandatory auditor contract periods, audit firm rotation, and "cooling-off periods" before clients can hire former auditors). A persistent concern is that many such interventions could reduce the amount of client knowledge that auditors can apply to the audit, as well as reducing a client's ability to dismiss auditors who do poor work. Previous research illustrates that it is possible to examine experimentally the effects of such interventions, using practicing auditors and examining cases that are designed to invoke the balance of incentives that auditors face in practice (e.g., Libby & Kinney, 2000; Kadous et al., 2003), or using abstract experiments that vary regulations and examine interactions over time (e.g., Dopuch et al., 2001). Such research could further inform policy makers' decisions.

References

American Institute of Certified Public Accountants (AICPA). (1999). *Audit Adjustments. Statement on Auditing Standards No. 89.* New York: AICPA.

American Institute of Certified Public Accountants (AICPA). (2000). *Audit Committee Communications. Statement on Auditing Standards No. 90.* New York: AICPA.

Antle, R. (1982). The auditor as an economic agent. *Journal of Accounting Research,* 20(2): 503–527.

Antle, R. (1984). Auditor independence. *Journal of Accounting Research,* 22(1): 1–20.

Antle, R., and Nalebuff, B. (1991). Conservatism and auditor-client negotiations. *Journal of Accounting Research,* 29 (supplement): 31–54.

Antle, R., Gordon, E. A., Narayanamoorthy, G., and Zhou, L. (2002). The joint determination of audit fees, non-audit fees, and abnormal accruals. Working paper, Yale University.

Arens, A. A., Elder, R. J., and Beasley, M. S. (2002). *Auditing and Assurance Services, An Integrated Approach.* Prentice Hall.

Ashbaugh, H., LaFond, R., and Mayhew, B. W. (2003). Do non-audit services compromise auditor independence? Further evidence. Working paper, University of Wisconsin–Madison.

Bazerman, M. H., Morgan, K. P., and Loewenstein, G. F. (1997). The impossibility of auditor independence. *Sloan Management Review* (Summer): 89–94.

Bazerman, M. H., Loewenstein, G. F., and Moore, D. A. (2002). Why good accountants do bad audits. *Harvard Business Review* (November): 97–102.

Beattie, V., Brandt, R., and Fearnley, S. (1999). Perceptions of auditor independence: U.K. evidence. *Accounting, Auditing and Taxation*, 8(1): 67–107.

Beeler, J. D., and Hunton, J. E. (2003). Contingent economic rents: Insidious threats to auditor independence. Working paper, Millsaps College.

Bloomfield, R. J. (1995). Strategic dependence and inherent risk assessments. *The Accounting Review*, 70(1): 71–90.

Bloomfield, R. J. (1996). The interdependence of reporting discretion and informational efficiency in labor markets. *The Accounting Review*, 71(4): 493–511.

Braun, K. W. (2001). The disposition of audit-detected misstatements: An examination of risk and reward factors and aggregation effects. *Contemporary Accounting Research*, 18(1): 71–99.

Butler, M. B., Leone, A. J., and Willenborg, M. (2002). An empirical analysis of auditor reporting and its association with abnormal accruals. Working paper, University of Rochester.

Calegari, M. J., Schatzberg, J. W., and Sevcik, G. R. (1998). Experimental evidence of differential auditor pricing and reporting strategies. *The Accounting Review* 73(2): 254–275.

Chung, H., and Kallapur, S. (2003). Client importance, non-audit services, and abnormal accruals. *The Accounting Review* 78(4): 931–955.

Cuccia, A. D., Hackenbrack, K. and Nelson, M. W. (1995). The ability of professional standards to mitigate aggressive reporting. *The Accounting Review* 70(2): 227–248.

DeAngelo, L. E. (1981). Auditor independence, "low balling," and disclosure regulation. *Journal of Accounting and Economics*, 3(2): 113–127.

DeFond, M. L., Raghunandan, K., and Subramanyam, K. R. (2002). Do non-audit service fees impair auditor independence? Evidence from going concern audit opinions. Working paper, University of Southern California.

Dopuch, N., and King, R. R. (1991). The impact of MAS on auditors independence – An experimental markets study. *Journal of Accounting Research*, 29: 60–98.

Dopuch, N., and King, R. R. (1996). The effects of lowballing on audit quality: An experimental markets study. *Journal of Accounting, Auditing and Finance*: 45–68.

Dopuch, N., King, R. R., and Schatzberg, J. W. (1994). An experimental investigation of alternative damage-sharing liability regimes with an auditing perspective. *Journal of Accounting Research*, 32: 103–130.

Dopuch, N., King, R. R., and Schwartz, R. (2001). An experimental investigation of retention and rotation requirements. *Journal of Accounting Research*, 39(1): 93–117.

Farmer, T. A., Rittenberg, L. E., and Trompeter, G. M. (1987). An investigation of the impact of economic and organizational factors on auditor independence. *Auditing: A Journal of Practice and Theory* 7 (1): 1–14.

Fellingham, J. C., and Newman, D. P. (1985). Strategic considerations in auditing. *The Accounting Review*, 60(4): 634–650.

Frankel, R. M., Johnson, M. F., and Nelson, K. K. (2002). The relation between auditors' fees for non-audit services and earnings management. *The Accounting Review*, 77: 71–105.

Gibbins, M., and Salterio, S. (2002). Modeling the auditor's intended strategy in auditor-client negotiation. Working paper, University of Alberta and University of Waterloo.

Gibbins, M., Salterio, S., and Webb, A. (2001). Evidence about auditor-client management negotiation concerning client's financial reporting. *Journal of Accounting Research*, 39(3): 534–563.

Goldman, A., and Barlev, B. (1974). The auditor-firm conflict of interests: Its implications for independence. *The Accounting Review*, 49(4): 707–718.

Hackenbrack, K., and Nelson, M. W. (1996). Auditors' incentives and their application of financial accounting standards. *The Accounting Review*, 71(1): 43–59.

Hronsky, J. J. F., and Houghton, K. A. (2001). The meaning of a defined accounting concept: Regulatory changes and the effect on auditor decision making. *Accounting, Organizations and Society*, 26 (2): 123–139.

Johnstone, K. M., Sutton, M. H., and Warefield, T. D. (2001). Antecedents and consequences of independence risk: Framework for analysis. *Accounting Horizons*, 15(1): 1–18.

Jones, J. J. (1991). Earnings management during import relief investigations. *Journal of Accounting Research*, 29 (Autumn): 193–228.

Kadous, K., Kennedy, J., and Peecher, M. E. (2003). The effect of quality assessment and directional goal commitment on auditors' acceptance of client-preferred accounting methods. Working paper, University of Illinois at Urbana-Champaign.

King, R. R. (1996). Reputation formation for reliable reporting: An experimental investigation. *The Accounting Review*, 71(3): 375–396.

King, R. R. (2002). An experimental investigation of self-serving biases in an auditing trust game: The effect of group affiliation. *The Accounting Review*, 77 (2): 265–284.

Kinney, W. R. (2000). *Information Quality Assurance and Internal Control for Management Decision Making*. McGraw-Hill.

Kinney, W. R., and Libby, R. (2002). Discussion of the relation between auditors' fees for non-audit services and earnings management. *The Accounting Review*, 77: 107–114.

68 *Mark W. Nelson*

Kinney, W. R., and Martin, R. D. (1994). Does auditing reduce bias in financial reporting? A review of audit related adjustment studies. *Auditing: A Journal of Practice and Theory*, 13(1): 149–156.

Kinney, W. R., Palmrose, Z. V., and Scholz. S. (2003). Auditor independence and non-audit services: What do restatements suggest? Working paper, University of Texas at Austin.

Kunda, Z. (1990). The Case for Motivated Reasoning. *Psychological Bulletin*, 108(3): 480–498.

Larcker, D. F., and Richardson, S. A. (2003). Corporate governance, fees for non-audit services and accrual choices. Working paper, University of Pennsylvania.

Lewis, B. L. (1980). Expert judgment in auditing: An expected utility approach. *Journal of Accounting Research*, 18 (2): 594–602.

Libby, R., and Kinney, W. R. (2000). Does mandated audit communication reduce opportunistic corrections to manage earnings to forecasts? *The Accounting Review*, 75(4): 383–404.

Libby, R., and Trotman, K. T. (1993). The review process as a control for differential recall of evidence in auditor judgments. *Accounting Organizations and Society*, 18(6): 559–574.

Libby, R., Bloomfield, R., and Nelson, M. (2002). Experimental research in financial accounting. *Accounting Organizations and Society*, 27 (8): 775–810.

Magee, R. P., and Tseng, M. C. (1990). Audit pricing and independence. *The Accounting Review*, 65(2): 315–336.

Mayhew, B. W. (2001). Auditor reputation building. *Journal of Accounting Research*, 39(3): 599–617.

Mayhew, B. W., Schatzberg, J. W., and Sevcik, G. R. (2001). The effect of accounting uncertainty and auditor reputation on auditor objectivity. *Auditing: A Journal of Practice and Theory*: 49–70.

Moore, D. A., Loewenstein, G., Tanlu, L., and Bazerman. M. H. (2003). Auditor independence, conflict of interest, and the unconscious intrusion of bias. Working paper, Carnegie Mellon University.

Neale, M. A., and Bazerman, M. H. (1991). *Cognition and rationality in negotiation*. The Free Press.

Nelson, M. W. (2003). Behavioral evidence on the effects of principles- and rules-based standards. *Accounting Horizons*, 17(1): 91–104.

Nelson, M. W., Elliott, J. A., and Tarpley, R. L. (2002). Evidence from auditors about managers' and auditors' earnings management decisions. *The Accounting Review*, 77 (Quality of Earnings Conference Issue): 175–202.

Nelson, M. W., Elliott, J. A., and Tarpley, R. L. (2003). How are earnings managed? Examples from auditors. *Accounting Horizons*, 17 (Supplement): 17–35.

Nelson, M. W., and Kinney, W. R. (1997). The effect of ambiguity on auditors' loss contingency reporting judgments. *The Accounting Review* 72 (2): 257–274.

Nelson, M. W., Smith, S. D., and Palmrose, Z.-V. (2003). Quantitative materiality perspectives and auditors' disposition of detected misstatements. Working paper, Cornell University.

Nichols, D. R., and Price, K. H. (1976). The auditor-firm conflict: An analysis using concepts of exchange theory. *The Accounting Review*, 51(2): 335–346.

Ng, T. B., and Tan, H. T. (2003). Effects of authoritative guidance availability and audit committee effectiveness on auditors' judgments in an auditor-client negotiation context. Working paper, Nanyang Technological University.

Ponemon, L. A. (1995). The objectivity of accountants litigation support judgments. *The Accounting Review*, 70(3): 467–488.

Russo, J. E., Medvec, V. H., and Meloy, M. G. (1996). The distortion of information during decisions. *Organizational Behavior and Human Decision Processes*, 66(1): 102–110.

Russo, J. E., Meloy, M. G., and Medvec, V. H. (1998). Predecisional distortion of product information. *Journal of Marketing Research*, 35(4): 438–452.

Russo, J. E., Meloy, M. G., and Wilks, T. J. (2000). Predecisional distortion of information by auditors and salespersons. *Management Science*, 46(1): 13–27.

Salterio, S., and Koonce, L. (1997). The persuasiveness of audit evidence: The case of accounting policy decisions. *Accounting, Organizations and Society* 22 (6): 573–587.

Schatzberg, J. W., and Sevcik, G. (1994). A multi-period model and experimental evidence of independence and "lowballing." *Contemporary Accounting Research*, 11 (Summer): 137–174.

Solomon, I., Rich, J. S., and Trotman, K. T. (1997). The audit review process: A characterization from the persuasion perspective. *Accounting, Organizations and Society*, 22(5): 481–505.

Teoh, S. H. (1992). Auditor independence, dismissal threats, and the market reaction to auditor switches. *Journal of Accounting Research*, 30(1): 1–23.

Thompson, L. (2001). *The mind and heart of the negotiator*. Prentice Hall.

Trompeter, G. (1994). The effect of partner compensation schemes and generally accepted accounting principles on audit partner judgment. *Auditing: A Journal of Practice and Theory*, 13: 56–71.

Trotman, K., Wright, A., and Wright, S. (2002). Auditor negotiations: An examination of the efficacy of intervention methods. Working paper, University of New South Wales.

Wilks, T. J. (2002). Predecisional distortion of evidence as a consequence of real-time audit review. *The Accounting Review* 77 (1): 51–71.

Wright, S., and Wright, A. M. (1997). The effect of industry experience on hypothesis generation and audit planning decisions. *Behavioral Research in Accounting*, 9: 273–294.

FOUR

Commentary

Conflicts of Interest in Accounting

Don A. Moore

Carnegie Mellon University

Mark Nelson has written a clear, interesting, and useful review of the research on conflict of interest in auditing. The review provides an insightful and critical review of a research literature that sheds light onto the role of conflicts of interest in auditing judgments, opinions, and reports. I see a number of noteworthy features of this chapter and of the research literature that it reviews. I will restrict my comment to three points, regarding (1) standards of proof; (2) selection of research participants; and (3) the relationship between researchers and professional accountants.

The first issue I want to raise has to do with standards of proof. In his review, Nelson mentions concern about the weight given to null results in the accounting literature on auditor bias. The chapter presents a number of articles that find no significant relationship between incentives and reports. As a rule, these papers have taken their null findings as evidence that no relationship exists. As a social scientist, I find this problematic. Personally, I have run more studies with null results than I care to admit, and most of them wind up in the trash because it is so difficult to know what to conclude from a null result – there is simply too much ambiguity. There are many ways to get a finding of no significant relationship between two variables, even when a relationship exists: small sample size, noisy data, bad measures, conservative statistical tests.

I realize that this complaint, if taken seriously, makes it difficult to show anything but bias as resulting from potentially biasing conditions. No bias means no relationship, and a null result. In psychology, we solve this by using so-called double-dissociation designs. The basic idea is that if you want to show that the independent variable has no effect on the dependent variable, you select a second dependent variable and show that it is influenced, as expected, by the independent variable, whereas the first is not. This solution may not be possible in the accounting context. Nevertheless, failing to find a relationship cannot be interpreted to mean that the two variables do not influence each other.

Accounting researchers often have wound up asking whether the balance of incentives faced by professional auditors are set up to reward honest reporting. The question is whether it is plausible that auditors' reports are actually unbiased – that they, on average, reflect the true state of the degree to which the client's financial reports comply with GAAP. How believable is it that the balance of incentives (including such varied motives as wanting more work for one's accounting firm; desiring promotion within the accounting firm; seeking future employment with the client; concern for future legal sanction; concern for the legal vulnerability of the audit firm; personal ties with client management; personal ties with fellow auditors; and accountability to shareholders, the investing public, management, and regulators) just happens to work out so that auditors' incentives lead them to report objectively? Assessing the objectivity of auditors' reports must depend on comparing those reports with the truth. In the field, we can really never know the truth, and that seems to make lab experiments, Nelson points out, more sensitive tools for testing hypotheses about auditor bias.

This brings me to the second issue I wanted to raise, namely, the selection of research participants in accounting research. Many scholars who study accounting are trained in an economic tradition and tend to be skeptical of psychological research. Even those accounting scholars who are trained in psychology may dismiss research that is not carried out on professional auditors with many years of experience. This has the effect of severely hampering behavioral research in accounting because the cost of obtaining these sorts of participants is often prohibitive. I believe that the evidence suggests that the expense of obtaining working professionals as subjects is rarely worth the cost, unless the study's intent is to elicit some aspect of expertise or response to incentives that is developed with experience and can only be invoked in a high-fidelity accounting context (see Libby, Bloomfield, & Nelson, 2002, for an exploration of these issues). Although professional auditors are likely to hold some knowledge that others do not, few would assert that, in the course of their training and professional socialization, auditors are made immune from the biases in judgment to which other human beings fall victim. Auditors are people, too. The history of research examining whether experts are vulnerable to biases in judgment is quite sobering, including research by Tversky and Kahneman (1974) showing that Ph.D. statisticians, just like undergraduate students, tend to make errors in Bayesian reasoning that are consistent with decision heuristics like the representativeness heuristic.

It is tempting to assume that working professionals will be different from the student samples that are studied most frequently: That auditors will be less easily biased, that lawyers will behave more rationally, that physicians will rely less on error-prone decision heuristics in their clinical decision making. But I believe that the evidence suggests instead that we should assume the opposite: that, unless there is a clear and compelling reason to expect a specific difference between two populations of people, that we should assume that they are the same, especially with regard to basic psychological processes in judgment and decision making. There is simply too much evidence showing that experienced professionals display the same decision-making biases as do less sophisticated individuals (Camerer, 2000; Kahneman, 2003; Kahneman & Tversky, 2000; Lichtenstein & Slovic, 1973).

Finally, I want to mention the role of accounting scholars in public discussions of governmental regulation of auditors and of the auditor–client relationship. Regulation of auditors is a public policy question of preeminent importance. Accounting fraud has cost American investors hundreds of billions of dollars in the last few years alone, and professional auditors have been found to be shockingly complicit with their clients in many of these cases, including the high-profile cases at Enron and WorldCom. While government regulators and elected officials have grappled with the question of reform, the scholarly accounting community has been remarkable in its hesitance to participate in this debate. This, despite the preponderance of evidence indicating that accounting firms' decisions and public reports have been tainted by conflicts of interest.

Auditors' conflicts of interest arise from the basic conflict of interest faced by managers. Auditors too often are selected by the managers whose work they are charged with assessing. If auditors were really hired and fired by the people who owned the corporation, rather than its managers, many of auditors' potential conflicts of interest would be eliminated. However, even where the hiring of auditors has been assigned specifically to the board of directors, few American companies have boards of directors that exercise truly independent control over management. Until shareholders gather the courage to stand up for their interests and wrest control from management, they cannot expect the firm's outside auditors to always report breaches of GAAP that will get them fired.

Accounting faculty, however, ought to be able to provide a voice of reason to temper the energetic self-interested advocacy of accounting firms. The large accounting firms have shown themselves to be willing to expend substantial resources to stave off regulation that they believe could reduce their profitability (Mayer, 2002). However, relatively few serious scholars of accounting have stood up to criticize the industry they study. Academic accounting departments are unique in the strength of their ties to the accounting profession. Few other academic disciplines are so clearly connected to a particular industry and a particular set of firms. As such, academic accountants would seem ideally positioned to be able to weigh in with authority on the question of audit regulation. However, active participation in public debates and the formulation of policy are often antithetical to the academic disposition. Academics are hired and tenured based on their ability to publish in academic journals, not their willingness to take stands on political issues.

References

Camerer, C. F. (2000). Prospect Theory in the Wild: Evidence from the Field. In D. Kahneman & A. Tversky (Eds.), *Choices, values, and frames* (pp. 288–300). Cambridge; New York and Melbourne: Cambridge University Press; New York: Russell Sage Foundation.

Kahneman, D. (2003). A perspective on judgment and choice: Mapping bounded rationality. *American Psychologist, 58*(9), 697–720.

Kahneman, D., & Tversky, A. (2000). *Choices, values, and frames.* New York: Russell Sage Foundation.

Libby, R., Bloomfield, R., & Nelson, M. W. (2002). Experimental research in financial accounting. *Accounting, Organizations, and Society, 27,* 775–810.

Lichtenstein, S., & Slovic, P. (1973). Response-induced reversals of preference in gambling: An extended replication in Las Vegas. *Journal of Experimental Psychology, 101*(1), 16–20.

Mayer, J. (2002, April 22 & 29). The accountants' war. *The New Yorker,* 64–72.

Tversky, A., & Kahneman, D. (1974). Judgment under uncertainty: Heuristics and biases. *Science, 185,* 1124–1131.

FIVE

Bounded Ethicality as a Psychological Barrier to Recognizing Conflicts of Interest

Dolly Chugh, Max H. Bazerman, and Mahzarin R. Banaji*

Harvard University

> But there is a more subtle question of conflict of interest that derives directly from human bounded rationality. The fact is, if we become involved in a particular activity and devote an important part of our lives to that activity, we will surely assign it a greater importance and value than we would have prior to our involvement with it.

> It's very hard for us, sometimes, not to draw from such facts a conclusion that human beings are rather dishonest creatures.... Yet most of the bias that arises from human occupations and preoccupations cannot be described correctly as rooted in dishonesty – which perhaps makes it more insidious than if it were.
> – Herbert A. Simon, 1983, pp. 95–96

Herbert Simon's perspective (1983) is broadly compatible with Moore, Loewenstein, Tanlu, and Bazerman's (2003) recent research on the psychological aspects of conflict of interest in the context of auditor independence. Moore et al. (2003) focus primarily on the work on self-serving interpretations of fairness. The current work broadens this theme, and develops a conceptual framework for understanding how unchecked psychological processes work against an objective assessment and allow us to act against personal, professional, and normative expectations when conflicts of interest exist.

* The authors are grateful for the feedback of the highly engaged participants in the NSF/CBI Conference on Conflict of Interest, hosted by Carnegie Mellon University. We especially thank Ann Tenbrunsel and Don Moore for their useful reviews, as well as Matt Cronin, Bill Keech, Scott Kim, and Kent Womack for their thoughtful written reactions to our conference presentation.

Our work pursues a more comprehensive treatment of Simon's informal notion through an integration of three critical psychological insights of the past century. We begin with Simon's own insight of bounded rationality, continue with subsequent insights offered in the work of Kahneman and Tversky regarding deviations from rationality, and then consider what we know today about the limitations of the conscious mind. In our assessment, these three literatures together provide robust support for the view that conflict of interest is not limited to explicit dishonesty. Rather, unconscious acts of ethically questionable behavior are more prevalent, more insidious, and as such, more in need of attention. The strands of these three insights weave together to form a powerful thread connecting what we know about basic human perception to cognitive, social, and, ultimately, ethical consequences. Thus, we develop the argument that the computational bounds on human cognition stretch further than previously assumed – they can influence the quality of ethical judgments, leading us to extend Simon's phrase "bounded rationality" to consider the possibility and consequence of "bounded ethicality." Bounded rationality refers to the limits on the quality of general decision making, and bounded ethicality is a strand that is used to refer to the limits on the quality of decision making with ethical import. In this chapter, we focus on the nature of bounded ethicality, and its psychological implications for recognizing conflicts of interest.

We propose that bounded ethicality places a critical constraint on the quality of decision making. We focus on one consequence of bounded ethicality, the limitation in recognizing the ethical challenge inherent in a situation or decision, such as a conflict of interest. Specifically, we argue that individuals view themselves as moral, competent, and deserving, and this view obstructs their ability to see and recognize conflicts of interest when they occur. Thus, ethicality is not bounded in unpredictable or nonsystematic ways but in systematic ways that unconsciously favor this particular vision of the self in our judgments. The self is an important construct in our argument, and we do not challenge the individual's capacity to recognize conflicts of interest in the abstract, or in the situations facing others, but rather in the situations involving the self.

We argue that conflicts of interests are even more prevalent than the "visible" conflicts traditionally assumed by that term. For example, visible conflicts of interest include the firm that collects both auditing and consulting revenues from the same client, as well as the investment bank that seeks investment banking business from the same companies rated by the firm's equity analyst. In contrast to these visible conflicts of interest, "invisible" conflicts of interests are rarely viewed as conflicts at all. Rather, these situations are opportunities, and even obligations, to demonstrate loyalty and generosity for one's nation, or team, or ethnic group. We argue that these opportunities are, in fact, potential conflicts of interest, and even more so when practiced by members of majority groups because of the large numbers of people within those groups who benefit.

THREE CRITICAL INSIGHTS OF THE PAST CENTURY

Simon offered bounded rationality as a "behavioral model (in which) human rationality is very limited, very much bounded by the situation and by human computational powers" (1983, p. 34; see also Simon, 1957). Fundamentally, Simon challenged economists' assumption of humans as rational creatures. Boundedness has since come to represent the distinction between economists' normative and psychologists' descriptive views of human decision making. Thaler (1996), for instance, extended Simon's thinking in describing the three ways in which "Homo Economicus" and "Homo Psychologicus" vary. People are "dumber, nicer, and weaker" than classical economic theory predicts (pp. 227, 230); that is, human beings have bounded rationality, self-interest, and willpower.

Building on Simon's work, Daniel Kahneman and Amos Tversky delineated the systematic patterns in which human beings demonstrate boundedness. From the 1970s to the present, the field of behavioral decision research has identified the systematic ways in which decision makers deviate from optimality or rationality in the use of information (Kahneman & Tverksy, 1973, 1979). This field has allowed researchers to predict, a priori, how people will make decisions that are inconsistent, inefficient, and based on normatively irrelevant information. The central argument of much of this literature is that people rely on simplifying strategies, or cognitive heuristics (Bazerman, 2002). Although heuristics are useful shortcuts, they also lead to predictable mistakes (Tversky & Kahneman, 1974). It is the systematic and predictable nature of these biases, and what they reveal about the human mind, that makes them so intriguing to researchers.

The roots of these traditions stretch back to cognitive psychology and basic visual and perceptual processes. Daniel Kahneman's acceptance speech for the Nobel Prize in Economics began, notably, with demonstrations of the primal limitations of our visual perception of lines and colors, followed by an extension of this limitation to more abstract forms of decision making (2002). Boundedness begins in perception and extends to cognition. Together, then, the insights of the bounded rationality and heuristics literatures have firmly established the universal computational limitations of the human mind.

In recent years, another important psychological insight has emerged, inviting us to consider boundedness from an even broader point of view. That is, we have seen rapid accumulation of evidence both for the limitations of the conscious mind and the power of the unconscious mind. The weight of this insight is demonstrated in the most recent *Handbook of Social Psychology*, which included a first-ever chapter about control and automaticity in social life (Bargh & Wegner, 1999). The limitations of the conscious mind are highlighted in Wegner's (2002) analysis of the role of consciousness in human thinking and action. He dramatically demonstrates "the illusion of conscious will" in which human beings not only claim responsibility but also intention for actions over which they had exactly no control. In a variety of tasks and contexts, humans tend to attribute their own behavior to premeditated intention, rather than to unconscious processes. Conscious will is consistently given more credit than is due, despite robust evidence about its limitations.

In parallel, the power of the unconscious mind in everyday life has become evident. In a growing, multimethod body of research, automaticity has been found to play some role in virtually every cognitive process studied, and its inevitability has been cleverly termed the "unbearable automaticity of being" (Bargh & Chartrand, 1999). The study of unconsciousness has been made possible by the growing commitment to the use and development of indirect measures (Greenwald & Banaji, 1995). Methodologically, unconscious processes present a challenge to observe directly, necessitating that researchers measure outcomes of those processes that are not directly accessible. Response latency is one of the most commonly used metrics in these methods,[1] relying on the relationship between speed of response and strength of unconscious cognitive associations, and can be measured through millisecond-level response times thanks to computer-based tasks. Another important metric is ease of recall, which relies on the relationship between the accessibility of a thought and the strength of an unconscious cognitive association, and can be measured by observing how a participant completes a word when only

---

[1] These have included, although not been limited to, the lexical decision task (LDT; e.g., Macrae, Bodenhausen, Milne, and Jetten, 1994), the sequential priming task (e.g., Fazio et al., 1995), word completions following unobtrusive priming (e.g., Gilbert & Hixon, 1991), and the Implicit Association Test (IAT; Greenwald, McGhee, and Schwartz, 1998).

a few letters are shown. Furthermore, by exposing participants to particular stimuli subliminally (known as priming), researchers can compare response times or ease of recall under different conditions, such as stereotypical primes versus counterstereotypical primes.

From these methods, data have emerged and converged that allows researchers to contrast implicit thinking with explicit thinking. Explicit processes are those of which the decision maker is aware and can consciously endorse. Implicit processes are those of which the decision maker is unaware, which are automatic, and which are not necessarily under the control of the decision maker. There is growing evidence that both types of mental processes have an impact on behavior, and growing evidence that we overstate the link between the conscious system and behavior, and understate the link between the unconscious system and behavior (Bargh, 1997; Chugh, 2004). It is with this insight that we return to where we began, for a fresh look at bounded rationality.

THE CASE FOR BOUNDED ETHICALITY

We begin with the well-established knowledge that boundedness and heuristics offer computational speed, critical to the survival of human beings with less than infinite time for decision making (Bazerman, 2002; Dawes, 1988). This "cognitive" perspective reflects humans' imperfections as statisticians and scientists (Dunning, 1999). In what has been presented as an opposing perspective by some (Dunning, 1999), the "motivational" perspective suggests that individuals' perceptions, judgments, and behaviors are biased toward the goal of maintaining self-worth, not just toward the more neutral goals of speed and efficiency. However, we see the two perspectives as complementary, not opposing, in the study of decision making (see Kunda, 1990). The particular decisions we discuss here, ethical decisions, bring social forces, and thus motivational forces, to bear on decision making.

So, we accept this motivational perspective as highly relevant to the domain of ethical decision making and will argue that motivational and social forces are a less studied but important cause of boundedness. But our attention to the motivational perspective should not be interpreted as an abandonment of the cognitive, computational perspective. In fact, we believe both computational limitations and motivation toward self-worth are at work in the domain of ethical decision making, consistent with the thread connecting perceptual, cognitive, and social bounds on decision making. Ethical decisions almost always involve consequences for self and/or others, and it is this social component that brings forth a surge of self-oriented motivations in ethical decision making. Bounded ethicality represents that subset of bounded rationality situations in which the self is central and, therefore, motivation is most likely to play a prominent role.

This particular feature of bounded ethicality brings us back to the roles of consciousness and automaticity in decision making. In the bounded rationality and heuristics literatures, which emerged from the cognitive perspective, the researchers' assumptions about the limitations of consciousness and the power of the unconscious are neither articulated nor disputed. In the motivational perspective, the drive toward maintaining self-worth is assumed to be unconscious. So, although the existence of unconscious processes may have been assumed by researchers, we attempt here to make such an assumption explicit, specific, and plausible. In fact, much insight into the nature and source of boundedness, and its role in ethical decision making, can be achieved by making consciousness and automaticity a focal point of our argument.

The use of bounded rationality to address a particular type of ethical decision making originated with Banaji and Bhaskar (2000). Arguing against the view that stereotyping is correct and rational, they linked the limitations of human cognition to memory and implicit stereotypes, demonstrating that such limitations lead to ethical failures. These ethical failures "reveal how the interaction of specific social experiences and a boundedly rational cognitive architecture jointly shape thought and behavior" (Banaji & Bhaskar, 2000, p. 154). Our notion of bounded ethicality emerges from this perspective, and importantly, picks up on the importance of implicit mental processes.

Specifically, social and ethical situations are particularly likely to trigger bounds on conscious thinking and biases in unconscious thinking, allowing us to more fully describe the richness of Simon's original insight about boundedness and subsequent insight about conflicts of interest. In the remainder of this chapter, we propose that bounded ethicality is a critical constraint on the quality of ethical decision making. We propose that ethicality is bounded in systematic ways that unconsciously favor a particular vision of the self in our judgments. Just as the heuristics and biases tradition took bounded rationality and specified a set of systematic, cognitive deviations from full rationality, we endeavor to take bounded ethicality and specify systematic, motivational deviations from full ethicality. Similarly to the bounded rationality tradition, bounded ethicality is characterized by computational speed that eases decision making complexity, but in addition, motivational forces are at work as well.

In the bounded ethicality model, the self processes work, unconsciously, to protect a particular view and this view bounds ethical decision making. Ethical decisions are biased by a stubborn view of oneself as moral, competent, and deserving, and thus, not susceptible to conflicts of interest. To the self, a view of morality ensures that the decision maker resists temptations for unfair gain; a view of competence ensures that the decision maker qualifies for the role at hand; and, a view of deservingness ensures that one's advantages arise from one's merits. An ethical blind spot emerges as decision makers view themselves as moral, competent, and deserving, and thus assume that conflicts of interest are nonissues. Thus, conflicts, particularly the Simon-esque variety mentioned at the start of this chapter, are unlikely to even be recognized as conflicts by the person at risk. The view of self that is preserved through bounded ethicality represents, in fact, exactly those qualities that one would require in order to be immune from conflicts of interest. In addition, it is this view of the self that prevents the decision maker from even recognizing the ethical situation in which he finds himself. And yet, ironically, a decision maker is made more susceptible to conflicts of interest because of the persistence of his or her self-image.

Furthermore, the evidence suggests that we are both particularly unaware of data that contradict this view of ourselves, and worse yet, particularly unaware of that unawareness. This unawareness is fundamental to the notion of the "totalitarian ego" (Greenwald, 1980). The ego (loosely equivalent to our use of "self" in this chapter) is an organization of knowledge, whereas the totalitarian ego displays three biases that correspond to the thought control and propaganda devices of a totalitarian political system. In a totalitarian political system, "it is necessary to remember that events happened in the desired manner ... and if it is necessary to rearrange one's memories or to tamper with written records, then it is necessary to forget that one has done so" (Orwell, 1949, p. 176). Similarly, the ego actively tampers and rearranges self-knowledge so as to ensure that a certain view is maintained, but retains no conscious belief that such tampering has taken place (Greenwald, 1980). Individuals are unaware of their unawareness. The limitations of the conscious mind are thus critical to the success of the totalitarian ego. Memory itself is distorted toward recollection of events "relevant to me" versus "not relevant to me," as well as a positive construal of those events.

The "egocentric ethics" (Epley & Caruso, 2004) of the totalitarian ego, combined with the power of the unconscious mind, make conflicts of interest difficult to recognize. In the following section, we consider the susceptibility of individuals to conflicts of interest because of the persistent views of self as moral, competent, and deserving.

SELF AS MORAL

People believe that they are more honest, trustworthy, ethical, and fair than others (Baumhart, 1968; Tenbrunsel, 1998; Messick & Bazerman, 1996). We give ourselves more credit for our good behaviors and take less responsibility for our moral lapses than others would be likely to do (Messick & Bazerman, 1996). We are motivated to see ourselves as ethical, and rate ourselves as more ethical than the average person (Tenbrunsel, 1998). When we engage in ethically questionable behavior, we often justify it as self-defense (Shapiro, 1991).

However, research suggests that humans continue to maintain an "illusion of objectivity" (Armor, 1998). Across a series of five studies, participants consistently rated their own objectivity higher than that of their average peer. In fact, approximately 85 percent of the participants believed themselves to be more objective than their average peer. Given the statistical improbability of 85 percent of participants being above their group's average, the illusion of objectivity is evident. And, participants were not simply seeing themselves as relatively less subjective than their peers. Participants' ratings of their own objectivity reflected a belief that they are not only viewing themselves as more objective relative to others, but also as objective in the absolute. These data suggest that at least some percentage of human beings must be perceiving the world less accurately than they believe they are. Yet, the illusion is also persistent, as participants retained their belief in their own objectivity even when made aware of the phenomenon taking place.

In one study, researchers explored the vulnerability of one's own objectivity by studying how perceptions of the world depend fundamentally on how the perception favors or disfavors the self (Kronzon & Darley, 1999). Participants observed an ethically questionable act of deception in a videotaped negotiation. Participants who were randomly allied with the victim of the ethically questionable behavior perceived the act as more reprehensible than did either partisans randomly allied with the perpetrator or neutral observers. Despite the influence that the situation has on perceptions, research suggests that people underestimate differences in construal, and thus are overconfident in the objectivity of their predictions of the behavior of both themselves and others (Griffin et al., 1990). This bias exaggerates a conflict of interest as the decision maker retains an unrealistic confidence in his or her perception of data about the situation.

In another study, researchers explored the conditions under which such unrealistically positive beliefs are maintained or loosened (Wade-Benzoni, Thompson, & Bazerman, 2003). Self-assessment of environmental sensitivity was found to depend on how much ambiguity surrounds the self-assessment. Specifically, individuals maintain unrealistically positive beliefs about their degree of environmental sensitivity when their self-evaluation is difficult to disconfirm, but possess more realistic assessments of themselves when they are constrained by the objectivity of the evaluation (consistent with earlier work, for example, Allison, Messick, & Goethals, 1989; Kunda, 1990).

For example, assessments of general beliefs such as one's awareness of, concern for, understanding of, and interest in environmental issues and problems are difficult to confirm or disconfirm. In contrast, assessments of how well one performs on specific activities such as recycling, donating money to environmental organizations, and using energy-saving lightbulbs can be checked against objective measures. If individuals define their environmental sensitivity in terms of general (not easily confirmable) behaviors instead of specific (objectively measurable) behaviors, their self-evaluations are likely to be inflated. Again, human beings maintain the illusion of objectivity, thus putting them at risk for not recognizing a conflict of interest when it presents itself.

Overall, this pattern of self-enhancement may provide people with an easy way out of engaging in more responsible societal behaviors. Thus, when the auditor hears of the Moore et al.'s (2003) concern that their audit might be biased in ways that they are not even aware, the auditor feels that his or her objectivity will make her immune from the problems. Babcock and Loewenstein (1997) demonstrated that even individuals' interpretations of these self-serving biases are self-serving. Study participants were taught about these biases, and the participants demonstrated a clear understanding of the bias by shifting their expectations of others' objectivity. Yet, the participants maintained a commitment to their own lack of bias, even while adjusting their expectations of the objectivity of others.

The bias toward believing that we are more objective than reality dictates leads us to the conclusion that our objectivity will keep conflicts of interests from influencing our judgment. In fact, in 2000, this is exactly the argument that Joseph Berardino, the CEO of Arthur Andersen, made while testifying before the SEC Commission. He argued that the professionalism and objectivity of professional auditors solved the issue of auditor independence. The SEC commissioners appeared to be influenced by this argument, despite its inconsistency with psychological research. The self-as-objective argument carried the day, the SEC failed to act sufficiently, and the lack of auditor independence contributed to many corporate failures. Professionals commonly sell their professionalism as immunity against being affected by conflict of interest. We believe that professionalism provides only partial immunity against intentional corruption, and little immunity from the unconscious processes that lead decision makers to succumb to conflicts of interest.

We also extend our idea of appropriate ethical behavior to others. Negotiators' expectations that their opponents will deceive them may be influenced by their own tendency to deceive. Tenbrunsel (1998) varied the amount of money participants could win for negotiating successfully. Participants who could win $100 expected significantly more deception from their opponents and were significantly more likely to deceive than those who could only win $1. However, participants' expectations of their opponents' deception depended both on their own level of temptation and the level of temptation of their opponents.

Individuals' perceptions of a situation can vary dramatically, even when given identical information, depending on their roles. This difference occurs because individuals begin with their preference for a particular outcome, as motivated by self-interests, and then justify this view on the basis of fairness through a biased perspective on what attributes constitute fairness (Messick & Sentis, 1983). The ethical failure is not in the commitment to fairness but in the biased interpretation of information (Diekmann et al., 1997; Messick & Sentis, 1983).

These limitations of the conscious mind are described by Jon Haidt (2001) as the "emotional dog and rational tail," in which "moral judgment is caused by quick moral intuitions, and is followed (when needed) by slow, ex-post facto moral reasoning." The moral reasoning essentially occurs after the fact. This sequence suggests that "automatic egocentrism" precedes an evaluative moral judgment (Epley & Caruso, 2004).

And, so, in such a tail-wagging-the-dog scenario, the view of oneself as moral is, at best, irrelevant (because morality occurs after the fact), and at worst, a psychological liability (because morality is rigged in our favor). The belief that the self is moral leads us to believe that conflicts of interests will not distort our judgment, thus bounding our ability to recognize the conflict when it occurs.

SELF AS COMPETENT

People perceive themselves as being better than others on a variety of desirable attributes (Messick, Bloom, Boldizer, & Samuelson, 1985), causing them to have unrealistically positive self-evaluations across a wide range of social contexts. Broadly, people have been found to perceive themselves as being superior to others across traits such as cooperativeness, decision making, negotiating, rationality, driving skill, health, and intelligence (Babcock and Loewenstein, 1997; Kramer, 1994).

Such inflated views are not based on abstract self-flattery. In fact, people tend to define concrete "performance standards" in ways that systematically favor their own unique set of attributes (Dunning, 1999). For example, Wade-Benzoni et al. (2003) found that people weight the environmental behaviors that they score high on to be more important than other environmental behaviors. In addition, a strong correlation exists between how subjects rate their actions regarding the environment and their judgments of the importance of that action to society. Positive illusions seem to enable people to believe that they are doing well relative to others on important activities, although they may admit to doing less well on activities they consider to be less important. These biases may cause individuals to think that their positive contributions to environmental issues are more important than the contributions of others. For example, an individual who puts effort into recycling, but refuses to take public transportation, may justify this decision by convincing him- or herself that recycling is the most important way of addressing the environmental crisis. Because individuals have the liberty to judge what they already do (which may be what is most convenient for them) as more important than behaviors that may call for inconvenient lifestyle changes, they are able to maintain positive views of themselves with minimal lifestyle adjustment.

By tilting performance assessments in favor of one's own competence, individuals who are paid to make sound decisions are unlikely to doubt their own competence in doing so. In many contexts, in fact, ethics and competence are intertwined. The auditing executive who believes herself to be honest may also make the claim that her competence allows for the assurance of appropriate behavior. The physician known for astute clinical decision making and deep commitment to patient well-being is likely to resist the notion that a pharmaceutical-funded trip to Hawaii might influence his clinical decision making. In a conflict of interest, competence is often viewed as sufficient for avoiding suboptimal decision making.

But, Taylor (1989) provides significant evidence that most people view themselves to be more competent than reality can sustain. In some cases, the positive illusion may have benefits, as Taylor and Brown (1988) argue that positive illusions about oneself enhance and protect self-esteem, increase personal contentment, help persistence in difficult tasks, and facilitate coping with uncontrollable events. Taylor (1989) also argues that positive illusions are beneficial to physical and mental health.

However, such positive illusions also put the self at risk in ethical decision-making contexts. The ability to maintain unrealistically positive beliefs about oneself may be constrained to some degree by the objectivity of these beliefs, their credibility, and the potential to disconfirm them (Allison, Messick, & Goethals, 1989). Thus, people can more easily maintain the view that they are more honest than others than maintain the belief that they are better tennis players or wittier cocktail party conversationalists. We rarely get accurate feedback on our comparative level of honesty. Allison et al. (1989) reason that it is harder to have optimistic illusions when they are inconsistent with easily available, objective data. In the same way, it may be easier for people to maintain the belief that they are fairer than other negotiators than to believe that they are more skillful at reaching profitable agreements.

Thus, although Taylor may be correct about certain advantages that positive illusions provide to the bearer of those illusions, such self-deception also can have less positive consequences. We argue that an additional harm that is created is that these illusions allow the illusion holder to act in his or her own self-interest, and against professional and normative demands. If our vision of self as competent is not always right, and if competence is intended to overcome conflicts of interest, then decision makers face a serious ethical challenge.

SELF AS DESERVING

In allocating resources, there exists a "tension between self-interest and the equality norm" (Diekmann et al., 1997). Allocators of resources and recipients of resources make sharply different fairness evaluations based on their role. Invariably, collaborators such as coauthors (Taylor, 1989), spouses (Ross & Sicoly, 1979), and *joint* Nobel Prize winners (Harris, 1946) who are asked to quantify their contribution to a joint effort generate a sum greater than 100 percent (Taylor, 1989).

This tendency extends from the self to one's ingroup. In the now-classic "they saw a game" study, Hastorf and Cantril (1954) showed student football fans from Princeton and Dartmouth a film of a football game between the two schools. Both sets of fans watched an identical film and, yet, both sets of fans rated the rival's team as playing less fairly and with less sportsmanship. Assessments of which team was deserving clearly varied by in-group.

This tendency is not limited to football fans. World leaders show the same bias, as in a failed Cold War arms race negotiation in which both leaders blamed the rigidity of the other side (Sutton & Kramer, 1990). President Reagan told reporters, "We came to Iceland to advance the cause of peace and although we put on the table the most far-reaching arms control proposal in history, the General Secretary rejected it." Speaking about the same negotiation, General Secretary Gorbachev stated: "I proposed an urgent meeting here because we had something to propose . . . the Americans came to this meeting empty handed." Kramer (1994) finds evidence in these leaders' memoirs that these perspectives are more than political rhetoric, but reflect the leaders' unconscious commitments to a particular view of self.

Diekmann et al. (1997) examined how the feeling of deservingness affects judgment in a simulation containing many characteristics of real-life conflicts of interest. MBA students were asked to allocate resources across two divisions of a company, and then assess the fairness of the allocation. "Advantaged" allocation recipients assessed these allocations as more appropriate than similar allocations that favored their rivals. In fact, advantaged allocation recipients made such assessments even when the imbalance in their own favor exceeded their own original assessment of an appropriate distribution. They relied on the fact that another decision maker had made the allocation to justify the favorable inequality. Finally, egocentrism in assessing fairness was greater when the information about the deservingness of various recipients was vague, leaving room for interpretations favoring the self. This study suggests that decision makers who rely on their own assessments of who is or is not deserving are at great risk of falling prey to a conflict of interest without realizing it.

DISTINGUISHING VISIBLE AND INVISIBLE CONFLICTS OF INTEREST

So far, we have argued that psychological barriers can prevent decision makers from recognizing conflicts of interest. First, individuals view themselves as more powerful than the situation (moral, competent), and then they view any gains incurred as appropriate (competent, deserving). The drive to maintain the view of oneself as moral, competent, and deserving is a barrier to recognizing otherwise visible conflicts of interest.

Visible conflicts of interest are those traditionally thought of by laypeople, economists, and regulators. In this view, the conflict is clearly in view (e.g., the auditor is charged with delivering a fair, potentially negative audit of the client, and simultaneously depends on the client for future earnings) and the decision maker explicitly vows to remain unbiased by the conflict. Evidence suggests that this vow ignores our basic understanding of how the human mind works, as we overestimate the influence of our own intention and we underestimate the influence of the psychological forces outside of our consciousness. This first type of conflict of interest – the visible, yet dismissed, conflict of interest – is the type referred to in the types of disclosures required by many organizations (e.g., disclosing a financial interest in a client).

A second kind of conflict of interest, less commonly described, is the invisible kind. These more insidious, inadvertent, and self-supporting biases are still considered to be nonobvious and therefore unchecked. The human tendency to favor the self and ingroup creates a gravitational pull toward one set of interests, even when that pull is quite invisible, even to the self. For example, the conflict for an employer is his unconscious tendency to prefer a particular race or gender, yet his fiduciary commitment to shareholders to hire the best talent and his moral commitment to be egalitarian. This invisible conflict of interest is even more pervasive than the visible variety. Here, the conflict of interest is invisible, and therefore, dismissed.

As an example, consider the role of a scholar to be a fair and objective assessor of ideas. In citing work, the scholar's obligation is to cite colleagues who have contributed to the current state of the understanding, rather than to favor oneself or one's group. Tony Greenwald and Eric Schuh (1994) studied the citation tendencies of social scientists, finding that "author's [ethnic] name category [Jewish or non-Jewish] was associated with 41 percent greater odds of citing an author from the same name category" (p. 623). This pattern even held up when the data set was limited to prejudice researchers. Presumably, these authors did not set out to exclude work by outgroup authors but, in essence, they did.

The insidious power of the self is evident in data captured on-line using the Implicit Association Test (IAT; Greenwald, McGhee, & Schwarz, 1998). A diverse 2.5 million tests have been taken through a publicly accessible Web site (http://implicit.harvard.edu) in which participants are asked to make split-second categorization decisions of words and pictures. The task is presented in two versions, one in which the categories are paired together in an attitudinally "compatible" way (flower and pleasant, insect and unpleasant) as contrasted with the "incompatible" version (flower and unpleasant, insect and pleasant). The difference in the participant's speed in making decisions under the two conditions reflects the individual's implicit bias (in this case, in favor of either flowers or insects). More socially and self-relevant versions of the test have examined implicit identity, using pairings such as "male and me" and "female and me" (Nosek, Banaji, & Greenwald, 2002). The results of test-takers' implicit identity tests are correlated with their results on other tests, such as implicit attitudes toward math. Implicit identity is shown to correlate highly with individuals' implicit attitudes toward math, and implicit gender stereotypes about math. That is, test-takers with a strongly masculine implicit identity were more likely to show implicit gender stereotypes associating men (not women) with math, despite the fact that self-reported, conscious attitudes toward gender and math did not reveal such patterns (Nosek, Banaji, & Greenwald, 2002).

A similar pattern was found in a study of implicit racial attitudes and identity. There, two findings are relevant. First, test-takers' group membership (in a race) is related to test-takers' attitudes toward race, particularly for majority group (white) test-takers, most of whom show a bias favoring whites. Second, the test-taker's degree of implicit race identity (black or white) was correlated with the individual's implicit attitudes toward blacks and whites, and implicit attitudes toward self (Greenwald, Banaji, Rudman, Farnham, Nosek, & Mellott, 2002). The centrality of self and group membership is evident, then, especially at the unconscious level, where implicit biases toward oneself are related to other attitudes. Again, this preference for self has important implications for conflicts of interest as decision makers are prone to invisible conflicts of interest in which their bias for themselves and their own group may distort their ethical decision making.

The impact of group membership also applies to individuals in a particular professional role, individuals affiliated with a particular side of an issue, or individuals advocating for a particular group. As we cited at the start of our chapter, Simon (1983) noted that "if we become involved in a particular type of activity, we will surely assign it a greater importance and value than we would have prior to our involvement with it" (p. 95). Moore et al. (2003) provide evidence that those in the auditing function are at risk when making related financial assessments. This tendency toward biased information processing prevails even when people on different sides of an issue are exposed to the exact same information (Babcock et al., 1997). Although many argue that professional auditors are less subject to these biases, research has found professionals to be vulnerable to the same motivated biases as are other people (Buchman, Tetlock, & Reed, 1996; Cuccia, Hackenbrack, & Nelson, 1995; Moore et al., 2003). When an auditor takes a partisan perspective, he is unlikely to objectively assess the data, and is likely to see ambiguous data consistent with the preferences of his client (Babcock et al., 1997; Messick & Sentis, 1979).

The invisible conflict of interest not only is hard to see but also deceptively easy to dismiss. In many instances, people are socially rewarded for explicit favoring of the ingroup, such as the support of sports teams (Banaji & Greenwald, 1995) or the willingness to do favors for similar others (Banaji, Bazerman, & Chugh, 2003). Human tendency toward such partisanship is strikingly powerful. The tendency to "take sides for no reason," or "implicit partisanship" (Greenwald, Pickrell, & Farnham, 2002) means that humans are always vulnerable to invisible conflicts of interest, even when performing altruistic acts.

Some organizations impose nepotism restrictions (e.g., immediate family members cannot work in the same division or the same company), to prevent conflicting family and organizational interests. Although most conflicts of interest commentaries have been role specific, the logic in this chapter also applies to situations in which individuals are claiming goods for their own group, selecting people for jobs, admitting students into school, and so on. Conflict of interest is a critical barrier to fairness in society.

Our claim that invisible conflicts of interest pervade every decision that involves our selves both buttresses and challenges the distributive justice notions of political philosopher John Rawls (1971). Rawls proposed that if an individual wore a "veil of ignorance" that cloaked his or her identity from himself or herself, the individual would make decisions as if to maximize the welfare of the worst-off member of society. This prediction represents the theoretical reverse of our empirical claim that individuals' decision making is always influenced by the interests of the self. In this sense, we are making a claim about invisible conflicts of interest that is consistent with the essence of Rawls' view of the importance of imposing a neutral stance. However, Rawls positioned the veil of ignorance as a thought experiment, or theoretical condition, and, in fact, the experimental evidence we have presented about the inescapability of the self suggests that the veil is only a theoretical, not actionable, construct. We ourselves have used the veil of ignorance as a powerful pedagogical tool (Banaji, Bazerman, & Chugh, 2003), but are less optimistic about the ability of individuals to truly don the veil. Psychologically, the veil of ignorance is inconsistent with our notions of human bounded ethicality.

Nonetheless, this is not to say that individuals from both advantaged and disadvantaged groups are equally susceptible to these invisible conflicts of interest. System Justification Theory (Jost & Banaji, 1994) demonstrates ways in which members of a lower-status group may support, rather than resist, the status quo. In these cases, the tendency to favor one's own group may be less likely. That said, if the tendency of the individual is to be implicitly partisan toward members of other groups, the risk of a conflict of interest still remains, but in an ironically non-self-supportive way. In our thinking about bounded ethicality, this scenario still represents a conflict of interest (or perhaps, it is better described as a "conflict of noninterest").

CONCLUSION

We have proposed that perceptual, cognitive, and social cognitive processes are bounded in similar, systematic ways that lead to gaps in observation and errors in decision making. Despite this robust evidence about boundedness, humans tend to view their own ethicality as unbounded. In fact, decision makers are psychologically motivated to maintain a stable view of a self that is moral, competent, and deserving, and thus, immune from ethical challenges. Because individuals view their immunity as more powerful than the situation (moral, competent) and view any gains incurred as appropriate (competent, deserving), this view is a barrier to recognizing and addressing conflicts of interest. So, ironically, decision makers' persistent view of their own ethicality leads to subethical decisions.

Although we have limited our application of the bounded ethicality concept to conflicts of interest in this chapter, the concept can be applied to a broad set of ethical decisions. Instances of power and corruption can be explained by the phenomenon as well, as when Bargh and Alvarez (2001) consider the roles of both conscious and nonconscious causes of power abuse. In the related domain of sexual harassment, one researcher has found that three out of four harassers "simply don't understand that they are harassers" (Fitzgerald, 1993, p. 22). Bounded ethicality limits the decision maker's capacity to recognize a wide range of morally problematic issues.

As such, decision makers are shown to be neither ethical, nor randomly unethical, nor fully aware of their unethicality. In distinctly different ways, three critical twentieth-century insights point to the surprising limitations of the conscious mind and the surprising reach of the unconscious mind.

In fact, consciousness may play a secondary role in determining judgments and decisions, whereas much of thought, feeling and motivation may operate in unconscious mode. Such pervasive operation of implicit or unconscious modes of thinking can compromise reaching intended ethical goals.

Our conception of conflicts of interest as instances of bounded ethicality implies that, unfortunately, many of the oft-discussed solutions are inadequate in the face of the robust psychological barriers to recognizing conflicts where they appear. Disclosure of interests addresses only visible conflicts and, even there, the conflict is not removed. Selecting better people is also unlikely to help, as the bias toward a particular view of self is not known to be easily pinpointed. Conventional approaches toward teaching ethics, borne of philosophical traditions, also are unhelpful, constrained by normative views of the ethicality rather than the more descriptive, psychologically based understanding of how the mind works.[2]

Although the focus of our chapter has not been prescriptive, we offer that preventive measures represent one important path for redress. The best way to remove the tendency to favor oneself and one's in-group in a decision is to remove oneself from the conflict, whether it be visible or invisible. Although such prevention may sometimes be impractical, we offer that the greater, immediate barrier to prevention is the illusion of objectivity that makes prevention seem unnecessary, rather than the practical difficulties of implementing the solution. Before solutions can truly be crafted, the need for a solution must be recognized. Our argument in this chapter is that this recognition is unlikely to occur, and poses a threat to ethical decision making in the face of conflicts of interest.

Although human bounded ethicality is not an issue of honesty, it has implications for the trustworthiness of our decision making. Simon (1983), we argue, was right in the quotation that opened this chapter: "Most of the bias that arises . . . cannot be described correctly as rooted in dishonesty – which perhaps makes it more insidious than if it were" (p. 96). Conflicts of interest sometimes pit one's honesty against one's corrupt intentions. However, we have argued that honesty is not the critical bound on ethical decisions, such as those posed by conflicts of interest. Rather, decisions where the self is central are highly prone to self-serving biases that obstruct the recognition of imminent ethical risks. Motivated psychological processes put the decision making of even "honest creatures" at risk.

---

[2] The philosophical tradition has begun, in some instances, to integrate the science of the mind. Owen Flanagan, for example, argues for "psychological realism" in ethics, which would constrain moral theories by what is psychologically possible.

References

Allison, S. T., Messick, D. M., and Goethals, G. R. (1989). On being better but not smarter than others: The Mohammad Ali effect. *Social Cognition*, 7, 275–296.

Armor, D. A. (1998). The illusion of objectivity: A bias in the perception of freedom from bias. (Dissertation abstract)

Babcock, L., Loewenstein, G., and Issacharoff, S. (1997). Creating convergence: Debiasing biased litigants. *Law and Social Inquiry-Journal of the American Bar Foundation*, 22(4), 913–925.

Babcock, L., and Loewenstein, G. (1997). Explaining bargaining impasse: The role of self-serving biases. *Journal of Economic Perspectives*, 11, 109–126.

Banaji, M. R., and Greenwald, A. G. (1995). Implicit gender stereotyping in judgments of fame. *Journal of Personality and Social Psychology*, 68(2), 181–198.

Banaji, M. R., and Bhaskar, R. (2000). Implicit stereotypes and memory: The bounded rationality of social beliefs. In Schacter and Scarry (Eds.), *Memory, Brain, and Belief* (pp. 139–175). Cambridge, MA: Harvard University Press.

Banaji, M. R., Bazerman, M. H., and Chugh, D. (2003). How (un) ethical are you? *Harvard Business Review*, 81(12), 56–64.

Bargh, J. A. (1997). The automaticity of everyday life. In R. S. Wyer, Jr. (Ed.), *The automaticity of everyday life: Advances in social cognition* (Vol. 10, pp. 1–61). Mahwah, NJ: Erlbaum.

Bargh, J. A., and Alvarez, J. (2001). The road to hell: Good intentions in the face of nonconscious tendencies to misuse power. In J. A. Bargh and A. Y. Lee-Chai (Eds.), *The use and abuse of power: Multiple perspectives on the causes of corruption* (pp. 41–55). New York: Psychology Press.

Bargh, J., and Chatrand, T. (1999). The unbearable atomaticity of being. *American Psychologist*, 54(7), 462–79.

Bargh, J. A., and Wegner, D. (1999). Control and automaticity in social life. In D. T. Gilbert, S. T. Fiske, and G. Lindzey (Eds.), *Handbook of social psychology* (pp. 445–496). New York: Oxford University Press.

Baumhart, R. (1968). *An honest profit: What businessmen say about ethics in business*. New York: Holt, Rinehart, and Winston.

Bazerman, M. H. (2002). *Judgment in managerial decision making* (5th ed.). New York: John Wiley and Sons.

Buchman, T. A., Tetlock, P. E., and Reed, R. O. (1996). Accountability and auditors' judgment about contingent events. *Journal of Business Finance and Accounting*, 23, 379–398.

Chugh, D. (2004). Why milliseconds matter: Societal and managerial implications of implicit social cognition. *Social Justice Research* 17(2).

Cuccia, A. D., Hackenbrack, K., and Nelson, M. W. (1995). The ability of professional standards to mitigate aggressive reporting. *Accounting Review*, 70(2), 227–248.

Dawes, R. M. (1988). Rational choice in an uncertain world. Chicago: Harcourt Brace Jovanovich.

Diekmann, K. A., Samuels, S. M., Ross, L., and Bazerman, M. H. (1997). Self-interest and fairness in problems of resource allocation. *Journal of Personality and Social Psychology*, 72, 1061–1074.

Dunning, D., Meyerowitz, J. A., and Holzberg, A. D. (2002). Ambiguity and self-evaluation: the role of idiosyncratic trait definitions in self-serving assessments of ability. In T. Gilovich, D. Griffin, and D. Kahneman (Eds.), *Heuristics and biases*. Cambridge: Cambridge University Press.

Dunning, D. (1999). A newer look: Motivated social cognition and the schematic representation of social concepts. *Psychological Inquiry*, 10, 1–11.

Epley, N., and Caruso, E. M. (2004). Egocentric ethics. *Social Justice Research* 17(2).

Fazio, R. H., Jackson, J. R., Dunton, B. C., and Williams, C. J. (1995). Variability in automatic activation as an unobtrusive measure of racial attitudes: A bona fide pipeline? *Journal of Personality and Social Psychology*, 69, 1013–1027.

Fitzgerald, L. F. (1993). Violence against women in the workplace. *American Psychologist*, 48(10), 1070–1076.

Flanagan, O. (1993). *Varieties of moral personality: Ethics and psychological realism*. Cambridge, MA: Harvard University Press.

Gilbert, D. T., and Hixon, J. G. (1991). The trouble of thinking: Activation and application of stereotypic beliefs. *Journal of Personality and Social Psychology*, 60, 509–517.

Greenwald, A. G. (1980). The totalitarian ego: Fabrication and revision of personal history. *American Psychologist*, 35, 603–618.

Greenwald, A. G., and Banaji, M. R. (1995). Implicit social cognition: Attitudes, self-esteem, and stereotypes. *Psychological Review*, 102, 4–27.

Greenwald, A. G., and Schuh, E. S. (1994). An ethnic bias is scientific citations. *European Journal of Social Psychology*, 24(6), 623–639.

Greenwald, A. G., Banaji, M. R., Rudman, L. A., Farnham, S. D., Nosek, B. A., and Mellott, D. S. (2002). A unified theory of implicit attitudes, stereotypes, self-esteem, and self-concept. *Psychological Review*, 109(1), 3–25.

Greenwald A. G., McGhee D. E., and Schwartz, J. L. K. (1998). Measuring individual differences in implicit cognition: The implicit association test. *Journal of Personality and Social Psychology*, 74(6), 1464–1480.

Greenwald, A. G., Pickrell, J. E., and Farnham, S. D. (2002). Implicit partisanship: Taking sides for no reason. *Journal of Personality and Social Psychology*, 83(2), 367–379.

Griffin, D. W., Dunning D., and Ross L. (1990). The role of construal processes in overconfident predictions about the self and others. *Journal of Personality and Social Psychology*, 59, 1128–1139.

Haidt, J. (2001). The emotional dog and its rational tail: A social intuitionist approach to moral judgment. *Psychological Review*, 108(4), 814–834.

Harris, S. (1946). *Banting's miracle: The story of the discovery of insulin*. Toronto: J.M. Dent and Sons.

Hastorf, A. H., and Cantril, H. (1954). They saw a game: A case study. *Journal of Abnormal and Social Psychology*, 49, 129–134.

Jost, J. T., and Banaji, M. R. (1994). The role of stereotyping in system-justification and the production of false consciousness. *British Journal of Social Psychology*, 33, 1–27.

Kahneman, D. (2002). *Acceptance speech for the Nobel Prize.* Retrieved June 1, 2003 from Nobel e-Museum Web site: http://www.nobel.se/economics/laureates/2002/.

Kahneman, D., and Tverksy, A. (1973). On the psychology of prediction. *Psychological Review*, 80, 237–251.

Kahneman, D., and Tversky, A. (1979). Prospect theory: An analysis of decision under risk. *Econometrica*, 47, 263–291.

Kramer, R. M. (1994). *Self-enhancing cognitions and organizational conflict.* Unpublished manuscript.

Kronzon, S., and Darley, J. (1999). Is this tactic ethical? Biased judgments of ethics in negotiation. *Basic and Applied Social Psychology*, 21(1), 49–60.

Kunda, Z. (1990). The case for motivated reasoning. *Psychological Bulletin*, 108, 408–420.

Lee-Chai, A., and Bargh, J. A. (Eds.). (2001). *The use and abuse of power.* Ann Arbor, MI: Sheldon Press.

Macrae, C. N., Bodenhausen, G. V., Milne, A. B., and Jetten, J. (1994). Out of mind but back in sight: Stereotypes on the rebound. *Journal of Personality and Social Psychology*, 67, 808–817.

March, J. G., and Simon, H. A. (1958). *Organizations.* New York: John Wiley and Sons.

Messick, D. M., and Sentis, K. (1983). Fairness, preference, and fairness biases. In D. M. Messick and K. S. Cook (Eds.), *Equity theory: Psychological and sociological perspectives* (pp. 61–64). New York: Praeger.

Messick, D. M. and Sentis, K. P. (1979). Fairness and preference. *Journal of Experimental Social Psychology*, 15, 418–434.

Messick, D. M., Bloom, S., Boldizer, J. P., and Samuelson, C. D. (1985). Why we are fairer than others. *Journal of Experimental Social Psychology*, 21, 480–500.

Messick, D. M., and Bazerman, M. H. (1996). Ethics for the 21st century: A decision making approach. *Sloan Management Review*, 37, 9–22.

Moore, D. A., Loewenstein, G., Tanlu, L., and Bazerman, M. H. (2003). *Auditor independence, conflict of interest, and the unconscious intrusion of bias.* Harvard Business School Working Paper #03–116.

Nosek, B. A., Banaji, M. R., and Greenwald, A. G. (2002). Harvesting intergroup attitudes and stereotypes from a demonstration website. *Group Dynamics*, 6, 1, 101–115.

Orwell, G. (1949). *1984.* New York: Harcourt, Brace.

Rawls, J. (1971). *A theory of justice.* Cambridge, MA: Harvard University Press.

Ross, M., and Sicoly, F. (1979). Egocentric biases in availability and attribution. *Journal of Personality and Social Psychology*, 37, 322–337.

Shapiro D. L. (1991). The effects of explanation on negative reactions to deceit. *Administrative Science Quarterly*, 36, 614–630.

Simon, H. A. (1957). *Models of man.* New York: Wiley.

Simon, H. A. (1983). *Reason in human affairs.* Stanford: Stanford University Press.

Sutton, R., and Kramer, R. M. (1990). Transforming failure into success. Impression management, the Reagan administration, and the Iceland arms control talks. In R. L. Zahn, and M. N. Zald (Eds.), *Organizations and nation-states: New perspectives on conflict and co-operation* San Francisco: Jossey-Bass.

Taylor, S. E. (1989). *Positive illusions.* New York: Basic Books.

Taylor, S. E., and Brown, J. D. (1988). Illusion and well-being: a social psychological perspective on mental health. *Psychological Bulletin*, 103, 193–210.

Tenbrunsel, A. E. (1998). Misrepresentation and expectations of misrepresentation in an ethical dilemma: The role of incentives and temptation. *Academy of Management Journal*, 41, 330–339.

Tenbrunsel, A. E. Justifying unethical behavior: The role of expectations of others' behavior and uncertainty (Dissertation).

Thaler, R. H. (1996). Doing economics without homo economicus. In Richard H. Thaler (Ed.), *How do economists do economics.* Warren Samuels.

Tversky, A., and Kahneman, D. (1974). Judgment under uncertainty: Heuristics and biases. *Science*, 185, 1124–1131.

Wade-Benzoni, K. A., Thompson, L. L. and Bazerman, M. H. *The malleability of environmentalism.* Unpublished manuscript.

Wegner, D. (2002). *The illusion of conscious will.* Cambridge, MA: MIT Press.

SIX

Commentary

Bounded Ethicality and Conflicts of Interest

Ann E. Tenbrunsel
University of Notre Dame

The focus on psychological processes, and their corresponding influence on unethical behavior, is incredibly important. Chugh, Bazerman, and Banaji intuitively note that these "unchecked processes" – including inflated perceptions of one's morality, competency, and deservingness – act as forces against objective assessments in situations involving conflicts of interest. The end result, they argue, is that individuals may not only be unaware of conflicts of interest but also that they are acting against professional and normative standards when faced with such conflicts.

This chapter is an essential component of a growing body of evidence that recognizes the human tendency to reconstruct ethical dilemmas so as to avoid any tension experienced by the individuals. Individuals, for example, are argued to engage in "ethical fading," a process that removes the difficult moral issues from a given problem or situation, hence increasing unethical behavior (Tenbrunsel & Messick, 2004). From this perspective, such unethical behavior occurs not because people are morally uneducated but, rather, because they do not see the "ethical" in the decision. Self-deception is identified to be at the root of this problem. Such deception involves avoidance of the truth, the lies that we tell to, and the secrets we keep from, ourselves (Bok, 1989). As illustrated later, the self-deception is insidious and therefore problematic:

This practice is common, normal, and accepted as constant and pervasive in individuals' lives. We are creative narrators of stories that tend to allow us to do what we want and that justify what we have done. We believe our stories and thus believe that we are objective about ourselves. (Tenbrunsel & Messick, 2004)

The discussion of the interplay between the conscious and the unconsciousness by Chugh, Bazerman, and Banaji speaks to this issue of self-deception. The descriptions of the psychological barriers to ethicality – including seeing the self as moral, competent, and deserving – are forms of self-deception, the way in which self-deception rears its ugly head. Recognizing these psychological obstacles is an important first step. Understanding how to break down these barriers is an essential next step. Taking that step, however, requires an informed understanding of several issues that were raised in the chapter. In the next section, several of those issues are discussed, including the relationships between inflated self-perceptions of morality, competency, and deservingness; the tension between ambiguity and specificity; and the reasons behind ingroup favoritism. The identification and resolution of these issues speaks to necessary future research, and in turn, to possible mechanisms to break down the psychological processes that are so aptly identified.

THE RELATIONSHIPS BETWEEN PERCEPTIONS OF THE SELF AS MORAL, COMPETENT, AND DESERVING

The discussion of the forms of self-deception – morality, competency, and deservingness – raises several interesting issues. One of those issues involves the relationships between these forms. More specifically, seeing oneself as moral seems to preclude the need to see oneself as competent and deserving. If I see myself as more moral than I should and, at the same time, believe that I am more objective than I really am, then I most likely see my decisions as more moral than they really are. If that is the case, then assessments of my competency and deservingness appear to be irrelevant. At the heart of this argument is the difference between seeing the self as moral versus seeing oneself as competent and deserving. Assessments of morality involve an overarching halo effect that one is an ethical person who makes ethical decisions. Assessments of competency and deservingness are notably different, appearing to come into play to justify why a seemingly unfair or unethical decision was made. If this is true, then assessments of competency and deservingness may only become important when the conception of the self as moral is threatened.

Of course, it is possible that an alternative relationship exists, namely that assessments of competency and deservingness convince oneself that one is ethical, which in turn increases self-assessments of morality. There is no doubt that these forms of self-deception are highly correlated. What is unclear is the interrelationships between them and how they interact to influence conflicts of interest. Investigating these linkages may therefore be worthwhile in understanding their contributions to such conflicts.

Furthermore, it is possible that the different forms of self-deception exist at different levels of consciousness. Although assessments of morality may be at the subconscious level, assessments of competency and deservingness, because they involve more justificatory processes, may exist more at the conscious level. If, for whatever reason, I do not see myself as particularly moral, then I must convince myself that my decisions are justified, and hence ethical. This process of convincing oneself may entail a more conscious calculation of competency and deservingness than that involved in morality. Gaining a better understanding of the extent to which each of these forms are "automatic" is therefore necessary if we are to identify mechanisms that will overcome the resulting self-deception.

THE "AMBIGUITY-SPECIFICITY PARADOX"

The tension between ambiguity and specificity, and their corresponding links to unethical behavior, is played out in the undercurrents of the chapter. Ambiguity is described as giving individuals too much freedom to construct their own "reality," hence contributing to the lack of objectivity highlighted in the chapter. Specificity, however, is viewed as overly restrictive, incorrectly limiting the perspective that individuals consider in identifying conflicts of interests. This inherent tension between ambiguity and specificity, termed the "ambiguity-specificity paradox," has been connected to unethical behavior (Tenbrunsel, 2000).

On the one hand, Chugh et al. portray ambiguity as a villain, associated with decreased objectivity and increased unethicality. In the definition of conflicts of interest, for example, the "Simon-esque" version, which identifies such conflicts as those in which personal interests interfere with organizations, is argued to be too vague. Such ambiguity, Chugh et al. argue, reduces the likelihood that a conflict of interest is recognized. Ambiguity is seen as equally troubling in self-assessments. In assessments of behavior, the more general the assessment, the less likely objectivity is to occur. Inflated self-perceptions are more prevalent, for instance, if one focuses on global beliefs or actions that do not have a clear benchmark (such as describing one's interest in environmental activities or one's honesty) rather than focusing on more specific actions and measurable attributes (amount of time recycling or one's success as a tennis player). Similarly, egocentric interpretations of fairness are exacerbated when there is uncertainty in the deservingness of the other party. Chugh et al. stand on firm ground in noting the connection between ambiguity and undesirable behaviors. Uncertainty has been linked to both opportunistic behavior (Fandt & Ferris, 1990) and, more central to this chapter, to unethical behavior and to expectations of others' behavior (Tenbrunsel, 1995).

Specificity, on the other hand, does not appear to be the solution. Adhering to a specific definition of conflict of interest is argued by Chugh et al. to send the message that conflicts of interest not covered by the definition are unimportant. Defining conflicts of interest as those that involve an existence of a significant financial interest for the individual, for example, is highlighted as too specific, ignoring other relevant dimensions of such conflicts. Furthermore, asking individuals to assess specific behaviors may not always increase self-objectivity. Wade-Benzoni, Thompson, and Bazerman (2004) found, for example, that the context of the rating mattered, such that self-ratings of environmental behavior were higher in assessments which involved denying harm to the environment than in assessments which focused on claiming to help the environment. This was true even though these assessments included very specific behaviors such as "neglecting to turn off the lights when you leave a room" (denying harm context) versus "turning off the lights when you leave a room" (helping the environment). The implications of this finding for situations involving conflicts of interest are potentially troubling. In self-assessments of very specific behaviors, people may believe erroneously that they do not deny harm to others when in fact they do.

Thus, it appears that although ambiguity may perpetuate inflated beliefs of oneself, specificity is not a quick fix. Although identifying the problem is useful, needed is insight into how to address this apparent dichotomy. The conclusion of this chapter provides some ideas on where we might get this insight.

FAVORING ONE'S INGROUP: THE ROLE OF NORMATIVE CONSTRAINTS

Associated with conflicts of interest is the tendency for one to favor one's in-group at the expense of one's out-group. Chugh et al. argue that subconscious processes are at work here as well, producing inflated perceptions of one's ingroup which in turn play a major role in the ensuing prejudicial process. Work on the role of relationships in matching markets suggests another factor – normative obligations – that may also contribute to such favoritism (Tenbrunsel, Wade-Benzoni, Moag, & Bazerman, 1999). In this research, relationships were found to impede market efficiency and individual profitability of high-powered players. In markets in which individuals were allowed to match (or form partnerships) with friends, market optimality and the individual profitability of high-powered players was lower than markets in which individuals were informed that they were not allowed to match with their friends. Although economic theory would argue that the imposition of a constraint (i.e., do not match with friends) reduces market efficiency, these results demonstrate the opposite. The explanation for these results was that, although a structural constraint was imposed, such an imposition actually removed a stronger psychological constraint, a normative constraint that individuals had to match with their friends, even when they did not want to or believe that they should.

Extending this research to the notion of ingroup favoritism suggests that in addition to enhanced perceptions of enhanced morality, competency, and deservingness, I may favor my ingroup because of a societal constraint, one that obligates me to favor them and perhaps even profess inflated perceptions. Even if I know that I should not favor my ingroup and really do not want to, I may feel that I have no choice. As discussed later, if this is the case, then structural constraints may provide some relief from the rampant ingroup favoritism that exists.

MITIGATING SELF-DECEPTION

The investigation of psychological processes and their relationship to conflicts of interest and unethical behavior is important but depressing for it reveals innate barriers that seem impermeable. Chugh, Bazerman, and Banaji recognize the difficulty in overcoming these psychological obstacles, identifying a single solution: "The best way to remove the tendency to favor oneself and one's in-group in a decision is to remove oneself from the decision." This certainly makes sense in situations in which removing oneself from the situation is possible, but what if extracting oneself is not an option? What do we do then?

Although there are no immediate answers, the issues that are raised in the chapter point to at least some possibilities where we might find solutions. One avenue is in the resolution of the ambiguity-specificity paradox. The resolution of this apparent dichotomy seems important if we are to construct mechanisms to overcome the psychological processes that encourage unethical behavior. What we really want to understand is how to reap the creative benefits of ambiguity and the directive benefits of specificity when doing away with their noted disadvantages.

On the surface, one obvious solution for reducing the negative impact of uncertainty on self-assessments is to be more specific about expected behaviors. One might, for example, set more specific goals about what one is expected to do or "should" do in situations involving conflicts of interest (Tenbrunsel, 2000). Other research, however, suggests that this may be equally problematic. In an examination of such standards in an environmental context, for example, it was found that setting a specific environmental standard distorted judgment and resulted in suboptimal decisions (Tenbrunsel, Wade-Benzoni, Messick, & Bazerman, 2000). Specific goals, although useful in directing attention toward the goal, also have been found to direct attention away from other more equally important objectives (Ilgen & Moore, 1987; Latham & Yukl, 1975; Shalley, 1991).

Thus, simply changing the degree of ambiguity or specificity inherent in the situational context may not be the answer. However, investigating how it is that people process multiple objectives, including ones that are in conflict, may be. If we can understand how individuals' process simultaneous objectives, for example, then perhaps we can understand how to manage goals that are naturally ambiguous (be ethical) with more specific directives (make money). A comparison of European organizations with U.S. organizations may provide some useful insight. European organizations are noted for their focus on a "triple bottom line," consisting of people, profit, and planet (Elkington, 2001). Organizations in the United States, in contrast, are well-known for their focus on a single bottom line: profit. An examination of how it is that European organizations are able to simultaneously process multiple objectives that often conflict may offer insights into how to address the ambiguity-specificity paradox. In turn, this knowledge will be useful in constructing policies, codes of conduct, and even the self-directed questions that we ask ourselves to justify our behavior.

The chapter provides a second possibility for mitigating some of the damaging effects of self-deception. One of the noted problems is that individuals "rarely get accurate feedback," perpetuating the cycle of such deception. Accurate feedback may prevent or at least slow down this process. In thinking about the role of feedback, it is important to note that different types of feedback can elicit different responses. It has been found that both the valence (positive or negative) and the type (ethicality versus ability) of feedback impact the response to that feedback

(Kim, Diekmann, & Tenbrunsel, 2003). For example, feedback that one is unethical (negative ethicality) leads one to become more ethical in future interactions whereas feedback that one is ethical (positive ethicality) has no noticeable impact on ethicality but does increase cooperative behavior; furthermore, feedback that one is incompetent (negative ability) increases competitive behavior and produces suboptimal outcomes. As this pattern of results illustrates, whether or not ethicality feedback impacts ethical behavior depends on the valence of that feedback. It is therefore important to make sure that a recommendation that encourages feedbacks incorporates the complex relationship between feedback type and valence. What is encouraging is that feedback does impact behavior, particularly ethical behavior, and therefore it may be an important mechanism in reducing the deleterious effects of self-enhanced perceptions.

At the group level, the effects of inflated perceptions are multiplied when they translate into group enhancement. Such enhancements may be cognitively driven, as noted by Chugh et al., but also may be driven by a sense of normative obligation (Tenbrunsel et al., 1999), an obligation that makes me feel as if I should favor my ingroup members above everyone. Increasing turnover within teams, such as those found in the accounting-client relationships, may reduce the strength of this obligation, both because it decreases the intensity of the ties that are formed and because it broadens the set of actors to which individuals feel obligated. Enlarging the pool of actors may have another positive effect – reducing the self-inflated assessments of one's ingroup members – which also should reduce ingroup favoritism.

The identification by Chugh, Bazerman, and Banaji of the psychological tendencies that allow unethical behavior to continue, unnoticed by the perpetrator, is an important first step in addressing conflicts of interests. If we do not acknowledge these tendencies, then structural solutions do not stand a chance. It is only in acknowledging these psychological processes that we can identify "smart" solutions that take the innate nature of humans into account.

References

Bok, S. (1989). *Secrets*. New York: Vintage Books.
Elkington, J. (2001). *The chrysalis economy*. Oxford: Capstone Press.
Fandt, P. M., & Ferris, G. R. (1990). The management of information and impressions: When employees behavior opportunistically. *Organizational Behavior and Human Decision Processes*, 45, 140–158.

Ilgen, D. R., & Moore, C. F. (1987). Types and choice of performance feedback. *Journal of Applied Psychology*, 72, 401–406.

Kim, P. H., Diekmann, K. A., & Tenbrunsel, A. E. (2003). Flattery may get you somewhere: The strategic implications of providing positive vs. negative feedback about ability vs. ethicality in negotiation. *Organizational Behavior and Human Decision Processes*, 90, 225–243.

Latham, G. P., & Yukl, G. A. (1975). A review of research on the application of goal setting in organizations. *Academy of Management Journal*, 18, 824–845.

Shalley, C. E. (1991). Effects of productivity goals, creativity goals, and personal discretion on individual creativity. *Journal of Applied Psychology*, 76, 179–185.

Tenbrunsel, A. E. (1995). Justifying unethical behavior: The role of expectations of others' behavior and uncertainty. Unpublished doctoral dissertation, Northwestern University, Evanston, IL.

Tenbrunsel, A. E. (2000). A behavioral perspective on codes of conduct: The ambiguity-specificity paradox. In O. F. Williams (Ed.), *Global Codes of Conduct*. Notre Dame, IN: University of Notre Dame Press.

Tenbrunsel, A. E. & Messick, D. M. Tenbrunsel (2004). Ethical fading: The role of self-deception in unethical behavior. *Social Justice Research*, 17, 223–236.

Tenbrunsel, A. E., Wade-Benzoni, K. A., Messick, D. M., & Bazerman, M. H. (2000). Understanding the influence of environmental standards on judgments and choices. *Academy of Management Journal*, 43, 854–866.

Tenbrunsel, A. E., Wade-Benzoni, K. A., Moag, J., & Bazerman, M. H. (1999). The negotiation matching process: Relationships and partner selection. *Organizational Behavior and Human Decision Processes*, 80, 252–283.

Wade-Benzoni, K. A., Thompson, L., & Bazerman, M. H. (2004). The malleability of environmentalism. Working paper. Duke University.

SEVEN

Coming Clean but Playing Dirtier

The Shortcomings of Disclosure as a Solution to Conflicts of Interest

Daylian M. Cain, George Loewenstein,
and Don A. Moore*

Carnegie Mellon University

ABSTRACT

Although disclosure is ubiquitous as a response to conflicts of interest, we suggest that it can have perverse effects. We show that disclosure can fail both because (1) although it may encourage the audience to discount advice, disclosed as problematic such discounting tends to be insufficient, and (2) it can lead advisors to give even more biased advice than they otherwise would. As a result, when an advisor's conflict of interest is disclosed, recipients of advice may be left worse off and providers of advice better off. We review existing psychological evidence that hints at the possibility that disclosure could be ineffective or even backfire, and then describe our own research which actually documents such perverse effects. We conclude that successful responses to conflicts of interest require more robust interventions than merely disclosing the conflicts.

It has become a truism on Wall Street that conflicts of interest are unavoidable. In fact, most of them only seem so, because avoiding them makes it harder to get rich. That's why full disclosure is suddenly so popular: it requires no substantive change.... Transparency is well and good, but accuracy and objectivity are even better. Wall Street doesn't have to keep confessing its sins. It just has to stop committing them.

– James Surowiecki (2002)

* The authors would like to thank Robyn Dawes, Colin Camerer, Mark Fichman, Christina Bicchieri, Rick Green, Jernej Barbic, Dale Miller, Kent Womack, and Mark Nelson for their insightful comments. We also would like to thank the Carnegie Bosch Institute and the National Science Foundation for generous funding.

Imagine that you want to purchase stock in a new company, but you are not sure how much to buy. Your stockbroker advises that you should put as much as you can afford into the stock, as it is almost sure to increase in value. The broker, who is honest, then reminds you that she gets paid based on your stockmarket activity. How should the disclosure of her conflict of interest influence your stock purchase? Could the disclosure itself have affected the advice she gave you?

There are many economic and social situations in which people must rely on advice from experts whose interests may not be perfectly aligned with their own. For example, an auto mechanic may recommend costly repairs; a physician may recommend expensive tests or procedures; a realtor may warn that a particular property is in great demand. This sort of advice ought to be taken with some skepticism because, although it may be informative and may be given in good faith, it also may be unintentionally biased or intentionally corrupt.

In situations like this, common sense suggests that we would make better use of the advice if we knew the incentives and motivations of the person giving it. Revealing the advisor's motivations, including their conflicts of interest, puts the advice giver and the advice receiver on a more level playing field with respect to information. This is the basic idea behind disclosure: Disclosure of one's conflicts of interest should allow the audience to discount the advice to the extent that it seems contaminated.

We question, however, whether disclosure can realistically be expected to solve the problems created by conflicts of interest. We begin by mentioning a few examples of the many situations in which forced disclosure has been implemented. We then consider disclosure's efficacy by reviewing evidence on how disclosure is thought to operate and by comparing this with empirical evidence. Our conclusion is that disclosure cannot generally be assumed to be an effective solution for the problems created by conflicts of interest; it may even make matters worse.

CONFLICTS OF INTEREST

As this volume attests, conflicts of interest are common among professionals in fields as diverse as medicine, real estate, investment banking, law, and accounting. Each one of these professions has struggled to balance its members' interest in self-enrichment with a responsibility to serve their clients and customers. Often, these conflicts of interests have been regulated by the industry's own norms and standards, but occasionally the conflicts of interest have produced problems so costly that lawmakers or governmental regulators have seen fit to intercede. Although there has always been uncertainty about the most effective policies for dealing with the problems created by conflicts of interest, often the first – or only – solution implemented involves disclosure. Here, we will consider a few of the more spectacular market failures brought about by conflicts of interest and how disclosure was implemented in each situation.

In 2001, the Enron Corporation was forced to declare bankruptcy after it revealed that its public financial reports had overstated profits by hundreds of millions of dollars – errors that Enron's auditor, Arthur Andersen, had failed to correct or expose. Although it was then the largest bankruptcy in U.S. history, the events at Enron were followed in quick succession by scandals at Adelphia, AOL Time Warner, Bristol-Myers Squibb, Global Crossing, Halliburton, Mirant Energy, Qwest, Rocky Mountain Electric, Tyco, Xerox, Shell Oil, and the even larger bankruptcy of WorldCom. Although the specifics of each of these scandals differed, there is at least one common element: In each case, the company's auditors were subject to conflicts of interest (Nelson, this volume). Perhaps the most significant source of such conflicts was a new practice: that accounting firms provide both auditing and consulting services to the same firm. By 2000, consulting revenues dwarfed those from auditing at many accounting firms.

In 2000, the U.S. Securities and Exchange Commission (SEC) was concerned enough about these actual and perceived conflicts of interest that it implemented a series of new rules and regulations. Predictably, these gave a prominent role to disclosure. Audit firms were required to reveal how much they were paid by the client firm and what services were provided in return. And the Sarbanes-Oxley Act of 2002, which was written in response to the accounting scandals, dedicates an entire section (Title IV) to increased disclosure requirements of various types.

Long before the ink had dried on these new laws and regulations, investment banks' stock analysts began to come under scrutiny for their own conflicts of interest. Many banks were simultaneously soliciting business from corporate clients and recommending their stocks to the investing public. Analysts such as Solomon Smith Barney's Jack Grubman found themselves under pressure to recommend losing stocks to their firms' customers so as to secure more business from client firms. Enron itself paid $323 million to investment banks in underwriting fees between 1986 and 2001 (Vickers et al., 2003). Many analysts continued recommending Enron stock even as its value plummeted: eleven out of sixteen analysts who followed Enron labeled it "Buy" or "Strong Buy" less than a month before Enron's bankruptcy filing (Vickers et al., 2002). In fact, across all stocks, analysts' "Buy" recommendations outnumbered "Sell" recommendations by about six to one in the early 1990s and, by the end of the decade, the ratio had soared to fifty to one (Michaely & Womack, 1999). What has the response been to these scandals? There have been a limited number of lawsuits and financial settlements, but the major policy response has been, again, disclosure. Major media sources of financial information, including CNBC and CNNfn, now require all stock analysts to disclose any conflicts of interest that they have when offering televised advice on stocks.

Medical doctors face a number of different conflicts of interest, but the issue that has received the most recent attention has to do with gifts and sponsorship from pharmaceutical companies (Choudhry, Stelfox, & Detsky, 2002; Dana & Loewenstein, 2003; Tenery, 2000). Whereas responses to these potential conflicts of interest are a matter of hot debate within the medical community (Kassirer, this volume), one measure that most medical societies have been able to agree on is disclosure: physicians should disclose their sources of funding when publishing research results or presenting them at conferences (although, one survey reported that less than 1 percent of conflicts are disclosed for scientific articles, including those in medicine; see Krimsky & Rothenberg, 2001).

Why is disclosure seemingly such an attractive policy? Part of the reason is that firms and individuals facing conflicts of interest often view it as the lesser of evils: they would rather have to tell about their conflicts of interest than have to get rid of them through divestiture or recusal. Although different types of policies are possible in different domains, disclosure tends to be the least intrusive possible policy in almost any domain. For example, the most obvious solution to the problems caused by gifts from pharmaceutical companies to physicians would be to bar such payoffs, but physicians are understandably reluctant to let go of the gravy-train. Disclosing gifts is a much less threatening policy. Likewise, the practice of accounting firms to offer auditing and consulting services to the same client creates obvious conflicts of interest which can only be truly eliminated by separating these lucrative services. Congress eventually barred accounting firms from providing auditing and consulting services to the same client, but only after a prolonged fight with regulators during which accounting firms insisted that disclosure would be adequate to solve the problem. Disclosure also has become an increasingly popular response to the growing number of conflicts of interest that have arisen as industry-academia connections proliferate (see, for example, American Association of Universities, 2001).

Disclosure, it seems, promises something for everyone. To professions facing conflicts of interest, disclosure promises minimal disruption from the status quo; it does not require professionals to sever financial relationships or change how they get paid. To regulators and policy makers, disclosure absolves them of some of their responsibility to limit market exploitation by transferring to advice receivers the responsibility of looking out for themselves. And to advice receivers, disclosure promises to give them the tools they need to look out for their own interests.

Those who support disclosure argue that it will contribute to market efficiency and to welfare by reducing information gaps between the informed and the uninformed (Gunderson, 1997). For example, Healy and Palepu (2000) write, "regulators may be concerned about the welfare of financially unsophisticated investors. By creating minimum disclosure requirements, regulators reduce the information gap between informed and uninformed."[1] When those receiving advice are aware of the advice giver's conflicts of interest, the argument goes, they have the knowledge they need to discount that advice appropriately and make better judgments themselves. Although this argument has numerous proponents and some intuitive appeal, we are suspicious of disclosure's promised benefits. We suspect, based on the existing psychological literature and our own recent research, that the benefits of disclosure may have been overstated, both through overestimation of its effects on advice receivers and underestimation of its effects on advice givers.

DISCLOSURE'S EFFECT ON ADVICE RECEIVED

For those receiving advice (we call them "estimators" in our studies), several different lines of reasoning suggest that people will have difficulty properly adjusting their beliefs based on knowledge of a conflict of interest. Such difficulties include: (1) difficulty of judgmental correction, (2) failure of evidentiary discreditation, and (3) lay dispositionism and the representativeness heuristic.

---

[1] Analytical research on disclosure is discussed by Verrecchia (2001) and Dye (2001). Empirical research on disclosure is discussed by Healy and Palepu (2000). Much of this research, however, discusses financial disclosures of many sorts, not merely disclosures of conflicts of interest.

First, regarding judgmental correction, the ability to undo a biasing in-fluence on one's own judgment depends on a number of preconditions that are rarely met (Mussweiler, Strack, & Pfeiffer, 2000; Strack & Mussweiler, 2001): (1) one must be motivated to make correct judgments, (2) one must be aware of the potentially distorting influence, and (3) one must be aware of the direction *and* magnitude of this influence. The third precondition for accurate judgmental correction is often the most difficult to meet, as the magnitude of biasing influence is often difficult to estimate. Given that even a researcher in the appropriate field would be hard-pressed to come up with a numerical prediction of the magnitude of bias in any par-ticular case, it seems unlikely that the average person would estimate the magnitude of bias with any precision. We would predict, then, that there tends to be more variability in the judgments of those who know about a conflict of interest. This is because although it may be apparent that the advice is biased and should be discounted, there remains a great deal of uncertainty about exactly how much it should be discounted. This uncer-tainty contributes variability to estimators' judgments which can by itself, in some cases, outweigh other benefits of disclosure (Cain, Loewenstein, & Moore, forthcoming).

The failure of judgmental correction in response to disclosure also can result from a process called "anchoring and insufficient adjustment" (Strack & Mussweiler, 1997; Tversky & Kahneman, 1974). Research on judgment suggests that the starting point in a judgmental process often holds undue sway over the eventual judgment, even when the anchors are known to be utterly irrelevant. For example, consider the following questions: What are the last three digits of your phone number? Now add four hundred to that number and think of the resulting sum as a year date. Now, consider whether Attila the Hun was defeated in Europe before or after that date. Finally, in what year would you guess that Attila the Hun was actually defeated?

The correct answer is 451 A.D. Russo and Shoemaker (1989, p. 90) found that responses to the above questions were strongly influenced by the "dates" computed from the respondents' telephone numbers – dates that were obviously irrelevant. The problem is that many valuations are not retrieved from memory directly, but instead are constructed *online*, in response to a query (Chapman & Johnson, 1999; Payne, Bettman & Johnson, 1992). Thus, uninformative starting points that are present at the time of questioning can powerfully influence valuations. Some have argued that biases in human judgment that are so powerful in the ex-perimental laboratory, are weaker in more information-rich naturalistic settings (Gigerenzer, 1991; Hogarth, 1981). Not so for the anchoring effect, which is extremely robust and affects both novice and expert alike (Northcraft & Neale, 1987), even when explicitly motivated to avoid these biases (Wilson, Houston, Etling, & Brekke, 1996).

Much of the previous research on anchoring dealt with numerical anchors shown to be completely irrelevant to the evaluation at hand. This arrangement makes any assimilation toward the anchor easy to identify as a bias. For example, most anchoring studies begin with a difficult question and then offer a possible answer (the anchor). This "advice" usually comes with a disclosure that says, in effect, "This number was randomly generated, so ignore it completely" (see Strack & Mussweiler, 1997; Tversky & Kahneman, 1974). We, by contrast, ask how judgments are influenced by biased anchors that are not completely *irrelevant* to the task at hand, but may nonetheless be *misleading*. Advocates of disclosure might suggest that disclosures of conflict of interest will alert the audience more than the discounting cues commonly used in the anchoring paradigm. After all, it makes sense that one might be more attuned to guard against manipulative influence than against randomly generated anchors; and most people will report that randomly generated anchors do not influence their judgment. By contrast, if we discover that someone is trying to manipulate us, we are more likely to be on our guard.

Contrary to this argument, however, Galinsky and Mussweiler (2001) have shown that even when anchors come from a source whose manipulative intent is common knowledge, they can still be influential. They found that first offers were powerful anchors that influenced final outcomes in negotiation. They manipulated who made the first offer and found that when buyers made the first offer, final sale prices were lower than when sellers made the first offer. Chapman and Bornstein (1996) also show assimilation to a manipulative anchor in a mock jury trial. The plaintiff requested an award for damages that was experimentally manipulated from $100 to $1 billion. The authors found that requests were strongly correlated with awards. Hastie, Schkade, and Payne (1999) conducted a similar study in which the plaintiff asserted that an award either "in the range from $15 million to $50 million" or "in the range from $50 million to $150 million" would be appropriate. The median awards were $15 million and $50 million respectively. This shows the power of the plaintiff's anchor, despite the judge's instructed that "The attorneys' recommendations are *not* evidence." In actual courtrooms, Ebbesen and Konecni (1975) found that criminal court judges set defendants' bail nearest the prosecuting attorney's recommendation, which happened to be the first formal proposal the judges heard. Finally, Northcraft and Neale (1987) found that manipulating the actual listing price of a piece of real estate had a consistent and large effect on professional real estate agents' appraisals, despite the fact that such appraisals are supposed to be based on more objective criteria, such as location, size, condition of property, and inputs on recent sale prices of comparable homes.

We conducted a study that examined the effect of disclosures of manipulative intent on anchoring (Cain, Loewenstein, & Moore, 2004). We began with the standard anchoring paradigm: 112 students answered a series of questions on such topics as the population of the United States. By answering more accurately, participants increased their chances of winning one of three $100 prizes. First, participants were provided with an anchor value that was either 50 percent higher (a U.S. population of 422 million people) or 50 percent lower (141 million people) than the true value (281 million people) and asked whether they believed the true value was above or below this anchor. Crossed with this anchoring manipulation was a manipulation of disclosing the putative source of the anchor value. Before they answered the questions, participants received one of four such disclosures: high, low, random, or boilerplate. Participants who received the high disclosure were warned, "When you answer, remember that the suggested answers were provided by someone who was trying to get you to give an answer that was artificially high." Those who received the low disclosure were likewise warned that the suggested answers came from someone who was trying to get them to answer low. The random disclosure, like previous anchoring studies, told participants that suggestions had been randomly generated. The boilerplate disclosure was designed to mimic the sorts of vague disclosures commonly used in industry, and warned participants, "When you answer, remember that the suggested answers were provided by someone who may have been trying to get you to answer one way or another."[2] The results showed a powerful effect of the anchoring manipulation. Participants' overall test scores were driven largely by the anchor suggested to them: Across all disclosures, the mean test z-score (.3453) of answers that were preceded by a

---

[2] Charles Schwab & Co., for example, has used the following boilerplate disclosure on its legal documents to cover every potential eventuality: "Schwab and/or its employees or directors as well as consultants to Schwab may have or may have had clients with positions in securities or companies referenced in Information, including Research Reports, and may, as principal or agent, buy from or sell to customers. From time to time, Schwab may perform investment banking or other services for, or solicit such services from, companies mentioned in Information."

high anchor was significantly higher than the mean test z-score (−.3520) of answers preceded by a low anchor. The disclosures had no significant main or interaction effect on participants' responses.

A second and related reason to expect that biased advice will nevertheless influence judgment has to do with the so-called failure of evidentiary discreditation: People sometimes have trouble "unlearning" false or misleading information, even when instructions are provided that should discredit that information (Tversky & Kahneman, 1974; Valins, 1966). Not only do people continue to be influenced by information that has been discredited, but also belief in information previously known to be false may actually increase over time (Pratkanis, Greenwald, Leippe, & Baumgardner, 1988). This "sleeper effect" occurs in situations in which memory of the information itself is more durable than the memory of the discounting cue or information source. When some fact is remembered but the unreliability of its source is forgotten, the fact is likely to gain in perceived veracity with time. This is somewhat similar to what happens when one forgets that a favorite story was a scene in a movie and is instead remembered as having been seen in real life. Thus, even a disclosure that discredits some information source as unreliable may lose its efficacy over time such that the source is forgotten but the message remains.

Along these lines, Allport and Lepkin (1945) asked why false wartime rumors were so often believed. Their study found that one of the most important predictors of belief in rumors was simply the number of times that the rumor had been heard, independent of the rumor's truth. Skurnik and his colleagues (Skurnik, Moskowitz, & Johnson, 2002; Skurnik, Park, & Schwarz, 2002) have likewise revealed that mere exposure leads to belief and that belief is bolstered by repetition. One reason for this effect appears to be that people use recognition as a heuristic for determining veracity, as if they assume that more familiar facts are also more likely to be true. However, when it happens that falsehoods are more familiar because they have been repeated more often, they also are more likely to be mistaken to be true (Skurnik, Moskowitz & Johnson, 2002). A second reason for this effect may have to do with a cause of the anchoring effect, namely, selective accessibility (Mussweiler & Strack, 1999; Strack & Mussweiler, 1997). When people consider a fact or an anchor, the general tendency towards positive hypothesis testing (Klayman & Ha, 1987) leads them to consider (however briefly) the hypothesis that the fact is true or that the anchor is the correct value. Consideration of this hypothesis tends to automatically activate knowledge consistent with it; this knowledge is then selectively accessible in memory, leading to subsequent judgments that are more consistent with the fact or anchor than they would have been otherwise (Loftus, 1979; Mussweiler, 2003). A final reason for the failure of evidentiary discreditation may have to do with the psychology of belief. Gilbert (1991) has argued that understanding and belief come together. After they have understood something, people can assent, reject, or even suspend judgment, but they do this only *after* initially accepting this new knowledge. Because this process of inferential correction requires effort and may be disrupted, there remains a residual tendency to believe information even after it is disclosed to be utterly false (let alone being suspect of bias).

Failure of evidentiary discreditation has been shown in many cases where the information is known to be false or misleading. The "curse of knowledge" (Camerer, Loewenstein, & Weber, 1989; Keysar, Ginzel, & Bazerman, 1995) describes the inability to disregard unhelpful information. In a recent study, Loewenstein, Moore, and Weber (2003) gave participants a puzzle to solve and asked them to predict how long others would take to solve the puzzle. Participants got paid more when they accurately predicted how long others would take. Some participants were given additional information: the solution to the puzzle. Those with the solution predicted that others would solve the puzzles significantly more quickly than the others actually did, and therefore these predictors earned less money than did predictors who were not told the solution. Moreover, because subjects were unaware of the curse of knowledge, many were actually willing to pay to acquire knowledge that made it more difficult to make optimal decisions and had false expectations that informed predictors would perform better. And, even when people are aware of the contaminating effects of misleading information, attempts to suppress thoughts can often result in ironic rebound effects, producing undesired thoughts more often than they would have appeared had there been no suppression attempt (Wegner, 1994); to experience this effect, try as has hard as you can *not* to think of a white bear. Thus, it may be difficult to ignore even what we know to be bad advice.

A third reason why estimators may insufficiently discount advice from biased advisors is highlighted by research on lay dispositionism and the representativeness heuristic: people tend to assume that behavioral outcomes are representative of the dispositions and character of the individuals who commit them, underplaying the role that the *situation* had in determining the behavior. Social psychology has documented people's general tendency to overestimate the correspondence between individual dispositions and behavior (Gilbert & Malone, 1995; Jones & Harris, 1967;

Ross, 1977). This "correspondence bias" leads people to assume that others will behave in ways that are consistent with their "true selves": their personalities, individual values, and personal beliefs. In the words of Ross and Nisbett (1991), we are "inveterate dispositionists," ascribing to dispositions behavior that is better explained by situational influences. This spells trouble for those trying to estimate the influence that a conflict of interest might have on a trusted other person: Estimating the extent to which advice has been biased by an advisor's conflict of interest necessitates estimating the effect of a situational inducement on behavior; and such situational effects generally tend to be underestimated. It does not seem to take much to induce even normally upstanding people to engage in appallingly bad behavior (e.g., Milgram, 1963), thus, it might take surprisingly little incentive to get advisors to skew their advice. It is not that our advisors might be of worse character than we suspect; it is that, in some situations, the average character is capable of surprisingly bad behavior.

In sum, a substantial body of research suggests that it is unlikely that estimators will be able to use disclosures of conflict of interest to correctly discount advice from biased sources, even if those disclosures are honest and thorough. Still, although the evidence discussed here suggests that estimators will not discount *enough*, we would still expect estimators to discount advice *more* when they know of an advisor's conflict of interest than when they do not. In two studies, this is what we find (Cain, Loewenstein, & Moore, forthcoming). Advice from advisors with conflicts of interest is discounted *more* when the conflict of interest is disclosed than when it is not. This increased discounting ought to leave estimators better off – and it might, except for one thing: disclosure's influence on the advice given.

DISCLOSURE DISTORTION: DISCLOSURE'S EFFECT ON ADVICE GIVEN

Advocates of disclosure generally assume that disclosure will either have no effect on the advice given or will improve advice by restricting experts' ability to indulge their own self-interest (Stark, this volume). To the extent that advisors themselves are influenced by disclosure, the anticipation of disclosure is assumed to compel more honesty by increasing the fear that biased advice will be recognized by more vigilant advisees. Much as accountability can reduce bias (Tetlock, 1992), disclosure is assumed to increase perceived scrutiny, thereby increasing the sense that one must be as objective as possible. However, we believe that the above arguments ignore two reasons to expect that disclosure might actually make advice *worse*.

The first is what we call "strategic exaggeration": if advisors fear that disclosure will cause their advice to be discounted (consistent with both naïve theory and empirical evidence), and if they wish to counteract this effect, they may try to compensate by further skewing their advice. This strategic exaggeration is similar to what happens in sales negotiations in which sellers inflate their asking price to compensate for the discounting and counteroffering that they expect to occur once bargaining begins. So, although it is possible that disclosure may increase perceived scrutiny and thereby promote less biased advice, there also is the possibility that strategic exaggeration will exacerbate bias. Although disclosure might warn an audience to cover its ears, it also may encourage advisors to yell even louder.

The second reason to expect disclosure to worsen advice involves what we call "moral licensing." Insofar as disclosure is perceived to level the strategic playing field, it may leave the advisor feeling less compelled to toe the ethical line and look out for the interests of those receiving their advice. Monin and Miller (2001) showed that such self-licensing can increase morally questionable behavior. They asked participants in their experiments whether a male or a female candidate would be most appropriate for a supervisory job at a cement manufacturing firm (a stereotypically male job). Before making this decision, however, some participants were given the opportunity to express their disagreement with blatantly sexist statements. When participants had been given this opportunity to show that they held egalitarian gender attitudes, they were more willing to endorse a man for the job. Having shown that they were not prejudiced people, participants were ironically *more* likely to behave in ways that were consistent with the prejudicial attitudes they had just denied. When participants in this experiment had been given the moral coverage provided by the ability to display nonsexist attitudes, they were subsequently more likely to express sexism.

When people lack the coverage of such a moral license, they are more likely to behave in ways that seek to certify their moral virtue. For example, Dutton and Lake (1973) began with a set of participants who rated themselves low in prejudice. They then showed participants slides of interracial couples and used false biofeedback to manipulate how participants believed they had reacted to seeing the images. Participants who were told that they had reacted negatively to the slides were subsequently more likely to give money when approached by a black panhandler than were participants who had not had their moral credentials likewise threatened. Thus, if disclosure provides some sort of moral license, perhaps a lack of disclosure will encourage advisors to exemplify their moral virtue and eschew the pecuniary benefits had by skewing their advice. And, perhaps disclosure will lead those who mislead their audience to think that such deception is "fair game."

In our research, we have found that advisors give more biased advice after disclosing that they have a conflict of interest. In one experiment (Cain, Loewenstein and Moore, forthcoming), participants were randomly assigned to the roles of advisor and estimator. Estimators were given the goal of accurately guessing how much money was in each of six jars of coins. The more accurate their estimates were, the more estimators were paid. However, estimators only saw each jar briefly and only from a distance. Advisors had much better information about each jar and its value. Some advisors were paid more when their estimators made accurate guesses, but other advisors had a conflict of interest. The latter got paid more when their estimators guessed high relative to the actual value of the jar of coins. This conflict of interest did significantly alter advice, as one might predict. But the more interesting result was that when these advisors knew that their advice would be sent along with a disclosure regarding their own incentives, their advice was higher (more in the direction of their financial incentives) than when there was no such warning.[3]

CONSEQUENCES OF DISCLOSURE

We have presented a number of reasons why we are skeptical of the potential for disclosure to eliminate the problems associated with conflicts of interest. But the question remains whether disclosure might possibly leave estimators better off in some situations. Even if advice gets worse and discounting is insufficient, it is nevertheless possible that the increase in discounting more than offsets the increased bias in advice. In our studies, however, we have not found this to be the case. For example, in our coin-jar study, conflicts of interest left estimators with worse estimates (compared to estimators whose advisors had no conflict of interest), whether advisors' incentives were disclosed or not. Furthermore, those receiving disclosures of conflicts of interest made significantly more error

---

[3] Likewise, in other research (Cain et al., 2004), we replicate the major findings of the coin-jar study using other stimulus materials involving the giving and receiving of advice concerning the market value of local Pittsburgh real estate.

than estimators whose conflicts of interest were not disclosed, whether we assess this error by comparing estimators' expected payoffs across condition, or by comparing estimates to what "accurate" advisors generally thought was in the jars, or by comparing estimates to what each estimator's own advisor thought was in the jars. These results persisted over several rounds that provided both experience and feedback on performance (Cain et al., forthcoming). Disclosure is supposed to warn people about possible bias, bring scrutiny to bear on information, and suggest that one should place less weight on the advice. On all of these points, we have found that disclosure falls short. In fact, when it came to the bottom line (estimator payoffs) in our studies, disclosure made matters worse.

Not all of these results will generalize to other settings. They depend on a number of situational features that are likely to vary, such as the strength of the conflict of interest, the suspiciousness of the estimator, and the nature of the disclosure. It is, of course, possible for disclosure to benefit estimators. From context to context, whether disclosure does more harm than good depends on the balance between the discounting it stimulates compared with the "disclosure distortion" (i.e., the distorting influence disclosure has on advice given) it induces. Rather than show that disclosures always exacerbate the problems created by conflicts of interest, our goal has been to argue that disclosure cannot be assumed to always help.

One of the moderating variables of the impact of biased advice is likely to be the estimator's trust in the advisor. One might think that disclosure of a conflict of interest would decrease trust, but it also is possible that disclosures will increase trust in the person giving the advice, especially if the person with the conflict of interest is the one who "warns" the estimator about it. Consider, for example, the doctor who points out that she is part owner of the clinic to which she refers her patients. Patients might then think (perhaps rightly) that the doctor is going out of her way to be candid when she discloses her conflicts of interest. Insofar as disclosure demonstrates advisor honesty, the disclosure could serve as an assurance of trustworthiness rather than serving as a warning. Such assurance might, then, actually *reduce* scrutiny, opening the estimator to further exploitation; and this might occur even if exploitation is unintentional on the doctor's part. Future research should examine different types of disclosures (such as those offered by the advisor or offered by someone else) and how they affect both attributions about the motivations of the advisor and discounting of the advice.

One additional consideration is how reliance on biased advice might be influenced when that advice is passed along by the original audience to a secondary audience. Unless the disclosure is also repeated to the secondary audience, their ability to discount the advice will be greatly compromised. The mass media's reporting of scientific studies exemplifies this problem: The headlines convey bold claims and expectations, often without clarifying the caveats and careful qualifications made by the original researchers. So, even if the initial qualifications might have led to some discounting of scientific claims, what is passed on may be unqualified claims and headlines. Furthermore, Gilovich (1987) has shown that those who receive advice secondhand come to more extreme conclusions than do their first generation counterparts. As accounts are retold, getting farther from the source, whatever distortions have been introduced become less likely to be corrected.

POTENTIALLY MITIGATING FACTORS

One may object that laboratory experiments have overstated the ability of conflicts of interest to bias advice because of the minimal incentives involved. In market settings, the incentives to offer accurate advice are great: establishing trust, building long-term relationships with clients, maintaining a reputation as an expert advisor, keeping one's job, and even staying out of jail; all might well depend on giving accurate advice. It does seem intuitively plausible that if the stakes are large enough, people will make fewer errors. But there is little supporting evidence for the hypothesis that financial incentives can eliminate either reliance on cognitive heuristics or the biases they produce (Thaler, 1991). Camerer and Hogarth (1999) report that the magnitude of incentives usually has no effect on average performance (though higher incentives can reduce variance) and note that "no replicated study has made rationality violations disappear purely by raising incentives." Certainly, even in the real world, with lots of money at stake, people have been consistently shown to exhibit many of the biases found in the lab (Camerer, 2000).

Even if the magnitude of incentives is a concern, material incentives to distort information are also commensurately greater for actual professionals than they were for any of the participants in the laboratory experiments discussed here. For example, when an increase in the company's stock can mean that the CEO's stock options are worth millions of dollars more, even the most honest executive is likely to see the value in making the firm's performance appear as good as it possibly can. And, as we have argued, the problem has less to do with outright and intentional corruption than with unconscious bias (Bazerman et al., 2002; Dana & Loewenstein, 2003; Gilovich, 1991; Kunda, 1990). Conflicts of interest can sway even the most honest advisors. Humans tend to be very good at justifying why self-serving behavior is fair, and experts can believe that they are giving objective, sound advice even while they are giving advice that aligns more closely with their incentives than with the truth (Messick & Sentis, 1979; Moore, Loewenstein, Tanlu, & Bazerman, 2003).

Feedback might be another factor that would help people learn to deal with the sorts of biases described here. If an audience can be biased by bad advice, repeated experience might alleviate this effect. After all, feedback from past errors could serve to correct future decisions (Hogarth, 1981). But serious doubts have been raised about the efficacy of feedback in correcting decision errors (Brehmer, 1980; Castellan, 1977; Einhorn, 1980; Einhorn & Hogarth, 1978). In our research (Cain et al., forthcoming), we find that bias persists even in the face of several rounds of feedback. Some research has even suggested the distressing possibility that feedback can exacerbate bias in some situations (Abelson & Levi, 1985). And, to the extent that advisors exaggerate their advice strategically, feedback may help them improve the influence of their advice: when estimators become more sophisticated, so might the advisor who wishes to manipulate them.

SUMMARY AND CONCLUSIONS

Those who advocate disclosure have relied on both lay psychological theory and economic models (Crawford & Sobel, 1982), which assume that disclosures allow advice to be appropriately discounted. We have catalogued a body of research that casts doubt onto this assumption. Furthermore, advocates of disclosure do not usually consider the potential influence that the disclosure has on the *transmission* of information. We have found that disclosures can further bias advice. The reader might object that these findings overestimate the effect, thinking that most working professionals are experts in managing conflicts of interest. And professions such as medicine, law, and accounting maintain high ethical standards (including rules on conflict of interest) that ought to alleviate the effects of conflicts of interest. For example, Gary Shamis, a leading figure within the American Institute of Certified Public Accountants, testified before the SEC, "We are professionals that follow our code of ethics and practice by the highest moral standards. We would never be influenced by our own personal financial well-being versus our professional ethics" (SEC, 2000). Similarly, the Code of Ethics of the American Medical Association (2002) states, "Under no circumstances may physicians place their own financial interests above the welfare of their patients." It would be nice to believe that writing down ethical guidelines and relying on the virtue of professionals is enough, but recent business scandals leave us less sanguine. We do not see it as our burden to prove that conflicts of interest are a real and present danger in the professions; we take this as a starting assumption.

It is not that we think that the professions are wildly corrupt. Our own previous work has challenged the assumption that intentional corruption explains the effects of conflicts of interest on advice. Self-interest affects the ways that people search for information, encode that information in memory, and evaluate evidence (Gilovich, 1991; Kunda, 1987, 1990). Self-interest can influence judgment at each stage, and this influence often operates outside of conscious awareness (Moore & Loewenstein, 2004). As Francis Bacon said, "Man prefers to believe what he prefers to be true." But this does not mean that we are unconstrained by objective evidence or the need to construct an argument that might persuade the dispassionate observer. The problem, as Kunda (1990, p. 10) describes it, is that "people do not realize that the [decision] process is biased by their goals, that they are only accessing a subset of their relevant knowledge, that they would probably access different beliefs and [decision] rules in the presence of different goals, and that they might even be capable of justifying opposite conclusions on different occasions." Indeed, even when people try to step out of their partisan roles in order to predict what an unbiased and objective outside party would see as right, their judgments are biased by their own self-interest (Babcock, Loewenstein, Issacharoff, & Camerer, 1995; Moore, Loewenstein, Tanlu, & Bazerman, 2003).

Because they are not aware of the ways in which self-interest biases their judgment, it is difficult for people to undo the influence of their own self-interest. The absence of such awareness can lead even experts to believe that they are being neutral and unbiased, when in fact they are giving advice that is biased and self-serving (Dana & Loewenstein, 2003). As a consequence, trying hard to be good (or wanting to adhere to high ethical principles; see Cain, 2004) may not be enough to achieve ethical behavior or unbiased advice.

Conflicts of interest can create substantial economic and social problems. Conflicts of interest lead to situations in which experts (who have the best information and the most relevant knowledge) have interests that are at odds with those who must rely on their advice. As a result, expert advice can be biased or even intentionally misleading. Those who must rely on the advice are likely to make worse decisions as a result. We argue that it is dangerous to assume that disclosure will be an effective solution to any of these problems.

References

Abelson, R. P., and Levi, A. (1985). Decision making and decision theory. In G. Lindzey and E. Aronson (Eds.), *The handbook of social psychology, 3rd edition, Vol. 1* (pp. 231–310). New York: Random House.

Akerlof, G. (1970). The market for lemons: Qualitative uncertainty and the market mechanism. *Quarterly Journal of Economics*, August, 488–500.

Allport, F. H., and Lepkin, M. (1945). Wartime rumors of waste and special privilege: Why some people believe them. *Journal of Abnormal and Social Psychology*, 40, 3–36.

American Association of Universities. (2001). *Report on individual and institutional financial conflict of interest*. http://www.aau.edu/research/coi.01.pdf.

American Medical Association. (2002, July 22). Code of medical ethics, section E-8.03, Available: http://www.ama-assn.org/ama/pub/category/8469.html

Babcock, L., Loewenstein, G., Issacharoff, S., and Camerer, C. (1995). Biased judgments of fairness in bargaining. *American Economic Review*, 85(5), 1337–1343.

Bazerman, M. H., Loewenstein, G., and Moore, D. A. (2002). Why good accountants do bad audits. *Harvard Business Review*, 80(1), 87–102.

Brehmer, B. (1980). In one word: Not from experience. *Acta Psychologica*, 45, 223–241.

Cain, D. M. (2004). Low quality compliance: Regulating behavior off the books. Unpublished manuscript. Carnegie Mellon University.

Cain, D. M., Loewenstein, G., and Moore, D. A. (forthcoming). The dirt on coming clean: Perverse effects of disclosing conflicts of interest. *Journal of Legal Studies*.

Cain, D. M., Loewenstein, G., and Moore, D. A. (2004). *Honesty and its discontents: Perverse effects of disclosing conflicts of interest*. Unpublished manuscript. Carnegie Mellon University.

Camerer, C. (2000). Prospect theory in the wild. In D. Kahneman and A. Tversky (Eds.), *Choice, values, and frames*, (pp. 288–300). New York: Cambridge University Press.

Camerer, C. and Hogarth, R. M. (1999). The effects of financial incentives in experiments: A review and capital-labor-production framework. *Journal of Risk and Uncertainty*, 19(1), 7–42.

Camerer, C. F., Loewenstein, G., and Weber, M. (1989). The curse of knowledge in economic settings: An experimental analysis. *Journal of Political Economy*, 97(5), 1232–1254.

Castellan, N. J. (1977). Decision making with multiple probabilistic cues. In N. Castellan, J. Pisoni, and M. Potts (Eds.), *Cognitive Theory*, Vol. 2 (pp. 288–300). Hillsdale, NJ: Erlbaum.

Chapman, G. B., and Bornstein, B. H. (1996). The more you ask for the more you get: Anchoring in personal injury verdicts. *Applied Cognitive Psychology*, 10, 519–540.

Chapman, G. B., and Johnson, E. J. (1999). Anchoring, activation, and the construction of values. *Organizational Behavior and Human Decision Processes*, 79, 115–153.

Choudhry, N. K., Stelfox, H. T., and Detsky, A. S. (2002). Relationships between authors of clinical practice guidelines and the pharmaceutical industry. *Journal of the American Medical Association*, 287(5).

Crawford, V. P., and Sobel, J. (1982). Strategic information transmission. *Econometrica*, 50(6), 1431–1451.

Dana, J., and Loewenstein, G. (2003). A social science perspective on gifts to physicians from industry. *Journal of the American Medical Association*, 290(2), 252–255.

Davis, M. (2001). Introduction. In M. Davis and A. Stark (Eds.), *Conflict of interest in the professions*, (pp. 3–19). Oxford: Oxford University Press.

Davis, M., and Stark, A. (2001). *Conflict of interest in the professions*. New York: Oxford University Press.

Dutton, D. G., and Lake, R. A. (1973). Threat of own prejudice and reverse discrimination in interracial situations. *Journal of Personality and Social Psychology*, 28(1), 94–100.

Dye, R. A., (2001). An evaluation of essays on disclosure and the disclosure literature in accounting. *Journal of Accounting and Economics*, (32), 181–235.

Ebbesen, E. B., and Konečni, V. J. (1975). Decision making and information integration in the courts: The setting of bail. *Journal of Personality and Social Psychology*, 32, 805–821.

Einhorn, H. (1980). Learning from experience and suboptimal rules in decision making. In T. S. Wallsten (Ed.), *Cognitive processes in choice and decision behavior*, (pp 1–20). Hillsdale, NJ: Erlbaum Associates.

Einhorn, H. and Hogarth, R. (1978). Confidence in judgment: Persistence of the illusion of validity. *Psychological Review*, 35(5), 395–416.

Galinsky, A. D., and Mussweiler, T. (2001). First offers as anchors: The role of perspective-taking and negotiator focus. *Journal of Personality and Social Psychology*, 81(4), 657–669.

Gigerenzer, G. (1991). How to make cognitive illusions disappear: Beyond Heuristics and biases. In W. Stroebe and M. Hewstone (Eds.), *European review of social psychology, Vol. 2* (pp. 83–115).

Gilbert, D. T. (1991). How mental systems believe. *American Psychologist*, 46(2), 107–119.

Gilbert, D. T., and Malone, P. S. (1995). The correspondence bias. *Psychological Bulletin*, 117(1), 21–38.

Gilovich, T. (1987). Secondhand information and social judgment. *Journal of Experimental Social Psychology*, 23, 59–74.

Gilovich, T. (1991). *How we know what isn't so: The fallibility of human reason in everyday life*. New York: Free Press.

Gunderson, M. (1997). Eliminating conflicts of interest in managed care organizations through disclosure and consent. *Journal of Law, Medicine, and Ethics*, 27, 5–15.

Hastie, R., Schkade, D. A., and Payne, J. W. (1999). Juror judgments in civil cases: Effects of plaintiff's requests and plaintiff's identity on punitive damage awards. *Law and Human Behavior*, 23, 445–470.

Healy, P., and Palepu, K. (2000). Information asymmetry, corporate disclosure, and the capital markets: A review of the empirical disclosure literature. *Proceedings of the JAE Rochester Conference* (http://papers.ssrn.com/sol3/papers.cfm?abstract_id=258514).

Hogarth, R. M. (1981). Beyond discrete biases: Functional and dysfunctional aspects of judgmental heuristics. *Psychological Bulletin*, 90, 197–217.

Jones, E. E., and Harris, V. A. (1967). The attribution of attitudes. *Journal of Experimental Social Psychology*, 3, 1–24.

Kahneman, D., and Tversky, A. (1972). Subjective probability: A judgment of representativeness. *Cognitive Psychology*, 3(3), 430–454.

Kassirer, J. P. (2003). *Physicians' ties with the pharmaceutical industry: A critical element of a wildly successful marketing network*. Unpublished manuscript. Boston: Tufts University.

Keysar, B., Ginzel, L. E., and Bazerman, M. H. (1995). States of affairs and states of mind: The effect of knowledge of beliefs. *Organizational Behavior and Human Decision Processes*, 64(3), 283–293.

Klayman, J., and Ha, Y. (1987). Confirmation, disconfirmation, and information in hypothesis testing. *Psychological Review*, 94(2), 211–228.

Krimsky, S., Rothenberg, L. (2001). Conflict of interest policies in science and medical journals: Editorial practices and author disclosures. *Science and Engineering Ethics*, 7, 205–218.

Kunda, Z. (1987). Motivated inference: Self-serving generation and evaluation of causal theories. *Journal of Personality and Social Psychology*, 53(4), 636–647.

Kunda, Z. (1990). The case for motivated reasoning. *Psychological Bulletin*, 108(3), 480–498.

Loewenstein, G., Moore, D. A., and Weber, R. (2003). Paying $1 to lose $2: Misperceptions of the value of information in predicting the performance of others. *Academy of Management Best Papers Proceedings*.

Loftus, E. F. (1979). The malleability of human memory. *American Scientist*, 67(May–June), 312–320.

Lord, C. G., Lepper, M. R., and Preston, E. (1984). Considering the opposite: A corrective strategy for social judgment. *Journal of Personality and Social Psychology*, 47, 1231–1243.

Messick, D. M., and Sentis, K. P. (1979). Fairness and preference. *Journal of Experimental Social Psychology*, 15, 418–434.

Michaely, R. and Womack, K. L. (1999). Conflict of interest and the credibility of underwriter analyst recommendations. *Review of Financial Studies*, 12, 653–686.

Milgram, S. (1963). Behavioral study of obedience. *Journal of Abnormal and Social Psychology*, 67, 371–378.

Monin, B., and Miller, D. T. (2001). Moral credentials and the expression of prejudice. *Journal of Personality and Social Psychology*, 81(1), 33–43.

Moore, D. A., and Loewenstein, G. (2004). Self-interest, automaticity, and the psychology of conflict of interest. *Social Justice Research*, 17(2), 189–202.

Moore, D. A., Loewenstein, G., Tanlu, L., and Bazerman, M. H. (2003). Conflict of interest, and the unconscious intrusion of bias. Unpublished manuscript. Pittsburgh, PA: Carnegie Mellon University.

Mussweiler, T. (2003). Comparison processes in social judgment: Mechanisms and consequences. *Psychological Review*, 110(3), 472–489.

Mussweiler, T., and Strack, F. (1999). Hypothesis-consistent testing and semantic priming in the anchoring paradigm: A selective accessibility model. *Journal of Experimental Social Psychology*, 35(2), 136–164.

Mussweiler, T., and Strack, F. (2001). Considering the impossible: Explaining the effects of implausible anchors. *Social Cognition*, 19, 145–160.

Mussweiler, T., Strack, F., and Pfeiffer, T. (2000). Overcoming the inevitable anchoring effect: Considering the opposite compensates for selective accessibility. *Personality and Social Psychology Bulletin*, 26, 1142–1150.

Northcraft, G. B., and Neale, M. A. (1987). Experts, amateurs, and real estate. *Organizational Behavior and Human Decision Processes*, 39, 84–97.

Payne, J. W., Bettman, J. R., and Johnson, E. J. (1992). Behavioral decision research: A constructive processing perspective. *Annual Review of Psychology*, 43, 87–131.

Pratkanis, A. R., Greenwald, A. G., Leippe, M. R., and Baumgardner, M. H. (1988). In search of reliable persuasion effects: The sleeper effect is dead: Long live the sleeper effect. *Journal of Personality and Social Psychology*, 54(2), 203–218.

Ross, L. (1977). The intuitive psychologist and his shortcomings: Distortions in the attribution process. In L. Berkowitz (Ed.), *Advances in Experimental Social psychology*, (Vol. 10, pp. 173–220). New York: Academic.

Ross, L., and Nisbett, R. E. (1991). *The person and the situation: Perspectives of social psychology*. New York: McGraw-Hill.

Russo, J. E., and Shoemaker, P. J. H. (1989). *Decision traps*. New York: Simon and Schuster.

SEC. (2000, September 13). Hearing on auditor independence. Available: *http://www.sec.gov/rules/proposed/s71300/testimony/shamis1.htm*.

Skurnik, I., Moskowitz, G. B., and Johnson, M. (2002). *Biases in remembering true and false information: The illusions of truth and falseness*. Unpublished manuscript. University of Toronto.

Skurnik, I., Park, D.C., and Schwarz, N. (2002). *How warnings become recommendations: Paradoxical effects of health warnings on beliefs of older adults*. Unpublished manuscript. University of Michigan.

Strack, F., and Mussweiler, T. (1997). Explaining the enigmatic anchoring effect: Mechanisms of selective accessibility. *Journal of Personality and Social Psychology*, 73(3), 437–446.

Strack, F., and Mussweiler, T. (in press). Resisting influence: Judgmental correction and its goals. In J. P. Forgas and K. Williams (Eds.), *The Sydney symposium of social psychology: Social influence*. Cambridge University Press.

Surowiecki, J. (2002). The financial page: The talking cure. *The New Yorker Magazine*, Dec. 9, 54.

Tenery, R. M. (2000). Interactions between physicians and the health care technology industry. *Journal of the American Medical Association*, 283(3), 391–393.

Tetlock, P. E. (1992). The impact of accountability on judgment and choice: Toward a social contingency model. In M. Zanna (Ed.), *Advances in experimental social psychology*, (Vol. 25, pp. 331–376). New York: Academic Press.

Thaler, R. H. (1991). The Psychology and Economics Conference Handbook. *Quasi rational economics*, (pp. 189–195). New York: Russell Sage Foundation.

Tversky, A., and Kahneman, D. (1974). Judgment under uncertainty: Heuristics and biases. *Science, 185*, 1124–1131.

Valins, S. (1966). Cognitive effects of false heart-rate feedback. *Journal of Personality and Social Psychology*, 4(4), 400–408.

Vickers, M., France, M., Thornton, E., Henry, D., Timmons, H., and McNamee, M. (2002, May 13). How corrupt is Wall Street? *Business Week*.

Verrecchia, R. E. (2001). Essays on Disclosure. *Journal of Accounting and Economics, 32*, 97–180.

Wegner, D. M. (1994). Ironic processes of mental control. *Psychological Review*, 101(1), 34–52.

Wilson, T. D., Houston, C., Etling, K. M., and Brekke, N. (1996). A new look at anchoring effects: Basic anchoring and its antecedents. *Journal of Experimental Psychology: General, 125*, 387–402.

EIGHT

Commentary

Psychologically Naive Assumptions about the Perils of Conflicts of Interest

Dale T. Miller

Stanford University

How problematic are conflicts of interest? As this volume documents, they are considerably more problematic than either those facing them or those vulnerable to them believe. In large part, people's misperceptions about conflicts of interest – which include the underestimation of their scope and the overestimation of the effectiveness of their purported remedies – reflect the public's psychological naivety about human motivation and human judgment.

To begin with, people are not good as they think they are at estimating how the opportunity for financial gain motivates people. Although there are many circumstances in which people err by assuming that material interest exercises more influence that it does (see Miller, 1999; Miller & Ratner, 1998), the most problematic cases of conflict of interest are those in which both parties, though especially the advisor, underestimate the influence of material interest on advice giving. As Cain, Loewenstein, and Moore's important chapter suggests, a wide range of psychological processes are implicated in this misjudgment.

People's naivete does not end with their assumptions about the need for addressing conflicts of interest, however. In their chapter, Cain et al. compellingly argue that people are also psychologically naive about the effectiveness of traditional remedies for the problems borne of such conflicts. The particular remedy they focus on in their chapter is disclosure. The rationale behind requiring advisors to disclose to clients that they have a material interest in the client taking a particular course of action – whether it is buying a particular stock or undertaking a particular course of medical treatment – is straightforward. Disclosure nullifies bias because it both serves to prevent advisors from giving skewed advice and provides the client with a corrective lens through which to view the advisor's potentially skewed advice. Neither of these assumptions is justified according to Cain et al. Consider first the claim that when it come to conflicts of interest, the old adage is true: to be forewarned is to be forearmed. A comforting thought but unfortunately an unduly optimistic one, assert Cain et al. First, as already mentioned, people's theories about the impact of vested interest on advice are notoriously inaccurate. Second, even when their theories are accurate their troubles, as Cain et al. point out, are often only beginning. Clients may know that they should be less confident in any judgment they make based on the advice they were given, but implementing that corrective is fraught with problems. Indeed, as Cain et al. claim, people's efforts to adjust for potentially biased advice are routinely and woefully inadequate.

I accept the authors' claim that people tend to adjust insufficiently for potential bias with one proviso. As the authors note, the task facing a client who has been told about an adviser's conflict of interest is essentially one of discounting. There are two types of discounting, however (see Fein, Hilton, & Miller, 1990; Hilton, Fein, & Miller, 1993). The first one, and the one emphasized by Cain et al., involves calibration. Consider their experiment in which participants had to estimate the number of coins contained in a jar. When participants were given an estimate by an adviser whom they were told had an incentive to induce them to give high/low estimates, they were faced with the task of recalibration or adjustment. They had to determine by how much the adviser had inflated/deflated his or her true estimate. The second type of discounting involves diagnosing which motive (e.g., greed or honesty) underlies the act rather than calibrating how much two or more different motives contributed to the act. The relevance of this distinction for the present discussion is that discounting is much more likely to be inadequate when the task facing the judge is one of calibration than one of diagnosis (Hilton et al., 1993). To illustrate, imagine a modified version of the coin estimation study. Imagine that instead of requiring participants to estimate the number of coins in a jar, they were required to predict which of two differently shaped jars (say one is traditionally shaped and one has an hourglass shape) contained more coins. Imagine further that in the disclosure condition, participants are told that the adviser has an incentive to convince them that one particular (unspecified) jar has more coins in it. Now the task is one of diagnosis. Does the adviser's claim that the hourglass-shaped jar contains more coins reflect her genuine belief or does it reflect motivated misrepresentation? I suspect that disclosure would have considerably more impact in this version of the task. In fact, if previous research (e.g., Hilton et al., 1993) is any guide, they might dismiss the advice out of hand, irrespective of such relevant information as that pertaining to the likelihood that their particular adviser does have a stake in their decision or to the magnitude of the stake that their adviser has in their decision.

Of course, clients' ability to discount sufficiently also will depend on their recognition of the need for discounting. Disclosures of interest, ironically, will sometimes, perhaps often, lead to the augmentation rather than to the discounting of confidence in the adviser's advice. This can be expected to the extent that the adviser's disclosure leaves the client more confident in the adviser's trustworthiness ("It was honest of her to tell me that") or in the adviser's expertise ("She must really believe in the stock if she invested in it"). This analysis suggests the perverse conclusion that advisers may sometimes wish to disclose conflicts they *do not have* as a means of establishing their bona fides with the client.

Cain et al. also make an excellent case that one should not be optimistic that forcing an agent to disclose a conflict of interest will eliminate or even reduce the degree of bias in the advice given by that agent. They offer two reasons for this. The first is that the adviser might, in their words, "strategically exaggerate" his or her advice following disclosure. To use their apt metaphor, the adviser, anticipating that the disclosure will lead the client to put her hands over her ears, may simply raise his voice. The second reason they offer is that the act of disclosing a conflict of interest may leave advisers feeling more confident in their ethicality and, hence "less compelled to toe the ethical line and look out for the interests of those receiving their advice." Their case and the data they offer in support of it are persuasive. I submit, however, that there is at least one other reason for expecting that the advice given by an adviser following disclosure might be more rather than less biased. The act of disclosure may liberate advisers from concerns about ethicality not only because it establishes in their mind, and perhaps in the mind of their client, their credentials as an ethical person but also because it leaves them feeling unfairly penalized. A person required to disclose a conflict of interest, especially one that she thinks is not material, may feel entitled to behave in ways that her personal ethical code might otherwise have prohibited. Much unethical behavior is justified by the sense of fairness or entitlement.

In summary, Cain and his collaborators make a strong case that it is psychologically naïve to assume that disclosing conflicts of interest will undermine their pernicious effects. One implication of this argument is that the remedy of divestiture is preferable to disclosure. Possibly, but I would end by pointing out that divestiture might not be the panacea it is assumed to be either. The rationale for divestiture is that once an adviser no longer has an incentive for promoting a particular concern, any advice he or she gives pertaining to that concern will no longer be biased. This is a reassuring assumption, but unfortunately it too is a psychologically naive one. A person whose self-interest was once, but is no longer, aligned with a concern cannot be said to be in the same psychological position as someone whose self-interest never coincided with that concern. For one thing, divesting yourself financially from a concern does not ensure that you will have divested yourself emotionally from that concern. Loyalty begot of material interest can persist long after the divestiture of the original self-interest. Second, divesting oneself of a financial interest in a concern will not erase the inevitable stake-consistent thoughts that were generated when one did have an interest in the concern (Kunda, 1990). Were it not for the problems so amply chronicled by Cain et al., I would be tempted to suggest that advisors be required to disclose their divested as well as nondivested interests.

References

Fein, S., Hilton, J. L., & Miller, D. T. (1990). Suspicion of ulterior motivation and the correspondence bias. *Journal of Personality and Social Psychology*, 58, 753–764.

Hilton, J. L., Fein, S., & Miller, D. T. (1993). Suspicion and dispositional inference. *Personality and Social Psychology Bulletin*, 19, 501–512.

Kunda, Z. (1990). The case for motivated reasoning. *Psychological Bulletin*, 108, 480–498.

Miller, D. T. (1999). The norm of self-interest. *American Psychologist*, 54, 1–8.

Miller, D. T., & Ratner, R. K. (1998). The disparity between the actual and assumed power of self-interest. *Journal of Personality and Social Psychology*, 74, 53–62.

PART TWO

MEDICINE

NINE

Physicians' Financial Ties with the Pharmaceutical Industry

A Critical Element of a Formidable Marketing Network

Jerome P. Kassirer, M.D.

Tufts University School of Medicine

In the course of an extensive examination of physicians' financial conflicts of interest with the pharmaceutical industry, I gradually became
aware that my perspective on this involvement had been naively narrow.
Although I knew that the industry had done more than just engage practicing doctors and academic physicians in its marketing efforts, I had only
a vague concept of the extent of the involvement or of the complex interactions between the companies, the doctors, and many others. My view of
these vast connections and their interactions developed after reading two
books on the evolving science of networks (Barbasi, 2003; Watts, 2003).
The concept that evolved posits that the pharmaceutical industry, either
deliberately or perhaps inadvertently, has combined willing physicians,
physicians' professional organizations, physician-run disease registries,
nurses, celebrities, health charities, and the lay public into an enormous
interlacing network that functions as a highly effective marketing tool for
prescription drugs. This marketing network is sufficiently successful to
help the pharmaceutical industry outperform all other industries in profitability. It appears that the network of physicians has reached critical
mass; most of us have had no idea that it even exists. In short, the whole
has apparently become far more powerful than the sum of its parts.

Advanced concepts of networks have evolved recently from studies of
complex systems that exist in nature, in technology, and in social systems.
Studies of networks of neurons of the brain, chemicals in the internal cell
milieu, sites on the World Wide Web, and relations between individuals
thousands of miles apart show that interconnectivity and communication
among element parts of a network are critical determinants of a network's
communicative success. The analogy between the nodes of any of these

networks and the enormous number of physicians involved in pharmaceutical marketing is striking, as is the reach of the industry throughout medicine.

Missing from discussions of physician–industry marketing connections has been some overview of the extent of this network, including the connections between the large number of individuals and organizations. Any consideration of the pharmaceutical marketing network must start with a description of its component parts.

Pharmaceutical marketing involves advertisements directed at physicians and the lay public, face-to-face encounters between drug salesmen and doctors, gifts to physicians, and engagement of physicians in the industry's activities. These activities include clinical and basic research, physician education, and product promotion. In virtually all of these activities, physicians have financial arrangements with pharmaceutical companies that have certain value in themselves (for example, they provide education), but they also foster the companies' marketing goals. The physicians involved include local respected practicing doctors who are "opinion leaders" as well as well-placed academic physicians who are leaders in clinical and basic research.

The extent of physicians' financial involvement with industry has only become evident recently. Although the financial arrangements that individuals have with industry are well hidden, about half of full professors and lesser fractions of more junior faculty who conduct life science research have substantial financial arrangements with industry (Campbell, Louis, & Blumenthal, 1998). Other sources, such as disclosures at medical meetings and in published journal articles, confirm the extent of involvement. During my tenure as Editor-in-Chief of the *New England Journal of Medicine* between 1991 and 1999, our policy allowed physicians (mostly academic physicians) to write review articles and editorials only if they were free of financial conflicts with any company whose products (or their competitors) were featured in the article. To ensure that there were no such arrangements, we required that potential authors disclose all of their industry connections before we could give them the go-ahead to submit the article. Finding authors without such conflicts seemed to get progressively more difficult during the 1990s. By the end of the 1990s, we often had to reject five or six prominent potential authors before we found one who had no conflicts. Indeed, my successor as editor softened the policy in 2001 because he found it extremely difficult to find authors who were free of conflicts (Drazen & Curfman, 2002). This experience alone suggests that individuals who have extensive relations with industry populate the upper echelons of academia.

In fact industry representatives inadvertently acknowledged that the involvement is extensive. The Washington Legal Foundation (WLF) is an organization devoted in part to protecting the pharmaceutical industry from excessive regulation. When the group that accredits organizations to provide doctors credits for continuing medical education (the Accreditation Council for Continuing Medical Education) tried to exclude physicians with a financial conflict of interest from involvement in physicians' educational activities, the WLF countered aggressively. They said that physicians' education would suffer if those with financial conflicts were excluded from teaching. They said, "It is widely acknowledged that most of the top medical authorities in this country, and virtually all of the top speakers on medical topics, are employed in some capacity by one or more of the country's pharmaceutical companies." They went on, "Indeed, it is difficult to understand how...CME [continuing medical education] providers will be able to locate speakers knowledgeable regarding the latest compounds in development – except among those medical professionals being compensated by the company that is financing the development" (Popeo & Samp, 2003). Additional evidence of such involvement comes from disclosure statements in published clinical trials in *JAMA* and the *New England Journal of Medicine*, in published consensus conferences in *JAMA*, and in pamphlets from drug company-sponsored "satellite" meetings held during major meetings of medical organizations. All of these sources paint a picture of extensive involvement between academic medicine and industry.

Practicing physicians are no less involved. Many get large chunks of their continuing medical education free from pharmaceutical company-sponsored programs, largely taught by physicians who themselves are paid members of drug company speakers' bureaus. In addition, drug salesmen who regularly show up at their offices to promote the latest and most expensive products treat them to lunches, dinners, and gifts of various sorts including free drug samples. Few people believe that their sales pitches are free from bias.

Physicians with financial conflicts of interest are engaged in producing materials for company-sponsored brochures and Web pages. Here are several examples: *Lipid Letter, Lipids Online*, and *Lipid Management* are publications that promote statin drug use for high blood cholesterol (and all are supported by statin manufacturers). All their authors (all prominent academicians) have financial ties with virtually all the companies that make statins (Anonymous [Lipid Letter], 2002; Anonymous [Lipids Online], 2002; Anonymous [Lipidhealth], 2002). Most of the authors of *Quick Consult: Guide to Clinical Trials in Thrombosis Management*, a handy little book on the diagnosis and management of venous thrombosis had financial ties to Aventis, the book's sponsor (Kleinschmidt et al., 2002). The book, which thousands of physicians received free, is a thinly veiled advertisement for Lovenox, an Aventis drug. The "ATS 2002 Conference Symposia Excerpts," a publication of the American Thoracic Society, selectively used speakers' quotes to lend credibility to assertions that strongly promote the use of drugs produced by the company that sponsored each of the four sections of the "Excerpts" (Anonymous [American Thoracic Society], 2002). The University of Pennsylvania prepared teaching slides for Berlex Laboratories, which makes a drug used to treat a complication of heparin therapy. All the authors of the teaching materials except one had a financial arrangement with Berlex (Anonymous [Managing HIT], 2002). The slide set that is being used to teach others is weighted toward early use of the Berlex drug and in favor of the Berlex drug over its competitor. NISE, the National Initiative in Sepsis Education, was founded in 2000 in part to "deliver information on new therapies [for severe sepsis]." Its programs are supported by an "unrestricted" educational grant from Eli Lilly and Company and accredited by Vanderbilt University. The Web site in December 2002 provided no conflict of interest information on the ten-member board of advisors (many do have financial ties to Lilly), but all "new content" dealt with information critical to the use of Lilly's very expensive product, Xigris (Anonymous [About NISE], 2002). Another publication, *Advances in Sepsis Online*, a "Current Awareness Journal," also sponsored by an "unrestricted" educational grant from Eli Lilly and Company, lists an international who's who in critical care medicine and sepsis, but provides no information on the editors' or authors' associations with Lilly. Its articles also deal with issues germane to Lilly's Xigris (Anonymous [Advances in Sepsis Online], 2003). An "unrestricted" grant from Wyeth Pharmaceuticals permitted the American Gastroenterological Association (AGA) to produce a glossy booklet called *Nocturnal GERD* (gastroesophageal reflux disease). The brochure says, "The program was launched in response to a Gallup survey, commissioned by the AGA, that revealed 79 percent of heartburn sufferers experience symptoms at night." In fact, Wyeth suggested the survey and paid for it. Not surprisingly, Wyeth makes one of the prominent proton pump inhibitors (Protonix), a mainstay of treatment for GERD and its complications. All but one of the authors of *Nocturnal GERD* has financial relations with Wyeth (Anonymous [Nocturnal GERD], 2002).

Physicians with financial conflicts of interest are also being allowed to write review articles for journals. The author of an article in *JAMA* that recommended Cox-2 inhibitors for postoperative pain (despite lack of any evidence) had a financial tie to both companies that made the drugs (Crews, 2002). The authors of an article in the *Annals of Internal Medicine* that suggested much wider use of an expensive drug for Fabry disease (a rare condition) had substantial financial ties to Genzyme, the drug's manufacturer (Desnick, 2003). A study of published articles on calcium channel blockers revealed that that almost all of the authors who had written favorably about the drugs had financial arrangements with the makers of the drugs. About two-thirds of those whose writing was neutral had such arrangements, and less than 40 percent of those who were negative about the class of drugs had financial connections to industry (Stelfox, Chua, O'Rourke, & Detsky, 1998).

Testimony at the FDA also may be influenced by financial conflicts. Dennis Cauchon, in *USA Today*, noted that the FDA waived federal restrictions on conflict of interest numerous times to allow experts to testify about drugs in the FDA's eighteen advisory committees. He found that in more than half of 159 advisory committee meetings, many of the committee members had financial interests in the topic being evaluated. Of the one hundred or so meetings that involved specific drugs, one-third of the committee members had a "financial conflict" (Cauchon, 2000).

Members of committees that formulate clinical practice guidelines are rarely free from financial conflicts. Except for the American College of Physicians, most major medical organizations allow physicians with financial conflicts to participate. Some allow them to disclose their arrangements privately, some publicly (often quickly at the start of deliberations), and some require no disclosures at all. Few disclose the conflicts when the guidelines are disseminated. When conflicts are disclosed, they often are extensive.

Recently, some companies have taken on the responsibility to develop national quality initiatives. One example is a registry originally sponsored by Millennium Pharmaceuticals (and more recently other companies) called CRUSADE. Hospitals send electronic data on patients with heart attacks to Duke University, the site of the CRUSADE database, and receive summaries of the data and comparative information about drug utilization at other medical centers. Interestingly, Millennium's product,

Integrilin, is given substantial space in the CRUSADE brochure, and the materials suggest that there is substantial underutilization of this expensive drug and its competitors (CRUSADE Executive Committee, 2002). The registry criteria are derived from American Heart Association clinical practice guidelines, which were created by physicians, many of whom had financial ties to the companies that made these drugs. Curiously, the registry data show that nearly all the drugs used in patients with heart attacks are underutilized. It seems quite apparent why drug companies are spending so much money to sponsor clinical registries.

Still another involvement by physicians is their participation in pharmaceutical industry-supported organizations that promote the medicalization of social conditions. Often a hidden agenda for these organizations involves the expansion of the market for drugs to treat social conditions that are being gradually converted into medical disorders. Some social conditions whose reach has been expanded recently with physician involvement include attention deficit disorder, adult anxiety, and male and female sexual dysfunction.

Physicians have engaged in a variety of other practices, all of which can influence the marketing of drugs or help a company avoid litigation. These practices include signing manuscripts for publication written by others (i.e., ghostwriting), slanting clinical tests to lessen the likelihood of litigation, and carrying out research with methods biased to achieve favorable outcomes.

The pharmaceutical industry has produced some remarkable drugs that save lives and reduce suffering. Yet, its appetite for the sale of new, more expensive drugs, for new drugs that compete with existing drugs with few demonstrated advantages (so-called me-too drugs), and for ever-expanding sales of existing drugs seems never to be sated. It must be acknowledged that the industry has produced an enormous number of useful drugs that alleviate suffering and save lives. At the same time, however, the industry has failed to develop drugs for many diseases that create huge burdens of human suffering but are not profitable (Angell & Relman, 2002). In addition, the strong promotion of the most expensive drugs with the collaboration of physicians has contributed importantly to a crisis in economics of health care.

The marketing efforts of the pharmaceutical industry are prodigious. Overall, the industry spends even more on marketing than it does on research and development. But we should not lose sight of the fact that patients do not order the industry's products; physicians do. And even though drug companies are increasingly marketing directly to patients, physicians still represent the major audience for the pharmaceutical industry's sales efforts. The physician network that the pharmaceutical industry has engaged in these marketing efforts is truly impressive. With minor exceptions, most of academic medicine seems to be involved in one way or another in industry's marketing efforts: carrying out research that sheds a good light on a drug, testifying about a drug's good qualities, writing papers and pamphlets, and developing clinical practice guidelines and registries that promote products. Although some stay uninvolved, industry's tentacles are everywhere in medicine, and the temptations to join up can be overwhelming.

The network of people who have joined up by industry to do its bidding is impressive. Because doctors order the drugs, the companies depend on their passive acquiescence or active participation in their marketing efforts. Many physicians are not just being compliant but also complicit.

Given the extraordinary success of the pharmaceutical industry, the complicity probably adds up to more than the sum of its parts. The network of involved, influential physicians in research and education creates a general buzz around pharmaceutical products that is fueled by advertising directed at nurses and at patients themselves. It is hard for an academic physician to turn down an opportunity to earn thousands of dollars extra by consulting or lecturing for a few hours or for a physician in practice to turn down the opportunity to make several thousand dollars for each patient he enrolls in a clinical trial.

At present, the national mood favors individualism, profits, and entrepreneurship. Medicine has gone along with this tide of free markets, but with the result that its reputation as a caring profession is threatened. Unless medicine is willing to give up its long legacy of public trust that avers that doctors are performing in their patients' best interests, the culture of ready acceptance of the industry's largesse must change. As one scholar said, "Conflicts of interest are institutional weeds. They take root below the surface and become pervasive problems often long before they show their ugliness" (Malinowski, 2001). Unfortunately, the weeds have long since broken through the surface.

Can anything be done to unravel this all-encompassing tangled web? For certain, it will not be easy. Several proposals should be considered immediately. Physicians should take *no* gifts from industry and should not engage in marketing of pharmaceuticals. All activities between physicians and industry should be clearly defined, and all marketing tasks eliminated, including speakers' bureaus and consulting involvement other than those related to purely scientific issues. Physicians should not be allowed to give lectures or publish review articles or educational materials if they have a financial relation to a company that makes a product mentioned in the lecture or the manuscript. "Prizes" including editorships, practice guideline committee memberships, and authorship of editorials should be reserved for nonconflicted physicians. These proposals are only meant as beginnings. Subsequent efforts would focus on fostering wide discussions about how to reduce the dependence of our practitioners, faculty, medical centers, and professional organizations on the largesse of the pharmaceutical industry.

References

Angell, M., & Relman, A. S. (2002). America's other drug problem. *The New Republic*, December 16.

Anonymous. About NISE: National Initiative in Sepsis Education, 2002. Accessed December 5, 2002, at http://nise.cc/about.php3.

Anonymous. Advances in Sepsis Online. Vol. 2003: Lilly Critical Care and Remedica Publishing Ltd. Accessed July 2, 2003, at http://www.sepsis.remedica.com/journal.asp?page = home.

Anonymous. American Thoracic Society. ATS 2002 Conference Symposia excerpts, Atlanta, GA, 2002. Medical Association Communications.

Anonymous. Lipidhealth. LipidManagement Newsletter. Vol. 2002: Thomson Professional Postgraduate Services.

Anonymous. Emerging science of lipid management. Lipid Letter. Vol. 2, 2002:1.

Anonymous. Lipids Online. Editorial Board Web Page. Vol. 2002. Accessed Dec 6, 2002 at http:www.lipidsonline.org/site/editorial.cfm.

Anonymous. Faculty Disclosure. Managing HIT: Preventing Life- and Limb-Threatening Thrombosis Slide Kit: University of Pennsylvania School of Medicine, 2002.

Anonymous. Nocturnal GERD. Bethesda, MD: American Gastroenterological Association, 2002.

Barabasi, A.-L. (2003). *Linked: How everything is connected to everything else and what it means for business, science, and everyday Life.* New York: Plume (Penguin Group).

Campbell, E. G., Louis, K. S., & Blumenthal, D. (1998). Looking a gift horse in the mouth: Corporate gifts supporting life sciences research. *Journal of the American Medical Association*, 279, 995–999.

Cauchon, D. (2000). FDA advisers tied to industry. *USA Today*, September 25, 1A.

Crews, J. C. (2002). Multimodal pain management strategies for office-based and ambulatory procedures. *Journal of the American Medical Association*, 288, 629–632.

CRUSADE Executive Committee (2002). A practical guide to understanding the 2002 ACC/AHA guidelines for the management of patients with non-ST-segment elevation acute coronary syndromes. Duke Clinical Research Institute, 1–42.

Desnick, R. J., Brady, R., Barranger, J., et al. (2003). Fabry Disease, and under-recognized multisystemic disorder: Expert recommendations for diagnosis, management, and enzyme replacement therapy. *Annals of Internal Medicine*, 138, 338–346.

Drazen, J. M., & Curfman G. D. (2002). Financial associations of authors. *New England Journal of Medicine*, 346, 1901–1902.

Kleinschmidt, K., Miller, A., Polack, C., Bosker, G. (Eds.). (2002). Quick consult: Guide to clinical trials in thrombosis management. In: Atlanta: American Health Consultants, 2002:452.

Popeo, D. J., & Samp, R. A. (2003). Comments of the Washington Legal Foundation to the Accreditation Council for Continuing Medical Education Concerning Request for Comments on the January 14, 2003 Draft "Standards to Ensure the Separation of Promotion From Education Within the CME Activities of ACCME Accredited Providers": Washington Legal Foundation, 1–11.

Stelfox, H. T., Chua, G., O'Rourke, K., & Detsky, A. S. (1998). Conflict of interest in the debate over calcium-channel antagonists. *New England Journal of Medicine*, 338, 101–106.

Watts, D. J. (2003). *Six degrees: The science of a connected age.* New York: W. W. Norton.

TEN

Commentary

How Did We Get into this Mess?

Peter A. Ubel, M.D.*

University of Michigan

I have been aware of the close ties between physicians and the pharmaceutical industry since the day I began medical school in 1984 and received a free stethoscope from a kind-hearted pharmaceutical company. Later that year, I received an expensive medical school textbook from another company, and, over the next several years, I ate more than a few donuts provided by sales representatives who set up meeting areas within the hospital at which I was training. When I left medical school and began residency training, I began to realize that some people thought it was inappropriate for doctors to get too cozy with the pharmaceutical industry. The Mayo Clinic, where I trained, banned pharmaceutical representatives from its grounds, to reduce industry influence on its physicians. In response to this policy, pharmaceutical representatives from several companies got together and rented a large hall in a hotel across the street from the clinic, where they provided food and conversation to Mayo Clinic physicians every week; we all, staff and trainees alike, gladly trudged across the cold Minnesota streets to receive free food and copies of important research articles that the sales representatives thought we should know about.

It is safe to say, then, that I have been aware of the close ties between physicians and industry for a long time. But until reading Dr. Kassirer's disturbing summary, I was unaware of the thoroughness of the pharmaceutical marketing network.

* Support: Dr. Ubel is a recipient of a Presidential Early Career Award for Scientists and Engineers (PECASE). This research also was supported by RO1 HD40789-01, R01 HD38963-02, and R01 CA87595-01A1.

Which leads me to ask: How did things get this way? This is a big question of course, which could be answered by looking at the economics of pharmaceutical marketing, at the regulatory atmosphere surrounding these relationships, and at the historical developments that led to the current situation. Indeed, if we want to fix these relationships, we need to understand as fully as possible why these relationships are so pervasive. However, in beginning to suggest some answers to this question, I am going to focus more narrowly on what I think is going on in physicians' heads. I am going to try to figure out why physicians – who are supposed to work in service of their patients' best interests, and who are not supposed to let their clinical judgements be influenced by their own financial interests – allowed themselves to be influenced by industry marketers, whose goals are to promote the bottom line of their companies.

I am going to paint a picture of how doctors' minds work. Some of my picture will be based on scientific evidence, some (I admit) on anecdotal evidence, and some is purely speculative. But my main goal is to show the importance of getting into doctors' heads, so that we can come up with solutions that take account of the way physicians think.

THE ILLUSION OF INVULNERABILITY

A key reason that relationships between industry and physicians are so pervasive is that physicians believe they are invulnerable to undue influence from industry. But when I have spoken with physicians about their interaction with sales representatives, they usually acknowledge that industry representatives hope to interact with them in order to influence their clinical decisions; they recognize that the information they receive from pharmaceutical representatives is not always balanced; they know that such information is selected to be favorable to industry products. But they say they still value conversations with representatives, in order to learn about new products, or new formulations of old products, or new combinations of medications. And they do not worry about any bias that sales representatives may introduce in their spoken comments, because they are convinced that their knowledge of the medical literature makes them impervious to industry influence. Studies show, in fact, that physicians believe they receive most of their information about medications from the medical literature. Near the bottom of their list of information sources are pharmaceutical representatives and advertisements (Avorn et al., 1982).

Some physicians are willing to admit that they might be influenced by sales representatives (McKinney et al., 1990), but these physicians often tell me that they can overcome such influence by visiting with sales representatives from multiple companies. For example, calcium channel blockers are profitable medicines that have captured a significant portion of the market for treating high blood pressure, in large part because they have been heavily promoted to physicians. A number of physicians I have spoken with argue that if they only spoke with a representative promoting Calcium Channel Blocker A, they might be unduly influenced to prescribe A. But if they meet with representatives promoting A, B, C, and D, they will get a balanced view of the Calcium Channel Blocker market and will prescribe medicines appropriately.

Many physicians believe that they are invulnerable to industry influence. But this belief is an illusion. A number of studies have shown the subtle ways that industry interactions influence physicians (Bowman, 1986; Bowman & Pearle, 1988; Caudill, 1996; Chren & Landefeld, 1994; Lurie, 1990). One study even showed that physicians' beliefs about medications are more closely aligned with pharmaceutical advertisements than they are with the scientific literature (Avorn, 1982).

The notion that meeting with sales representatives from multiple companies will reduce any undue influence is also an illusion. To take the Calcium Channel Blocker example a little further: these medications are more expensive, and have less proven efficacy in preventing heart attacks and strokes, than inexpensive, generic water pills (Hansson, 2000; Materson, 1993; Neaton, 1993). But pharmaceutical companies have little incentive to market water pills. So even if doctors talk to representatives from a wide range of companies who promote Calcium Channel Blockers, they are unlikely to get much information about the relative merits of Calcium Channel Blockers versus diuretics.

In a nationally representative survey of primary care physicians in the United States, my colleagues and I found out that many physicians hold beliefs about blood pressure medicines that do not mirror the scientific literature (Ubel, 2003). They incorrectly believe that newer, more expensive blood pressure medicines are more effective or better tolerated than less expensive medicines. In addition, we found that many physicians recommend expensive medicines as first line agents in treating high blood pressure, despite consensus guidelines from academic experts that generic medications should be the first line of treatment (Siegel & Lopez, 1997).

Especially concerning in our study was evidence that provision of free medication samples to patients might influence physicians' prescribing

habits. Many physicians say they shun gifts from pharmaceutical representatives but still meet with them in order to receive medication samples
that they can offer to patients who have difficulty paying for expensive
medicines (Backer, 2000). In our survey, we found that those physicians
who say that they offer free medication samples to some of their patients
with high blood pressure were more likely to recommend more expensive
medications as first line agent in treating uncomplicated hypertension.
This supports other research, demonstrating that discussion with sales
representatives, or familiarity with products resulting from use of the free
samples, unduly influences physicians' prescribing habits (Chew, 2000).
This is not surprising. Physicians treating high blood pressure can choose
from among dozens of effective medicines. Under such circumstances,
they are likely to prescribe those medicines that come to mind most easily.
In addition, it is doubtful that pharmaceutical companies would provide
so many free samples to physicians if they thought it would not influence
physician prescribing habits.

Heightening physicians' sense of invulnerability is their ignorance of
the social psychology of gift exchanges. Physicians do not realize the kind
of psychological indebtedness they will feel by accepting gifts from the
pharmaceutical industry (Dana & Loewenstein, 2003). Physicians I have
spoken to are quick to dismiss the chance that a 10¢ pen, or even a
$30 baseball ticket, could ever influence their prescribing patterns. They
ignore the likelihood that when they accept even small gifts from sales
representatives, they are going to feel some obligation to have sustained
conversations with theses sales representatives, and that they might sub-
consciously think more favorably upon the pharmaceutical industry than
they otherwise would have.

M – E – D – S IN THE USA!

The illusion of invulnerability is very important in fostering relationships
between physicians and industry, because if physicians felt they were vulnerable, few would be so willing to interact with industry. Nevertheless,
this illusion is not enough to explain the unusually pervasive relationship
between physicians and the pharmaceutical industry in the United States.
I do not think such pervasiveness occurs because U.S. physicians feel they
are more invulnerable to pharmaceutical influences than other physicians
do. Instead, I think it results from some unique aspects of the U.S. health
care system.

The U.S. health care system is more free market based than any health care system in the developed world. The U.S. government plays little role in trying to influence physicians' prescription habits. The passivity of the U.S. government results largely because the U.S. government does not bear the brunt of most pharmaceutical costs. Most people in the United States receive health care insurance from non-government sources. In addition, the largest government health insurance program, Medicare, did not pay until recently for outpatient medications. And only in the Veterans Administration Healthcare System has it been very aggressive in trying to control prescription costs. Most U.S. physicians, then, have not been pressured to save money on prescriptions, and see no reason to do so. By contrast, many developed countries offer health care insurance to the majority of their populations through their governments. Thus, they have pressured physicians to hold down medication costs, and this has limited the incentive for pharmaceutical companies to try to influence physicians' prescribing habits. The pharmaceutical industry even charges more in the United States for most medicines than it does elsewhere, and gets away with these high prices because of huge political lobbying.

The free market focus of the U.S. health care system, and of the U.S. economy more generally, clearly influences physician's thinking. For example, consistent with free market thinking is the belief that advertising is a right. Also consistent with free market thinking is the idea that more information is better than less information, and that the high cost of health care in the United States is not an important issue, as long as people are spending health care dollars freely. The majority of physicians in the United States, in fact, show little concern about the rising cost of health care (Ubel, 2000). They tend to perceive health care as a business, not as a public good, and thus see no reason to do anything other than pursue patients' best interests, regardless of costs.

In a survey of primary care physicians in the United States, my colleagues and I presented physicians with hypothetical scenarios that posed tradeoffs between the costs and quality of various cancer screening tests. For example, we presented some physicians with hypothetical scenarios of women who desired screening for cervical cancer, and asked them whether they would recommend screening such a woman every three years, at a cost of approximately $17,000 per year of life gained, or annually, at a cost of close to $800,000 per life year gained. Across a wide range of such scenarios, we found that the majority of physicians were hesitant to offer anything other than the most expensive and most effective tests to their patients (Ubel, 2003). More relevant to the topic at hand, we also discovered that those physicians who recommended the more expensive tests did so in part because they believed that any money they would have saved by offering the less expensive test would not have benefited patients, by lowering insurance premiums. Instead, they felt little inclination to save money because they were convinced that any savings would have simply gone to the insurance industry – toward higher executive salaries, or toward higher profits for shareholders (Asch, 2003). Economic theory tells us that ultimately all this money has to come from patients' pockets, and therefore that when physicians act to save money on medical expenses, it will reduce overall health care expenditures for all patients. But many physicians in the United States are focused primarily on the belief that there is no reason to consider the cost of health care, because the only entity who benefits from reducing health care costs are for-profit insurance companies. This is a belief, I predict, that would be far less common outside of the United States.

In understanding what is unique about the U.S. health care system, it is probably also important to think about the psychological impact of the economic boom of the 1990s. Lots of people in the United States made a lot of money in that decade – the media was filled with stories of twenty-five-year-old multimillionaires. Now imagine that you are a middle-aged gastroenterologist, who graduated near the top of his college class, and then went through ten years or more of hellacious medical training, and finally began to make the kind of money doctors are supposed to make, only to find out, in the 1990s, that managed care organizations, insurance companies, and public payers wanted to reduce your income. Your income has fallen from $300,000 per year to $275,000. Would you still be happy with that income? If you compared yourself to European gastroenterologists, you would be ecstatic about your income. If you compared yourself to 90 percent of Americans, you would realize how wealthy and fortunate you are. But instead you see a bunch of your friends, in industry or law, getting 15–25 percent increases in their income on an annual basis, and you read about all the dot-commers making it rich, and you are not happy with your current situation. Even more importantly, you feel strongly that your income should not decrease as you age (Loewenstein, 1992). If your income had just risen from $250,000 to $275,000, you would be much happier than you are now.

Perhaps nowhere were financial pressures greater on physicians than in academia. In the 1980s, academic physicians in the United States usually were given time to read medical journals, to prepare lectures for medical students, and to be . . . scholarly. But, as the 1990s progressed, academic physicians found themselves increasingly pressured to find ways to pay for every minute of their time. This pressure arose because academic medical centers were having financial difficulties. Insurance companies were less willing to give academic centers carte blanche to charge more for their services than they had previously. Consequently, academic physicians were pressured to see more patients, to find more grant money, or to do something else to pay their salary.

In the 1990s, academic physicians in the United States were under a psychological triple whammy – their incomes were declining, dot-commer incomes were rising, and they were under pressure to generate an increasing percentage of their academic salaries – and they felt a strong, psychological need to make more money.

Now enter industry. Industry can be a source of relatively easy money for physicians. Industry pays physicians well to enroll patients into clinical trials – more than covering the cost of enrolling the patients. Industry funds grants with much less rigorous peer review and much faster turnaround time than federal funding agencies. But perhaps just as important as these financial issues, industry simply knows how to make beleaguered academic physicians feel special again. I have had very little experience with this myself, having not accepted any research grants from industry during my ten-year academic career. But I did give a talk once at an industry meeting. I was met at the airport by a driver holding up a sign with my name on it. (I had always wanted someone to do that for me.) I was taken out to a nice meal, I was paid a nice honorarium for my one-hour talk, and when I got back home, I received a wonderful gift from the company – a signed copy of *The Double Helix*, a book written by Nobel laureate James Watson, one of the other speakers featured at this company's meeting. I had not been treated like this in years! How can physicians not respond positively to this kind of treatment? After being beaten upon by their department chairs, hounded by insurance companies, nit-picked by NIH study sections, why would not physicians want to be treated this way once in a while? Industry understands this psychology very well.

DISTINGUISHING BETWEEN DEEDS AND PEOPLE

I want to discuss one final phenomenon that I think plays a role in relationships between physicians and industry. It is a failure to distinguish between deeds and people. It is the fallacious belief that if good people do X, then X must be a good thing to do. I recently explored this phenomenon in a study exploring medical students' attitudes toward practicing pelvic examinations on anaesthetized women. It is a common practice in many medical schools to offer medical students an opportunity to practice pelvic examinations in the operating room, after women are put asleep to undergo gynecologic surgery. Pelvic examinations, it should be noted, are very difficult parts of the physical exam. In a manual pelvic examination, physicians try to feel the shape and size of a woman's uterus and her ovaries. Medical students are often quite nervous about doing such examinations, and this nervousness is often transmitted to patients, who tighten their abdominal muscles in response, making it even harder to palpate the internal anatomy. Therefore, a pelvic examination on an anaesthetized woman is a potentially helpful learning opportunity, because the woman's muscles are relaxed, and the medical student can feel internal anatomy more easily. Nevertheless, such examinations are clearly inappropriate unless women have given permission to let medical students practice on them.

Unfortunately, the practice in many medical schools is to do such examinations without asking permission from women. In our study, we wondered how such experiences would affect medical students' attitudes toward the importance of asking permission before conducting such examinations. We found that as medical students progressed through medical school, they thought it was less and less important to ask permission before conducting such examinations. In addition, we found specific erosion in their attitudes toward asking permission for such examinations among students who had completed OB/GYN rotations (Ubel, 2003). The experience of doing their gynecologic training was associated with medical students' attitudes toward asking permission before doing such examinations. I think the most plausible explanation for this is the following – medical students train with OB/GYN specialists who they recognize as caring deeply for the benefit of their patients. They are asked by these highly respected people whether they want to practice a pelvic exam on an anesthetized woman. And they conclude that if such good and decent people are asking them to conduct such an examination, then it must be okay to do such an examination.

I think the same kind of reasoning is probably contributing to the pervasive relationship between industry and physicians. As I have progressed throughout my academic career, I have encountered an increasing number of colleagues who have worked closely with industry. I know these colleagues are smart and well-intentioned. I know they are trying to do research that will improve the world. And, over time, seeing such good and decent people working with industry is inevitably going to make most people think that such relationships are acceptable.

LOOKING IN PHYSICIANS' HEADS FOR SOLUTIONS

I have speculated a fair amount about why we are in this mess. And it would clearly be nice to have a little more evidence to back up a lot of what I say. But my main goal is to suggest that if we are going to find a solution to the mess that we are in, we need to take account of what is going on in physicians' heads. If physicians are interacting with industry because industry makes them feel special, maybe we need to find other ways to make them feel special, or maybe we need to find ways to make them feel ashamed of interacting with industry. If they are unwilling to consider the cost of prescription medicines when taking care of patients, because they assume that such costs are only going to be borne by insurance companies, then maybe we need to find a way to make people feel like we are all in this together – maybe we need to offer universal health coverage so that everyone recognizes that expensive medications are going to either lead to larger federal deficits or to higher taxes. If physicians are incorrectly assuming that industry relationships are acceptable because they see so many people having such relationships, maybe we need to get a critical mass of opinion leaders who vocally argue that such relationships are not proper.

References

Asch, D. A., Jepson, C., et al. (2003). When money is saved by reducing healthcare costs, where do US primary care physicians think the money goes? *American Journal of Managed Care* 9(6), 438–442.
Avorn, J., M. Chen, et al. (1982). Scientific versus commercial sources of influence on the prescribing behavior of physicians. *American Journal of Medicine* 73(1), 4–8.
Backer, E. L., Lebsack, J. A., et al. (2000). The value of pharmaceutical representative visits and medication samples in community-based family practices. *Journal of Family Practice* 49(9), 811–816.
Bowman, M. A. (1986). The impact of drug company funding on the content of continuing medical education. *Mobius* 6, 66–69.
Bowman, M. A., & D. L. Pearle (1988). Changes in drug prescribing patterns related to commercial company funding of continuing medical education. *Journal of Continuing Education in the Health Professions* 8(1), 13–20.
Caudill, T. S., Johnson, M. S., et al. (1996). Physicians, pharmaceutical sales representatives, and the cost of prescribing. *Archives of Family Medicine* 5(4), 201–206.
Chew, L. D., O'Young, T. S., et al. (2000). A physician survey of the effect of drug sample availability on physicians' behavior. *Journal of General Internal Medicine* 15(7), 478–483.

Chren, M. M., & Landefeld, C. S. (1994). Physicians' behavior and their inter-actions with drug companies: A controlled study of physicians who requested additions to a hospital drug formulary. *Journal of the American Medical Association* 271(9), 684–689.

Dana, J., & Loewenstein, G. (2003). A social science perspective on gifts to physi-cians from industry. *American Medical Association* 290(2), 252–255.

Hansson, L., Hedner, T., et al. (2000). Randomised trial of effects of calcium antagonists compared with diuretics and beta-blockers on cardiovascular mor-bidity and mortality in hypertension: The Nordic Diltiazem (NORDIL) study. *Lancet* 356(9227), 359–365.

Loewenstein, G. (1992). The fall and rise of psychological explanations in the economics of intertemporal choice. *Choice over time*. G. Loewenstein & J. Elster (Eds.). New York, The Russell Sage Foundation: 3–34.

Lurie, N., Rich, E. C., et al. (1990). Pharmaceutical representatives in academic medical centers: Interaction with faculty and housestaff. *Journal of General Internal Medicine* 5(3), 240–243.

Materson, B. J., Reda, D. J., et al. (1993). Single-drug therapy for hypertension in men. A comparison of six antihypertensive agents with placebo: The De-partment of Veterans Affairs Cooperative Study Group on Antihypertensive Agents. *New England Journal of Medicine* 328(13), 914–921.

McKinney, W. P., Schiedermayer, D. L., et al. (1990). Attitudes of internal medicine faculty and residents toward professional interaction with pharmaceu-tical sales representatives. *Journal of the American Medical Association* 264(13), 1693–1697.

Neaton, J. D., Grimm, Jr., R. H., et al. (1993). Treatment of mild hypertension study, final results. Treatment of mild hypertension study research group. *Jour-nal of the American Medical Association* 270(6), 713–724.

Siegel, D., & Lopez, J. (1997). Trends in antihypertensive drug use in the United States: do the JNC V recommendations affect prescribing? Fifth Joint Na-tional Commission on the Detection, Evaluation, and Treatment of High Blood Pressure. *Journal of the American Medical Association* 278(21), 1745–1748.

Ubel, P. A. (2000). *Pricing life: Why it's time for health care rationing.* Cambridge, MA: MIT Press.

Ubel, P. A., Jepson, C., et al. (2003). The influence of cost-effectiveness infor-mation on physicians' cancer screening recommendations. *Social Science & Medicine* 56, 1727–1736.

Ubel, P. A., Jepson, C., et al. (2003). Misperceptions about beta blockers and diuretics: Are they related to the provision of free drug samples? *Journal of General Internal Medicine.*

Ubel, P. A., Jepson, C., et al. (2003). Don't ask, don't tell: A change in medical student attitudes after obstetrics/gynecology clerkships toward seeking con-sent for pelvic examinations on an anesthetized patient. *American Journal of Obstetrics and Gynecology* 188(2), 575–579.

ELEVEN

Why Are (Some) Conflicts of Interest in Medicine So Uniquely Vexing?

Andrew Stark

University of Toronto

Over the past decade, four kinds of biomedical conflict of interest – two besetting academic researchers, and the other two physicians – have proved unamenable to any substantial consensus as to their seriousness. For researchers, they are the conflicts inherent in (a) grants from pharmaceutical or biotech companies and (b) peer review. For doctors, they are the conflicts created by (a) gifts of professional travel or equipment from pharmaceutical or medical-device manufacturers and (b) self-referral.

Organizations and institutions have adopted a gamut of different policies on these conflicts. Each of the four continues to provoke "deep divisions" (Moore, 1996, p. 173) or "endless debate" (Grace, 1998, p. A12), with some commentators demanding that they be "proscribed" (Kassirer & Angell, 1993, p. 570) and others insisting that they pose "no problem" (McDowell, 1989, p. 75). In what follows, I step back from these debates and, aided by comparisons with other professions, ask why they are so contentious. As I shall argue, these four conflicts all share a characteristic not found *in the same pronounced way* in any other professional conflict of interest, whether in medicine or elsewhere. My goal here is not to take sides on the question of whether these conflicts are to be prohibited or permitted. It is to analyze the debates surrounding them and to explain, by examining underlying issues of comparative professional structure, why those debates seem so relatively polarized.

TYPES OF CONFLICT OF INTEREST

A conflict of interest, as I use the term, arises when a professional, and more specifically a medical practitioner or a medical researcher, possesses an interest that could impair her in executing her professional, fiduciary obligations to the principal. By "principal," I mean the patient in the case of medical practice and the public in the case of medical research. For purposes here, I do not use the term "fiduciary" in a legalistic sense. By "fiduciary" or "trust" obligations, I mean simply a heightened duty of commitment or devotion, a duty that one assumes to particular principals by entering certain professional roles, a duty that goes beyond the ordinary moral obligations that we bear toward anyone, no matter what role we assume. I am operating here in the tradition of Rodwin (1993, p. 184), who says of physicians that "the medical ethos of acting in patients' interests embodies the fiduciary ideal"; and of Witt and Gostin (1994, p. 538), who speak of biomedical researchers' "fiduciary duty to the public."

To see what is comparatively unique about the four central biomedical conflicts of interest under discussion, consider first some biomedical conflicts that provoke less controversy, either because they are universally recognized to be deeply troubling or else because they are widely seen to bear enough redeeming aspects to be permissible. On the one hand, a physician's or a scientist's exercise of her professional role might be influenced by a private interest that arises outside of that role, an interest *external* to the relationship that she enjoys with her principal. In the case of medical practice, think of a gift of cash or the loan of a yacht from a third party external to the physician–patient relationship, say a medical-device manufacturer, which the manufacturer hopes will influence the way the physician carries out her professional role (Relman, 1985). Or think of a biomedical researcher's decision within her professional role (perhaps concerning experimental design) that might affect her private, external holding in a biotech company, but which could also compromise her "fiduciary duty to the public" to objectively pursue scientific knowledge. Such conflicts are "external" or "private" or "out-of-role" (I will use these terms interchangeably) in two senses. First, they originate in a source, often a private third party – a medical-device manufacturer, a biotech company – external to the professional–principal relationship. And, second, they advance interests that the physician or researcher enjoys external to her professional role: private interests we all have in acquiring cash or consumables. Many commentators have argued that such "external" or "private" biomedical conflicts be prohibited, and no one (even among those who prefer that they simply be disclosed) argues that they are unproblematic (Boyd, Cho, & Bero, 2003, p. 773; Cho, Ryo, Schissel, & Rennie, 2000; Frankel, 1996; Krimsky & Rothenberg, 1998).

On the other hand, a physician or scientist might be placed in conflict by interests *internal* to her professional role, interests *intrinsic* to the relationship she enjoys with her principals. A biomedical researcher might want her experiments to yield positive results, and therefore might be influenced as she exercises her role, because she knows that positive results will bring her greater professional stature. Or maybe those results would vindicate a theoretical approach that she has long advocated, against those advanced by rival fellow-professionals. Or a fee-for-service physician might order more tests than necessary, knowing that the patient (or the patient's insurer) will pay her for each one. Or a doctor facing capitation and withholding might order fewer tests than necessary, knowing that her professional, in-role remuneration will increase as a consequence. Such conflicts are "internal" or "professional" or "in-role" (I use these terms interchangeably) in two senses. First, they originate internally to the professional relationship between the researcher or physician and her principals; no external source or third party is needed to initiate them. And, second, they advance interests that the researcher or physician enjoys internal to, and only because she occupies, her professional role: interests in professional remuneration or status. For some purposes, one might deem a capitating HMO to be a third party external to the doctor–patient relationship; but not for purposes here, since the HMO, unlike the medical-device manufacturer, is also an agent of the patient's, being ultimately paid by him. Of course, HMOs face their own well-publicized internal conflicts of interest in carrying out that agency role.

Without denying that conflicts of interest of the internal type can adversely affect professional judgment, many observers argue that by comparison with external conflicts of interest, they can actually be functional, in all professions and not just medical research or practice (Ad Hoc Committee, 1990; Donaldson & Capron, 1991; Levinsky, 2002; Thompson, 1993). We want professionals to provide unstinting service to their principals even if (as in fee-for-service practice) they earn more professional income in doing so. By the same token, we also want them to avoid unnecessary service provision, even if (through capitation) they earn more professional income by doing so. We want them to aspire to professional esteem, even if their doing so gratifies their egos. And we want them to pursue particular professional beliefs or theories to which they subscribe, even if their doing so advances a vested interest they have in professional vindication. As Arnold S. Relman (1989, p. 934) puts it, "professional ambition in medical scientists, whatever its danger, has a redeeming social value absent from the pursuit of" private, external interests. Indeed, private external interests, such as the interests in getting gifts from or increasing the value of shares in external third parties, seem wholly unrelated to, or unnecessary for, any aspects of professional conduct that we value.

But it is not just that conflicts posed by internal interests, serious though they may be, can avail themselves of a mitigating or redeeming functionality. There is another difference: by comparison with external conflicts of interest, internal conflicts of interest can be extremely difficult to remedy.

Think of the two traditional conflict-of-interest remedies. The first is recusal, which relieves the professional from executing her role in situations where she has chosen to retain conflicting interests. The second is divestiture/blind trust, which removes any conflicting interests from the professional as long as she is exercising her role. These two remedies work tolerably well for conflicts that involve external, private interests. Consider, for example, requirements that university researchers recuse themselves from clinical tests of products made by companies in which they have invested; or else, if they participate in the test, to divest themselves of their holdings (Shipp, 1992; Johns, Barnes, & Florencio, 2003, p. 743).

But, with internal interests, ones integral to the professional–principal relationship, such as the desires for professional esteem or for professional remuneration, the remedies of recusal and divestiture become far less availing. Consider the fee-for-service physician, who, as Stephen R. Latham (2001, pp. 285–286) observes, "diagnoses the patient's illness, prescribes some course of action and bills the patient." "[A]lready in this simplest of cases," Latham continues, "we find conflict of interest" of the in-role sort, internal to the professional–principal relationship, because the doctor "has a pecuniary interest in advising [his patient] to make rather more extravagant purchases than a disinterested prudence would counsel." Of course, we could in theory eliminate such conflicts by requiring physicians who occupy a diagnostic role in any given case to recuse themselves from treating; or else a diagnostician might divest herself of a treatment practice altogether. But, as Latham says, "the costs of creating such a world would be enormous." Instead, for such internal conflicts of interest, we must, and do, rely on "the honorable physician [who] would resist [the] temptation" to over-treat.

True, we can supplement this reliance with requirements for disclosure (Solitto et al., 2003), although, with a few exceptions, disclosure does not tend to get recommended for internal conflicts of interest simply because the interest in question, such as the researcher's pet theories or the doctor's fee-for-service imperatives, already are fairly evident. But, in any event, disclosure is not a conflict-of-interest remedy *per se*. Unlike recusal and divestiture, disclosure leaves any conflict undisturbed, requiring only that it be transparent (Sage, 1999, p. 1750). And so, ultimately, even disclosure relies on the honorable character of the individual professional concerned. Faced with disclosure, some professionals, whether in medicine or elsewhere, will scrupulously avoid any conflict: a decision that will depend entirely on their individual senses of propriety. Others will continue executing their role while remaining possessed of conflicting interests, in which case all that disclosure can do is invite the principal to determine whether the conflict is influencing the professional's conduct. In other words, disclosure ultimately invites the principal to judge the professional's character. What former senator Philip Hart once said of legislators is true of all professionals: Disclosure works not by eliminating but by "revealing the possibility of . . . conflict, leaving it to the voter to decide whether the conflict has influenced the officials acts of the congressman . . . " (Gunderson, 1997; Miller and Sage, 1991; Rodwin, 1993, pp. 213, 216; Sage, 1999, pp. 1759, 1767; U.S. House of Representatives, 1988, pp. 112, 122; disclosure has other problems, too; see Cain, Moore, & Loewenstein, this volume; Dana and Loewenstein, 2003).

One point of clarification: obviously, both internal and external interests can take pecuniary form. Hence, the professional who pursues his internal interest in greater professional remuneration can use that increased compensation to pursue his external, private interest in owning a yacht. This is why the difference between an internal and an external interest does not hinge on any distinction between them in their form, which might be pecuniary in either case. Rather, their differences lie in an internal interest's greater functionality, lesser remediability and, most fundamentally, in its particular origins: in the twin facts that an internal interest in professional remuneration or prestige (a) arises within the professional–principal relationship and not at the instigation of an external third party; and it (b) exists for a person only because she occupies a particular professional role, whereas external interests, in cash and consumables, exist for anyone.

All professions, of course, lend themselves to both kinds of conflicts: those that involve less remediable but often functional internal, professional interests, and those that involve dysfunctional but more remediable external, private interests. So then wherein lies the uniqueness of the four central biomedical conflicts of interest that I mention at the outset? The answer is that, in ways seen in no other profession (indeed, not even elsewhere in medicine), these central conflicts routinely blur the boundary between the internal and external types. So much so that it will often be intensely debatable as to which of the two, internal or external, really is at stake in any given case. It is this boundary-blurring that explains why these four medical conflicts of interest are so singularly contested, with one side in any given debate vehemently insisting that the interest in question is the dysfunctional, external, private kind, hence necessitating divestiture or recusal. And it accounts, equally, for how the other side just as genuinely manages to see the interest at issue as the often functional internal, professional sort, necessitating instead a reliance on the scientist's or doctor's personal integrity.

In what follows, I will not look at conflicts that might occur because an individual holds two different professional roles (in particular, both a medical-research and a medical-practice role), which are generally termed "conflicts of roles," not "conflicts of interest." Nor will I discuss conflicts that arise because an individual might bear professional, fiduciary obligations to two different principals, as some have claimed HMO physicians do, to their patients and to their investors. Nor, most crucially, do I mean to suggest that there never exist instances of such border-blurring conflicts in other professions, only that as a systemic matter, having to do with the structure of the different professions, they are far less evident elsewhere than in medicine. My points are meant to be comparative, not absolute.

MEDICAL RESEARCH

Private Funding for Researchers

Consider a university (clinical, hospital) scientist who, though holding no equity or contracts with a pharmaceutical (biotech, medical device) company, receives research funding from it. On the one hand, any conflict – any temptation the scientist faces to compromise her research agenda or findings – resembles the external kind (Blumenthal et al., 1996; Korenman, 1993; McNutt, 1999, p. 2). It originates in a third party, a private company, external to the relationship between researcher and public. On the other hand, such conflicts resemble the internal type, because researchers "do not ... gain increased personal [i.e., dividend, royalty] income from these ... arrangements"; instead, such arrangements assist researchers in "recruiting large numbers of technical staff [and] building special facilities," thereby "boost[ing their] academic career[s]" through increased professional "recognition [and] promotion" (Omenn, 1982, p. 25; see also Bero, 1998; Parmley, 1992).

These kinds of conflicts, posed as they are by internally useful research funding from external third parties, can arise in "basic science as well as clinical science" (Pisetsky, Hunder, & Gravallese, 2003, p. 874), and they confront research institutions, too, and not just individual scientists (Johns, Barnes, & Florencio, 2003). Of course, institutions (universities, hospitals) themselves also hold equity interests in external, private third-party biotech and pharmaceutical companies. But institutions do not as a rule have private, external interests in cash or consumption in the way an individual scientist does: anything they earn from their portfolio of external holdings generally goes into furthering their task of in-role research. Thus for institutions, it is not only research grants from private companies, but also equity holdings in private companies, that straddle the external–internal divide.

Most institutional and professional codes restrict scientists in using their role to affect external, private entities which have boosted their external, private interests, either via equity holdings or consulting contracts. But "policies vary considerably" when it comes to scientists exercising their roles to affect external, private entities that have supported their internal, professional interests through research funding (Boyd, Cho, & Bero, 2003, p. 769).

This external/internal hybrid conflict is relatively unique. Any gifts that a stockbroker, say, might get from a private third party external to the broker–client relationship, from (for example) a mutual-fund salesman seeking to influence the broker, typically take the form of cash or stocks: items that advance the broker's external interests in private consumption or accumulation. Any gifts that a contracting engineer, say, might get from (for example) a private third-party cement supplier external to the contractor–client relationship, in similar fashion, typically take the form of a kickback of cash, or perhaps supplies for the engineer's private use: items that advance the engineer's external interests in private accumulation or consumption (West Bank Bureau, 2001; Wilson, 2002). There is no record of such external third-party gifts to brokers, or lawyers or accountants or engineers, taking the form of dedicated support for equipment or travel meant to advance their internal interests in professional success.

True, in other *academic* fields, researchers often advance their internal interests via the receipt of gifts, in particular research grants, from corporations or firms. But although it is reasonable to say that these researchers, whether sociologists or mathematicians, conduct activity that is in the public interest, the term "fiduciary obligation" gets applied, within academia, almost exclusively to the relationship between the biomedical researcher and the public (Rennie, Flanagin, & Glass, 1993; U.S. House of Representatives, 1989, p. 79; Witt & Gostin, 1994; Wyngaarden, 1982). And this usage heightens the sense in which the pharmaceutical-company grantor is an external third party, a third party external to an identifiable fiduciary relationship between researcher and public, to an extent that is not the case for grantors in other academic fields. Indeed, some have even described medical professionals as occupying a "quasi-official" role: further testimony to the idea that medical research bears a singular relationship of trust to the public (Friedman, 1990, p. A48).

The term "fiduciary," I stress, need not be understood legalistically; it simply betokens a sense that biomedical researchers, among all academic researchers, bear a singular relationship of trust to the public. Certainly, not every member of the biomedical community holds such a view. But to a degree that exceeds other fields, biomedical research does lend itself to the vocabulary of "trust" and "fiduciary responsibilities." Possibly, this is because medicine deals with life-and-death issues. Or possibly it is because of a sense that "academic physician experts direct the decisions of specialist [and] family physicians and ultimately of the patients" (Patterson, 2002). It is because of a belief that the "duty of a biomedical [researcher] is to render all possible assistance to the physician," which bestows on researchers a direct "responsibility to patient care" (Horrobin, 1989, p. 24).

Analogous comments would less frequently, if ever, be made of academic researchers in sociology or mathematics; nor even in law or accounting. Their journal articles are much more (if not wholly) meant for one another, not for a practitioner community that would then regularly deliver their findings to principals in the form of professional services rendered (see, e.g., Fogarty and Ravenscroft, 1999). And, more so than in other comparable academic fields, such as law, accounting, or engineering, those with research positions in medicine are also themselves active practitioners. All of which testifies to the transmission belt from medical researchers to the public, and hence the unique fiduciary link between them, in the form of the intermediating connector of professional practice.

In fact, the extent to which the principals themselves, that is, the public, now directly access medical research findings in order to better understand and challenge their practitioners is just beginning to be explored. But it, too, has no significant counterpart in law, engineering, or accounting. And, unlike researchers in these other fields, biomedical researchers periodically find themselves being investigated by those representatives of the public, congressional committees (U.S. House of Representatives

1985, 1989), precisely for conflict of interest. All of which justifies observations such as David Korn's: "the relationship between the public and academic medicine is special, different from any other in academe, and rooted in trust that is nowhere more evident or fragile than in medical research" (Korn, 2000, p. 2236).

So, other professionals, such as engineers, lawyers, or accountants, may well bear fiduciary obligations to identifiable principals. But if those obligations are threatened by gifts from private third parties external to that fiduciary relationship, it is almost always by gifts that directly advance the engineer's, lawyer's or accountant's private, external interests in cash or consumables, not her professional, internal interests in staff-hiring, equipment or travel. Such gifts are generally regarded as bribes.

By the same token, other academics, such as anthropologists, physicists, or legal, engineering or accounting scholars, may get gifts of research funding that advance their internal interests in staff hiring, equipment or travel. But these gifts are rarely said to threaten a "fiduciary" or other relationship of trust with a principal, the public. When corporate gifts of research support advance (say) a sociologist's internal, professional interests, any resultant conflict may well be a problem for fellow professionals – academics – internal to the field, who generally comprise the readership of his research, but not for a fiduciary-style principal such as the public. In other words, the gifts might not advance external, private interests, but then neither is the giver an external third party to a professional–principal relationship.

Only biomedical researchers so consistently find themselves in a position to receive gifts from private third parties *external* to what is seen as a fiduciary relationship with their principal, the public, but that advance those researchers' *internal*, professional interests. It is this external/internal hybrid that explains why observers have noted "a lack of consensus about the gravity of the problem [of privately-sourced biomedical research funding] . . . professional societies and journals have also differed substantially, reflecting the controversy underlying the proposals for reform" (Bekelman, Li, & Gross, 2003, p. 464).

I have excluded government funding from discussion here because, though such funding advances scientists' internal professional interests, government arguably is not an external intervenor in the researcher–public relationship; rather, it represents the public. And speaking of government, it is the only other profession in which private third parties external to the professional's (i.e., an official's) relationship with the principal, which also happens to be the public, might give gifts that advance the professional's in-role interests. Some federal agencies have a "gift-acceptance authority," which nominally allows them to receive gifts for in-role, professional purposes (usually, official travel but sometimes salary-supplementation or equipment) from private sources. However, this practice is far less routine than it is in biomedical research, and almost always involves gifts from nonprofit private entities, whose interests (as attested by their tax-favored status) are deemed "compatible with those of the Government" or the public (U.S. Office of Government Ethics, 1986). Far more severe strictures apply to in-role, professionally useful gifts from "profit-making enterprise[s]," whose interests are deemed separate from the public's, and that can therefore appropriately be described as private "third parties" external to the fiduciary relationship between officials and their public–principal. But of course the right to give in-role gifts does extend, in biomedical research, to private for-profit enterprises extrinsic to the relationship between researcher and public.

Peer Review

Consider "outside" peer review (in other words, review by colleagues outside of one's own institution) in biomedical grant or publication decisions. On the one hand, the attendant conflicts resemble the internal kind; peer reviewers routinely have their own professional interests – biases, rivalries, axes-to-grind, and interests in their own professional standing – at play. On the other hand, although such biases, rivalries, or axes-to-grind may (in and of themselves) be functionally internal for the biomedical scientist in his professional role as a researcher, when he steps into a different role – that of peer reviewer of the way other scientists conduct their research – such formerly internal biases and rivalries can take on the flavor of external, hence more troubling interests. This situation is comparatively unique, both relative to the professions and to other academic fields.

Think first of all about peer review in professions such as law, engineering, or accounting. Generally, peer review here takes place *post facto*, after the professional being reviewed has completed a job or obtained a contract, to make sure that it has been or is being executed properly. Sometimes the peer review takes place in a disciplinary hearing to assess, say, a lawyer's handling of a particular principal's (i.e., a particular client's) affairs. And sometimes peer review takes the form of a compliance or monitoring procedure in which a principal, a client, hires an accounting or an engineering firm to make sure that another accounting or engineering firm, one that the client has engaged to do some work, is executing its contractual responsibilities in accordance with the client's interests (Business Editors, 2002; Lewis, 2002; Mancuso, 1991).

Now, on the one hand, in this kind of professional peer review, it certainly is the professional's conduct of his fiduciary relationship with his principal that is being reviewed; and the peer reviewer herself, consequently, is acting on behalf of that principal. But, on the other hand, such peer reviewers in law, accounting, or engineering rarely have internal professional rivalries, axes-to-grind, or interests in increasing their own professional remuneration or prestige at stake. After all, peer reviews in the professions are, as I have noted, conducted *post facto*, after a job has been completed or a contract awarded, unlike in academia, where peer review far more crucially takes place *ex ante*, as a condition of securing a grant or publication. And so peer review in the professions provides much less scope for professional rivalries to play through. It is relatively easy to select peer reviewers who have no competitive professional interests at stake in the outcome of a particular disciplinary or compliance review in law, accounting, or engineering and also, incidentally, in medical practice (Scanlon, 2003). Certainly, that task is easier than selecting peer reviewers who have no competitive professional interests at stake in the outcome of an academic grant proposal or publication review.

Now, let us turn from peer review in the professions to peer review in other academic fields, apart from the biomedical, such as sociology, mathematics, or literary studies. Here, the reverse is the case. Reviewers systematically *do* have internal interests in their own professional success, such as biases and rivalries of various sorts, at play. But reviewers in scholarly fields apart from the biomedical are rarely, if ever, said to be reviewing aspects of a fiduciary relationship between the researcher being reviewed and a principal: namely, the public. Instead, nonbiomedical academic peer reviewers essentially represent fellow researchers, whether sociologists or mathematicians, who will use the research that the reviewer reviews as a factor of production in their own work. Any internal interests that the nonbiomedical peer reviewer has at stake, such as biases or rivalries, remain internal ones precisely because she is acting on behalf of fellow academics inside the field.

In biomedical research, however, there exists a uniquely heightened fiduciary link between the researcher and the public. And so peer reviewers are meant, much more so than in the case of nonbiomedical research, to represent as well the reviewee's principal: the public, along with the public's interest as the ultimate consumers of biomedical science. As former *JAMA* editor George Lundberg told a 1989 congressional committee hearing, peer reviewers for a biomedical journal "have a trust relationship with...the public as patients...the peer review process [is] looking to the public interest as the principal interest" (U.S. House of Representatives, 1989, pp. 33, 79). Peer reviewers in other academic fields are simply not as likely to be so described.

All of this makes for the dilemma lying at the core of debate over biomedical peer review conflicts. Axes to grind, rivalries, and biases may well be interests of the internal, professional, functional sort for the biomedical scientist in her role as a researcher. And axes to grind, rivalries, and biases may even remain of the internal, professional, functional sort for the nonbiomedical academic in his role as peer reviewer, representing as he does other academics inside the profession. But axes to grind, rivalries, and biases can still be seen as unacceptably external, as originating outside of the role, when the role is that of a biomedical peer reviewer with a fiduciary responsibility to the public. "The importance of distinguishing between [editors or reviewers of] biomedical research and those carrying out such research is gaining acceptance in...the biomedical communities," Johns, Barnes and Florencio (2003: 744) write. Axes to grind, biases, and rivalries are, on this view, external and dysfunctional for the proper exercise of the biomedical peer reviewer's role, even if they are internal and functional for the proper exercise of the biomedical researcher role, in much the same way that being partisan encumbers a judge but aids a lawyer. Editors at *The Lancet* (James & Horton, 2003) have written that they carefully "consider whether it is wise, and it usually is not, to seek review from a known antagonist or supporter of an author's work." There "is some concern," the editors of *Nature Cell Biology* (2003, p. 584) state, "that a researcher might agree to review a manuscript, despite the fact that they have an axe to grind and cannot provide an impartial review."

But this is only one side of the argument, the side that looks at rivalries, axes to grind, and biases operating on the biomedical peer reviewer and sees them as external to her role, as they would be in legal, accounting, and engineering peer review. There are also those who view such rivalries, axes to grind, and biases as functionally internal to the biomedical peer reviewer's role, as they can be for nonbiomedical peer reviewers. "If the editor [of a biomedical journal] has done a good job," Rennie, Flanagin, and Glass (1991, p. 267) write in flat contradiction of the concerns expressed by the editors of *The Lancet* and *Nature Cell Biology*, "he or she will have found the person who knows most about the subject, and that person not only will have an intellectual conflict, but *should* have one . . . [such a] reviewer is likely to give a critical review that ultimately will help the author" (see also Rothman, 1993; Smith, 1994). It is the unique internal/external quality of the axes-to-grind, biases, and rivalries operating on the biomedical peer reviewer that accounts for the fact that, as commentators have observed, biomedical "peer review [is] an exceedingly contentious field" (Lock, 1994; Rennie, 1993, p. 2857). The interests in question originate internally within academic science, within the scientist's role as a researcher. But as the researcher moves into a different role, that of peer reviewer, they can be seen as both internal and external; and debate remains polarized.

MEDICAL PRACTICE

Private Gifts to Doctors

Pharmaceutical (or medical-device) firms routinely give gifts to doctors of pens, textbooks, stethoscopes, salary defrayal for nurses and technicians, "professional travel [to continuing medical education conferences] or supplies and equipment" (Shimm & Spece, 1991, pp. 148, 151). On the one hand, such items seem to pose internal conflicts. They do not advance the external private interests of doctors, as do gifts of movie passes or golf balls, which the pharmaceutical industry has recently subjected to prohibitive guidelines (Hensley, 2002). Rather, they are "related to the physician's work" or "related to patient care" (Council of Ethical and Judicial Affairs, 1991; Lexchin, 1993; Shimm, Spece, & DiGregorio, 1996, p. 327). On the other hand, they resemble external conflicts, because they originate with a private third party external to the fiduciary doctor–patient relationship. Not surprisingly, physicians have deeply "mixed feelings about the effects of gifts from the industry" (Steinman, 2000, p. 2243).

Again, this hybrid is comparatively unique. If an external third party wants to induce a lawyer to throw a client's case, or an accountant to fix an audit, he will offer an exclusively external, privately useful gift of cash, stock, or consumables (Kravetz, 2000; Sadovi, 2002). Conversely, when a lawyer or accountant does get gifts of internally, professionally useful equipment or travel, the giver is generally in the equipment or travel business. And the point is to entice the lawyer/accountant to make professional equipment or travel purchases *on behalf of the lawyer's or accountant's firm* from the giver. A computer distributor, for example, might give a lawyer a free office computer to check out, hoping that the lawyer will place a bulk order for his firm. But here, it would be the lawyer's partners, not his principals (i.e., his clients), who would suffer if the gift impairs the lawyer's judgment. In such situations, although the gift advances the lawyer's internal interests, the computer distributor is not an external third party interfering in a fiduciary relationship between professional and principal, but rather in an internal matter within the firm. In medical practice, by contrast, the external third-party pharmaceutical firm is not in the equipment or travel business. And the point of giving gifts of internally functional equipment/travel is precisely to entice the doctor to prescribe to his principals, his patients, drugs to be purchased from the third party.

It is true that pharmaceutical companies sometimes give gifts of the product they *are* in the business of manufacturing, in the form of samples, to physicians for the purpose of inducing them to prescribe a particular drug to their patients, just as a publisher might give a textbook to an instructor with the hope that he will "prescribe" it to his students. But the recipient physician, not being a pharmacist, would not (unlike with gifts of stethoscopes or conference travel) otherwise have had an interest in purchasing such drugs for internal, professional purposes (although, of course, by dispensing them *gratis*, she cements the gratitude of her patients and thus strengthens her professional practice). Nor would such drug samples generally be of use to the physician personally or external to role, unless the she or her family happen to have a condition that the drug addresses (Berger, 2003, p. 56). Apart from that, though, drug samples do not routinely constitute a judgment-encumbering interest. This is not to deny that they might constitute extremely effective, and perhaps troublingly effective, advertising. But unless the physician converts them to cash, and such conversions are prohibited, they generally do not affect her interests.

Of course, drug companies not only regularly give gifts of free drug samples to physicians, but they also occasionally sell drugs to physicians at a discount, enabling those doctors to resell them to patients and make a profit. Some may view this practice as nothing more than a contribution to the physician's internal interests in professional remuneration. After all, drugs are medically required and the doctor is selling them out of his professional office. There is no difference between the doctor diagnosing a need for a return visit, and then supplying it, and his diagnosing a need for a drug, and then supplying it. If we allow the first, as we must, then why not the second? Others, though, see in the sale of drugs more of a dysfunctional external interest for physicians. Traditionally, dispensing drugs is an activity that not only falls outside the doctor's role, but it is also one that belongs to an entirely different professional role, that of pharmacist. Any temptation the doctor faces to prescribe drugs in order to boost his external revenue as a pharmacist is therefore, on this view, as troubling as any temptation a judge faces to decide a case in a particular way in order to affect his external interest in a company in which he owns stock. Which interpretation is the better one is very much an open, and a polarizing, question. My argument here, though, would simply be that one's willingness to accept physician drug-resale will depend very much on whether one sees it as an internal or an external interest.

When it comes to pharmaceutical company gifts of equipment and travel to physicians, a further blurring of internal and external interests arises for those doctors who own or co-own their own practices. In such cases, to benefit the physician professionally, in-role, is in a sense to benefit the physician personally, out-of-role. After all, she herself would have had to pay for that professional, in-role equipment/travel out of income that would otherwise have been at her disposal to spend on personal, out-of-role consumption, on anything from yogurt to yachts. "I fail to see the moral distinction between a $100 golf bag and a $100 stethoscope that frees up physician income so he or she can buy the $100 golf bag," Goodman (2003, p. 57) says.

To counter this claim, others describe the stethoscope not as a gift from a private third party but as a form of professional remuneration for which the physician has rendered something of value in return. "Time spent with a pharmaceutical representative is time that is not spent treating a patient; it thereby constitutes both a professional and a financial 'opportunity cost,'" Morin and Morse (2003, p. 54) argue; "[i]n this regard, courtesy alone might justify some form of gift-giving, so long as the gift meets reasonable guidelines and does not result in undue influence." On this argument, the gift doesn't free up physician income but rather compensates for lost income, such that it is more appropriately interpreted as a form of professional, in-role remuneration, not an external, private gift (Mansfield, 2003, p. 47). Similar internal/external ambiguities arise in the context of pharmaceutical-company payments to physicians for entering patients into clinical trials. As Shimm and Spece (1991, p. 149) note, such reimbursements are meant to support "professional travel [or] purchase supplies and equipment," but they can thereby spill over into the physician "appropriating... excess money for personal use."

In sum, in other professions, the professional, say a lawyer, might receive external gifts of cash or consumables, from a third-party external to the lawyer–client relationship, to throw a case. Or an accountant might receive external gifts of cash or consumables from an external third party to fix an audit. In such instances, the fiduciary obligation to the principal is threatened by an outside party, a party external to the professional–principal relationship. But the interests posing the conflict are also un-ambiguously external ones, so there is little controversy as to their nefar-iousness. Conversely, a lawyer or accountant might receive gifts of pro-fessional equipment or travel from an equipment manufacturer or travel agent, in which case the interests posing the conflict are internal ones. However, the lawyer or accountant would generally be acting on behalf of partners internal to the firm in considering whether to buy equipment or travel services, and hence is not risking the betrayal of a principal. In other words, the gifts might not advance external interests, but then neither is the giver an external third party to a professional–principal re-lationship. Here, there is little ambiguity as to their innocuousness. Pretty much alone among professionals, the physician is in a position to receive gifts from private third parties external to the professional–principal re-lationship, but that advance her internal interests in staff accumulation, equipment modernization, and professional travel.

The only proximate exception is journalism, but – although this was not always the case – journalists are now generally prohibited from being taken out to dinner, or from attending events, courtesy of the individuals or organizations they are covering. I conjecture that there is less room for a defense of such gifts in journalism than in medicine because the journalist, during such dinners and events, is unequivocally engaged in the practice of journalism; part of what it means to *do* journalism is to interview and observe. Doctors who attend continuing medical education seminars at desirable locations or under enjoyable circumstances are not, in a comparable way, engaging in the practice of medicine when they do so, and so there is more room for debate as to whether they are acting in their professional role. This, I believe, might explain why it is not a matter of controversy in journalism that such freebies be prohibited, while it remains one in medicine.

Professional Self-Referral

Consider a physician who refers a patient to a lab/clinic she owns or co-owns. On the one hand, any attendant conflict would seem to resemble the internal kind, because the interests at stake, being remunerated by a patient for medical services such as blood tests or X-rays, are part and parcel of the profession of medicine. Indeed, the doctor could as easily have supplied such services herself within her own practice. This makes any attendant conflicts resemble the internal type inherent in all fee-for-service professions, in which the professional both diagnoses a problem and then, along with his firm or partnership, provides professional services to resolve it. Consider an accountant who performs an audit and then offers her firm's forensic assistance to deal with any shortcomings she discovers. Or a lawyer who reviews a client's estate and then suggests that he and his partners arrange a series of interlocking trusts. These internal interests are so endemic to the professional role that we would find it impossible to prohibit them through recusal and divestiture.

To say that blood tests and X-rays are part and parcel of the profession of medicine is not to suggest that (only) doctors can provide these services. Rather, they are part of the services one expects when one accesses the medical profession, just as paralegal and clerical services are part of the services one expects when one accesses the legal profession. Indeed, from the patient's point of view, the advantage entailed in her making use of a clinic co-owned by her doctor arises precisely because, so the patient assumes, that clinic will "provide better quality care as a result of the physician's involvement" (Zientek, 2003, p. 124); in other words, because the patient will still come under her doctor's professional ambit.

And yet, on the other hand, when a doctor diagnoses a need that a lab/clinic she owns then serves, the interest she is abetting, although it may be internal to the profession, is nevertheless external to her office/organization. Here, it begins to look like the doctor's interest in an external third party is impinging on her relationship with the patient. It begins to look like impermissible self-dealing, as when a professional uses her diagnostic role to affect not her internal, professional interests in remunerative professional service-provision, but her external, private interests. For example, an agriculture-department official might diagnose a departmental requirement for warehouse space and then, in his external capacity as a warehouse owner, supply it (*Smith v. U.S.*, 1962). Such self-dealing is generally subject to recusal or divestiture requirements.

This kind of blur between internal, professional interests (after all, the services performed by a lab or clinic are part of the medical profession) and external, private interests (after all, those services are not being provided by the physician's office) would seem to exist in no other major profession: at least, not as systematically. In other major professions, a professional either refers her principal to somewhere within both her profession and her office/firm/organization, and that is simply tolerable and irremediable fee-for-service conflict, or else to an interest she holds outside of both, which is intolerable and remediable self-dealing. Only in medicine do professionals *so regularly* have the opportunity to refer principals to somewhere internal to the profession but external to the organization, which is why no other profession seems to have spawned a comparably "significant disagreement" (Zientek, 2003, p. 115) over self-referral. Although reports of controversy over the topic in medical practice are widespread, they are documented in other professions with comparative infrequency.

Consider, for example, the legal profession, which offers an interesting counterpoint, essentially inverting the structure of self-referral in medicine. Big "diversified law firms" now offer "non-legal [services] beyond the range of the traditional law firm," services such as accounting, lobbying, financial consulting, or insurance (Moore, 1996, pp. 175, 177). This means, however, that the lawyer is in a position to refer clients to services outside the profession of law but inside her organization and not, as with medical self-referral, inside the profession of medicine but outside the organization. Consequently, the debates and concerns in law have less to do with a blurring between internal fee-for-service and external self-dealing, and more to do with conflicts between different professional norms. Lawyers and accountants within the same firm, for example, might operate according to different standards of client confidentiality.

In sum, from this broad comparative perspective, we can see what it is that is unique about the conflicts that arise when a doctor refers patients to a lab or clinic she owns. On the one hand, the services rendered are internal to the medical profession (blood tests, X-rays, and the like), such that from the referring physician's perspective, she is simply affecting her own in-role, professional interests, not her external, private ones. And yet, on the other hand, unlike the situation where the accountant or lawyer diagnoses a need that her firm then serves, when the doctor diagnoses a need that a clinic or lab she owns then serves, she is abetting an interest she possesses outside her office or organization. Here, it starts to look more like self-dealing, more like the situation in which the professional uses her role to favor an external, private interest, not an internal, professional one. Understandably, federal regulations governing physician self-referral of Medicare/Medicaid patients get stricter as the organizational links between the physician's office and the lab or clinic attenuate (Taylor, 1999). It is as a result of this internal/external blur that physician self-referral provokes "endless debate" (Grace, 1998, p. A12) within the medical community, with participants recommending everything from "complete prohibition" to "complete freedom regarding self-referral" (McDowell, 1989, p. 75). The interests in question originate internally within the profession of medicine, but as the service provider moves into a different organization, they can be seen as both internal and external; and debate remains polarized.

COMPETING PERSPECTIVES

I have argued that the four biomedical conflicts discussed here, by comparison with those arising in other professions, blur the external–internal boundary. I now want to show that this explains why each of the four provokes fierce debates. For, if you look at those debates closely, you will see that the arguments made by those who deem the conflict in question untroubling focus, invariably, on those of its aspects that resemble the functional and irremediable internal kind. Those who see the conflict as troubling, by contrast, fix on those characteristics that resemble the dysfunctional and remediable external kind.

So, for example, those who remain relatively unconcerned about research grants from pharmaceutical companies emphasize the internal, and hence functional, nature of the interests abetted. They focus on the fact that "professional ambition in medical scientists, whatever its danger, has a redeeming social value" (Donaldson & Capron, 1991, pp. 62–63; Relman, 1989, pp. 933–934; Rothman, 1993). After all, even researchers who do not rely on private research support have exactly the same interests at stake in their professional decisions (Davidoff, 1997, p. 986). Those seeking or getting funding from government (in other words, the public principal) can, as well, easily be imagined to skew their research topics or findings in order to attract or maintain the government monies necessary to advance their in-role interests in laboratory equipment, fame, or glory. "[B]oth government and academic scientists," Kenneth Rothman (1993, p. 2783) says, "may well have an interest in obtaining provocative results, since publicity and prominent publication may bring the rewards of promotion and further research funding." It is true that externally funded scientists might have an interest in withholding or falsifying their data, but so, notoriously, do scientists whose only interests are internal ones in promotion or esteem. Such internal interests are so endemic and ingrained, these observers feel, that there is no possibility of a researcher recusing himself from research decisions that affect them. Nor is there any possibility of divesting them. Instead, we have to rely on the researcher's personal integrity to prevent such in-role interests from adversely (as opposed to positively) affecting her path of inquiry.

Similarly, those who see peer-review conflicts as relatively untroubling also stress the internal, hence functional, characteristics of the interests at play. The ideal peer reviewer, as Rennie, Flanagin, and Glass (1991, p. 267) put this argument, will be "the person who knows most about the subject, and that person not only will have an intellectual conflict, but *should* have one ... [such a] reviewer is likely to give a critical review that ultimately will help the author." Moreover, such peer-review conflicts are irremediable. If every peer with an in-role interest at stake recused herself, there would arguably be no one left to do the reviewing. Alternatively, it is impossible to divest oneself of such in-role interests without ceasing to be a research peer. Instead, those who take this view say, we must rely on the "moral integrity" or "intellectual integrity" of reviewers (see comments of John Silber, U.S. House of Representatives, 1985, p. 96). We must depend on their ability to read a proposal or a paper fairly and with sufficient self-awareness to surmount whatever biases they may have, perhaps for good measure disclosing them to the grantmaker or editor.

Likewise, those who remain unperturbed by the conflicts caused by pharmaceutical-company gifts to doctors invariably note their internal functionality, the ways in which they promote the physician's professional, in-role interests. Defenders of the practice will underscore how such gifts are "related to the physician's work" or "related to patient care" or "im-prove the recipient physician's practice of medicine" (Bernat, Goldstein, & Ringel, 1998; Gibbons, 1998; Shimm & Spece, 1991, p. 149). In this vein, one recent survey showed, "71 percent [of physicans] don't think that accepting gifts, trips, and hospitality diminishes their objectivity" (Murray, 2002, p. 119). Another reports that "physicians believe that most [gifts of work-related nature] do not pose major ethical problems" (Brett, Burr, & Moloo, 2003, p. 2216). Indeed, to attempt to divest themselves of pharmaceutical-industry assistance, whether that assistance comes in the form of equipment or travel/accommodation for continuing medical education events, would be virtually impossible, given their endemic en-tanglement with the practice of medicine. On this view, we simply have to rely on doctors having sufficient character that they cannot be inappro-priately influenced by interests that help them professionally, and which in any case are both functional for the patient and irremediable (Hodges, 1995; see also Gibbons et al., 1998; McKinney et al., 1990).

Finally, those who remain unperturbed by physician self-referral fo-cus on the fact that, as in fee-for-service, the interests the doctor has at stake are internal ones functional for the patient: "[I]f we are reluctant to refuse patients the advantages of in-office laboratories and x-rays," E. Haavi Morreim (1996, p. 255) writes, "Then we are hard pressed to justify refusing them whatever advantages they might enjoy by using their physicians' free-standing facilities." Or as Bradford H. Gray (1991, p. 198) puts this argument, "If the physician who invests in facilities to which he refers cannot be trusted to resist economic temptation and to put the patient's interest first, then why should fee-for-service physicians – who are faced with analogous decisions daily – be trusted?" Fee-for-service conflicts are irremediable, and so we necessarily rely on the professional's integrity, supplemented perhaps by disclosure to the patient (Miller & Sage, 1999), to surmount them. Since on this view self-referral is but a variant of fee-for-service, we must rely on the physician's integrity here too. There should, on this view, be "complete freedom regarding self-referral" (McDowell, 1989, p. 75; Wilkinson, 1993).

But there are those who look at the same four conflicts and insist they be prohibited, subjected to recusal or divestment. These observers focus on how the interests at play resemble the external, dysfunctional sort. Those disturbed by research funding from pharmaceutical companies, to begin with, stress that such companies are external intervenors impinging upon the relationship between biomedical researcher and public. Many such critics, if they had their way, would ultimately prefer such funding be prohibited and replaced entirely by government or non-profit support (Cho & Billings, 1997; Cho, Ryo, Schissel, & Rennie, 2000; Emanuel & Steiner, 1995; Witt & Gostin, 1994). At the very least, a scientist should recuse herself from any research that affects the third-party funder's interests, or else divest herself of the funding (Bernat, Goldstein, & Ringel, 1998; Blake, 1992; Brody, 1996; Friedberg et al., 1999; Krimsky, 1999; U.S. House of Representatives, 1989, p. 77).

When it comes to peer review, those troubled by biases, axes to grind, and rivalries can concede that such interests might be functionally internal to a role in which the biomedical scientist acts as a researcher herself. But such interests can, they worry, become dysfunctionally external to the role in which the biomedical scientist acts on behalf of the public, the principal, as a reviewer of other scientists' research. In other arenas in which a professional bears fiduciary responsibilities, such as law or accounting, the internal interests that compel him to be a zealous partisan are functional as long as he is practicing the profession, but definitely not if he is reviewing the performance of other professionals. Hence, biomedical peer reviewers who harbor such interests in any particular case should recuse themselves (King et al., 1997, p. 163; McNutt, 1999, p. 1; Southgate, 1987). Or else, in effect, editors or grant makers ought to divest themselves of biased reviews. As Mary E. Clutter, senior science adviser at NSF, told a 1986 congressional hearing (and it is noteworthy that peer review in no other academic field has sparked congressional hearings), "when you...spot the one where somebody is biased...we simply [would not] use that review in making our decisions" (U.S. House of Representatives, 1986, p. 169).

Likewise, those who would prohibit gifts to doctors from pharmaceutical firms emphasize that such firms are private third parties external to the physician–patient relationship; and so, as Jerome Kassirer once argued, there should be "no free lunch. No free dinner. Or textbooks. Or even a ballpoint pen" (Kassirer, 2000). Because they sway the professional's judgment, such gifts are dysfunctional. They "undermine medicine as a moral activity," Allman (2003, p. 167) says; "surely," Brett (2003) claims, "we can buy our own pens and notepads" (see also Chren & Landefeld, 1994; Stelfox, Chua, O'Rourke, & Dresky, 1998). If the educational contents of drug-company-sponsored seminars are as unbiased and informative as the industry claims; if they are indeed effective in promoting the internal, professional interests that doctors have in developing their own "human capital," then physicians should be willing to pay for them, or charge patients more to attend them. They have no need to rely on an external third party to defray them as a gift. For these critics, it is eminently possible for physicians to remedy the conflict by just saying no, in effect divesting themselves of industry gifts and freebies.

Finally, those troubled by physician self-referral stress that when in fee-for-service, the physician refers the patient to other professionals within his organization, here there is an additional set of professionals involved: those external to the organization. This makes it seem more like self-dealing; like an interest in an external third party is impinging on the physician's relationship with his patient. "What is troubling," as Ronald Green (1990) expresses this view, "is the self-dealing or conflict of interest created when [physicians] refer patients to a facility in which they have an interest." Critics of self-referral thus argue for "complete prohibition" (McDowell, 1989, p. 75). Green, as do others (Babcock, 1993; Pretzer, 1998), recommends that physicians either recuse themselves from making diagnostic recommendations that point patients to their outside labs or clinics, or else divest themselves of such holdings.

CONCLUSION

My goal has not been to take sides on these four hybrid conflicts, to stamp one as ultimately "internal" and another "external." Indeed, my goal has been to offer an explanation as to why such resolution is not ready to hand. I have tried to show why these central debates over biomedical conflict of interest are so deeply polarizing, why it is that researchers and physicians have "been prompted to adopt positions at either end of the regulatory spectrum" (Johns, Barnes, & Florencio, 2003, p. 742). There may of course be other factors at play. But there does seem to be a consistent thread running throughout this central set of medical conflicts of interest, namely, their hybrid internal-professional/external-private nature. And this is a thread that dominates in medicine to a degree seen nowhere else.

My aim, then, has not been to try to resolve this polarization by siding with one party or another. Rather, it has been to ease that polarization by placing a comparative mirror alongside the four debates; to assist those holding any given view to better understand and appreciate the structural roots of the opposing perspective. No matter how plausibly and deeply a participant in any one of these debates insists on the correctness of her position, whatever it may be, it cannot have escaped her notice that there are others who just as passionately take precisely the opposite view. I have tried to abet a process of mutual and self-understanding by making explicit the extent to which issues of comparative professional structure shape and allow for such divergent convictions, so that their relatively unique contestability might be better appreciated.

It is typically said of medical patients that awareness of the problem is the first step toward some kind of cure. I would say that the same applies here. If medical researchers and practitioners are ever to find some acceptable middle ground in these debates, an awareness of the structural reasons as to why central conflicts of interest in their profession are so singularly polarizing might well be the first step toward it.

References

Ad Hoc Committee on Misconduct and Conflict of Interest in Research. (1990). Guidelines for dealing with faculty conflicts of commitment and conflicts of interest in research. *Academic Medicine*, 65, 488–496.

Allman, R. L. (2003). The relationship between physicians and the pharmaceutical industry. *HEC Forum*, 15, 155–170.

Barrett, D. (2000). Lawyer busted in stocks bribe. *New York Post*. November 21.

Bekelman, J. E., Li, Y., and Gross, C. P. (2003). Scope and impact of financial conflicts of interest in biomedical research. *Journal of the American Medical Association*, 289, 454–464.

Berger, J. T. (2003). Pharmaceutical industry influences on physician prescribing: Gifts, quasi-gifts, and patient-directed gifts. *American Journal of Bioethics*, 3, 56–57.

Bernat, J. L., Goldstein, M. L., and Ringel, S. P. (1998). Conflicts of interest in neurology. *Neurology*, 50, 327–331.

Bero, L. A. (1998). Disclosure policies for gifts from industry to academic faculty. *Journal of the American Medical Association*, 279, 1031–1032.

Berton, L. (1986). CPA self-regulation: A contradiction in terms? *Wall Street Journal*, August 19: 1.

Blake, D. A. (1992). The opportunities and problems of commercial ventures: the university view. In R. J. Porter and T. E. Malone (Eds.), *Biomedical Research: Collaboration and Conflict of Interest*. Baltimore and London: Johns Hopkins.

Blumenthal, D., Causino, N., Campbell, E., and Louis, K. S. (1996). Relationships between academic and industry in the life sciences – an industry survey. *New England Journal of Medicine*, 334, 368–373.

Boyd, E., Cho, M., and Bero, L. (2003). Financial conflict-of-interest policies in clinical research: issues for clinical investigators. *Academic Medicine*, 78, 769–774.

Brett, A. S. (2003). Cheap trinkets, effective marketing: small gifts from drug companies to physicians. *American Journal of Bioethics*, 3, 52–53.

Brett, A. S., Burr, W., and Moloo, J. (2003). Are gifts from pharmaceutical companies ethically problematic? *Archives of Internal Medicine*, 163, 2213–2218.

Brody, B. A. (1996). Conflicts of interest and the validity of clinical trials. In R. G. Spece, D. S. Shimm, and A. E. Buchanan (Eds.), *Conflicts of interest in clinical research and practice*. New York: Oxford University Press.

Business Editors. (2002). Technical findings for water program reaffirmed. *Business Wire*, March 2: 1.

Cantekin, E., and McGuire, T. W. (1989). Biomedical information, peer reviews, and conflict of interest as they influence public health (abstract). In *Guarding the guardians: Research on peer review*. The First International Congress on Peer Review in Biomedical Publication, May 10–12: 19–20.

Cho, M. K., and Billings, P. (1997). Conflict of interest and institutional review boards. *Journal of Investigative Medicine*, 45, 154–159.

Cho, M. K., Ryo, S., Schissel, A., and Rennie, D. (2000). Policies on faculty conflicts of interest at US universities. *Journal of the American Medical Association*, 284, 2203–2208.

Chren, M. M., and Landefeld, C. S. (1994). Physicians' behavior and their interactions with drug companies. *Journal of the American Medical Association*, 271, 684–689.

Council of Ethical and Judicial Affairs of the American Medical Association. (1991). Gifts to physicians from industry. *Journal of the American Medical Association*, 256, 501.

176 *Andrew Stark*

Dana, J., and Loewenstein, G. (2003). A social science perspective on gifts to physicians from industry. *Journal of the American Medical Association,* 290, 252–256.

Davidoff, F. (1997). Where's the bias? *Annals of Internal Medicine,* 126, 986–988.

DeAngelis, C. D. (2000). Conflict of interest and public trust. *Journal of the American Medical Association,* 284, 2237–2238.

Donaldson M. S., and Capron, A. M. (1991). *Patient outcomes research teams: Managing conflict of interest.* Washington, D.C.: National Academy Press.

Editors. (1991). Whistle blows at BCCI: Sounds of silence. *Bank Systems and Technology,* 28, 30–32.

Editors. (2003). Editorial procedures reviewed. *Nature Cell Biology,* 5, 583–584.

Emanuel, E. J., and Steiner, D. (1995). Institutional conflict of interest. *New England Journal of Medicine,* 322, 262–268.

Fogarty, T., and Ravenscroct, S. (1999). Making accounting knowledge: Peering at power. *Panopticon,* California State University at Stanislaus, 1–18.

Foster, R. S. (2003). Conflicts of interest: Recognition, disclosure and management. *Journal of the American College of Surgeons,* 196, 505–517.

Frankel, M. S. (1996). Perception, reality and the political context of conflict of interest in university-industry relationships. *Academic Medicine,* 71, 1297–1304.

Friedberg, M. Saffran, B., Sinson, T. J., Nelson, W., and Bennett, C. L. (1999). Evaluation of conflict of interest in economic analyses of new drugs used in oncology. *Journal of the American Medical Association,* 282, 1453–1457.

Friedman, P. J. (1990). We need to find new ways to help scientists avoid ethical problems without overly limiting research. *Chronicle of Higher Education,* October 31: A48.

Gatehouse, J. (2001). Journals push back at drug giants. *National Post,* August 13: A1.

Gibbons, R. V. et al. (1998). A comparison of physicians' and patients' attitudes toward pharmaceutical industry gifts. *Journal of General Internal Medicine,* 13, 151–154.

Goldrick, B. A., Larson, E., and Lyons, D. (1995). Conflict of interest in academia. *Image the Journal of Nursing Scholarship,* 27, 65–69.

Goodman, B. (2003). All rationalizations large and small. *American Journal of Bioethics,* 3, 57–58.

Grace, S. (1998). Physicians disagree on the ethics of self-referral. *Times-Picayune,* May 10:A12.

Gray, B. H. (1991). *The profit motive and patient care: The changing accountability of doctors and hospitals.* Cambridge, MA: Harvard University Press.

Green, R. M. (1990). Physicians, entrepreneurism and the problem of conflict of interest. *Theoretical Medicine,* 11, 287–300.

Gunderson, M. (1997). Eliminating conflicts of interest in managed care organizations through disclosure and consent. *Journal of Law, Medicine and Ethics,* 25, 5–15.

Hensley, S. (2002). Drug group sets guidelines to curb hard-sell tactics. *Wall Street Journal,* April 19: A2.

Hilts, P. J. (2000). Medical-research official cites ethics woes. *New York Times.* August 17: A20.

Hodges, B. (1995). Interactions with the pharmaceutical industry: experiences and attitudes of psychiatry residents, interns and clerks. *Canadian Medical Association Journal*, 153, 553–559.

Horrobin, D. (1989). The philosophical basis of peer review (abstract). *In guarding the guardians: Research on peer review*. The First International Congress on Peer Review in Biomedical Publication. May 10–12: 24.

Horton, R. (1997). Conflicts of interest in clinical research: opprobrium or obsession. *Lancet*, 349, 1112–1113.

James, A., and Horton, R. (2003). *The Lancet*'s policy on conflicts of interest. *Lancet*, 361, 8–9.

Johns, M. M. E., Barnes, M., and Florencio, P. S. (2003). Restoring balance to industry-academic relationships in an era of institutional financial conflicts of interest. *Journal of the American Medical Association*, 289, 741–746.

Kassirer, J. P. (2000). Financial indigestion. *Journal of the American Medical Association*, 284, 2156–2157.

Kassirer, J. P., and Angell, M. (1993). Financial conflicts of interest in biomedical research. *New England Journal of Medicine*, 329, 570–571.

Katz, D., Caplan, A. L., and Merz, J. F. (2003). All gifts large and small. *American Journal of Bioethics*, 3, 39–46.

King, C. R., McGuire, D. B., Longman, A. J., and Carroll-Johnson, R. M. (1997). Peer review, authorship, ethics and conflict of interest. *Image*, 29, 163–167.

Korenman, S. G. (1993). Conflicts of interest and commercialization of research. *Academic Medicine*, 9: S18–S22.

Korn, D. (2000). Conflicts of interest in biomedical research. *Journal of the American Medical Association*, 284, 2234–2237.

Kraus, W. (1999). Certification – improvement thanks to peer review. *Cost Engineering*, 41, 22–24.

Kravetz, A. (2000). Judge to rule on bribery charge in Mitsubishi case. *Peoria Star Journal*. January 21.

Krimsky, S., and Rothenberg, L. S. (1998). Financial interest and its disclosure in scientific publications. *Journal of the American Medical Association*, 280, 225–226.

Krimsky, S. (1999). Conflict of interest and cost-effectiveness analysis. *Journal of the American Medical Association*, 282, 1474–1475.

Latham, S. (2001). Conflict of interest in medical practice. In M. Davis and A. Stark (Eds.), *Conflict of interest and the professions*. New York: Oxford University Press.

Lemmens, T. L., and Singer, P. A. (1998). Bioethics for clinicians: Conflict of interest in research, education and patient care. *Canadian Medical Association Journal*, 159, 960–965.

Levinsky, N. G. (2002). Nonfinancial Conflicts of Interest in Research. *New England Journal of Medicine*, 247, 759–761.

Lewis, R. (2002). Rules stall quick hire of Boston Highway megaproject reviewer. *Knight Ridder Tribune Business News*, February 26: 1.

Lexchin, J. (1993). Interactions between physicians and the pharmaceutical industry: What does the literature say? *Canadian Medical Association Journal*, 149, 1401–1407.

178 *Andrew Stark*

Lock, S. (1994). Does editorial peer review work? *Annals of Internal Medicine*, 121, 60–61.

McDowell, T. N. (1989). Physician self referral arrangements: Legitimate business or unethical "entrepreneurialism." *American Journal of Law and Medicine*, 15, 61–109.

McKinney, W. P. et al. (1990). Attitudes of internal medicine faculty toward professional interaction with pharmaceutical sales representatives. *Journal of the American Medical Association*, 264, 1693–1697.

McNutt, K. (1999). Conflict of interest (nutrition research). *Journal of the American Diet Association*, 99, 1–4.

Mancuso, A. J. (1991). The road to quality. *CPA Journal*, 61, 94.

Mansfield, P. R. (2003). Bribes for doctors: A gift for bioethicists? *American Journal of Bioethics*, 3, 47–48.

Marshall E. (1992). When does intellectual passion become conflict of interest? *Science*, 257, 621.

Miller, T. E., and Sage, W. M. (1999). Disclosing physician financial incentives. *Journal of the American Medical Association*, 281, 1424–1430.

Moore, N.J. (1996). Entrepreneurial doctors and lawyers: Regulating business activities in the medical and legal professions. In R. G. Spece, D. S. Shimm, and A. E. Buchanan (Eds.), *Conflicts of interest in clinical research and practice*. New York: Oxford University Press.

Morin, K., and Morse, L. J. (2003). The ethics of pharmaceutical gift-giving: The role of a professional association. *American Journal of Bioethics*, 3, 54–55.

Morreim, E. H. (1996). Conflict of interest for physician entrepreneurs. In R. G. Spece, D. S. Shimm, and A. E. Buchanan (Eds.), *Conflicts of interest in clinical research and practice*. New York: Oxford University Press.

Murray, D. (2002). Gifts: What's all the fuss about? *Medical Economics*, October 11.

Omenn, G. S. (1983). University-corporate relations in science and technology. In *Partners in the research enterprise: A national conference on university-corporate relations in science and technology*. University of Pennsylvania, Dec. 14–16, 1982; Philadelphia: University of Pennsylvania Press.

Parmley, W. W. (1992). Conflict of interest: An issue for authors and reviewers. *Journal of the American College of Cardiology*, 20, 1017.

Parmley, W. W. (2000). Full disclosure: The antidote to conflict of interest. *Journal of the American College of Cardiology*, 25, 1693.

Patterson, K. (2002). What doctors don't know (almost everything). *New York Times Magazine*, May 5.

Pisetsky, D. S., Hunder, G. G., and Gravallese, E. (2003). New policy on disclosure of interest for American College of Rheumatology journals. *Arthritis and Rheumatism*, 48, 863–875.

Porter, R. J. (1992). Conflict of interest in research: Personal gain – the seeds of conflict. In R. J. Porter and T. E. Malone (Eds.), *Biomedical research: Collaboration and conflict of interest*. Baltimore and London: Johns Hopkins University Press.

Relman, A. S. (1985). Dealing with conflicts of interest. *New England Journal of Medicine*, 313, 749–751.

Relman, A. S. (1989). Economic incentives in clinical investigation. (1989). *New England Journal of Medicine*, 320, 933–934.

Rennie, D., Flanagin, A., and Glass, R. M. (1991). Conflicts of interest in the publication of science. *Journal of the American Medical Association*, 266, 266–267.

Rennie, D. (1993). More peering into editorial peer review. *Journal of the American Medical Association*, 270, 2856–2858.

Rhodes, R., and Capozzi, J. D. (2003). The invisible influence of industry inducements. *American Journal of Bioethics*, 3, 65–67.

Rodwin, M. (1993). *Medicine, money, and morals*. New York: Oxford University Press.

Rodwin, M., and Okamoto, A. (2000). Physicians' conflict of interest in Japan and the United States: Lessons for the United States. *Journal of Health Politics, Policy and Law*, 25, 343–375.

Rothman, K. J. (1993). Conflict of interest: The new McCarthyism in science. *Journal of the American Medical Association*, 269, 2782–2784.

Rumsey, T. S. (1999). One editor's views on conflict of interest. *Journal of Animal Science*, 77, 2379–2383.

Sadovi, C. (2002). Lawyer accused of seeking bribe. *Chicago Sun-Times*, April 4.

Sage, W. M. (1999). Regulating through information: Disclosure laws and American health care. *Columbia Law Review*, 99, 1701–1829.

Scanlon, B. (2003). Safety versus secrecy; Physician peer reviews conflict with patients' right to know, critics say. *Rocky Mountain News*, Dec. 6: 25A.

Shimm, D. S., and Spece, R. G. (1991). Industry reimbursement for entering patients into clinical trials: Legal and ethical issues. *Annals of Internal Medicine*, 115, 148–151.

Shimm, D. S., Spece, R. G., and DiGregorio, M. B. (1996). Conflicts of interests in relationships between physicians and the pharmaceutical industry. In R. G. Spece, D. S. Shimm, and A. E. Buchanan (Eds.), *Conflicts of interest in clinical research and practice*. New York: Oxford University Press.

Shipp, A. C. (1992). How to control conflict of interest. In R. J. Porter and T. E. Malone (Eds.), *Biomedical research: Collaboration and conflict of interest*. Baltimore and London: Johns Hopkins University Press.

Smith, R. (1994). Conflict of interest and the BMJ. *British Medical Journal*, 308, 4–5.

Smith v. U.S. 1962. 305 F. 2d 197 (9th Circuit).

Sollitto, S. et al. (2003). Intrinsic conflicts of interest in clinical research: A need for disclosure. *Kennedy Institute of Ethics Journal*, 13, 83–91.

Southgate, M. (1987). Conflict of interest and the peer review process. *Journal of the American Medical Association*, 258, 1375.

Steinman, M. A. (2000). Gifts to physicians in the consumer marketing era. *Journal of the American Medical Association*, 284, 2243.

Stelfox, H. T., Chua, G., O'Rourke, K., and Dresky, A. S. (1998). Conflict of interest in the debate over calcium-channel antagonists. *New England Journal of Medicine*, 338, 101–106.

Taylor, M. (1999). Healthcare struggles with Stark reality. *Modern Healthcare*, July 5: 30–31.

Thompson, D. F. (1993). Understanding financial conflicts of interest. *New England Journal of Medicine*, 329, 573–576.

U.S. House of Representatives. (1989). Committee on Government Operations, Subcommittee on Human Resources and Intergovernmental Relations. *Hearings: Is science for sale? Conflicts of interest vs. the public interest.* 101st Congress, 1st Session, June 13.

U.S. House of Representatives. (1988). Committee on the Judiciary. Subcommittee on Administrative Law and Governmental Relations. *Post-employment restrictions for federal officers and employees.* 100th Congress, 2nd Session, May 4.

U.S. House of Representatives. (1986). Committee on Science and Technology, Task Force on Science Policy. *Hearings.* 99th Session, 2nd Congress. April 8–10.

U.S. House of Representatives. (1985). Committee on Science and Technology, Task Force on Science Policy. *Hearings: Science in the political process.* 99th Congress, 1st Session, June 25, 26.

U.S. Office of Government Ethics. (1986). *Letter to an employee* (86 × 10), August 8.

Wazana, A. (2000). Physicians and the pharmaceutical industry: Is a gift ever just a gift? *Journal of the American Medical Association*, 19, 373–380.

Welch, S. J. (1997). Conflict of interest and financial disclosure. *Chest*, 112, 865–867.

West Bank Bureau. (2001). Engineer receives fine, 3 years probation. *New Orleans Times Picayune*, July 21: BW1.

Wilkinson, P. (1993). "Self-referral": A potential conflict of interest. *British Medical Journal*, 306, 1083–1084.

Wilson, C. (2002). Contractor to pay back $145,000; Woman sentenced in bribery case. *South Florida Sun-Sentinel*, March 10: 5B.

Witt, M., and Gostin, L. (1994). Conflict of interest dilemmas in biomedical research. *Journal of the American Medical Association*, 271, 547–551.

Wyden, R. (1987). When doctors sell drugs: A conflict of interest. *Washington Post*, April 28: Z6.

Wyngaarden, J. (1983). Government, industry and academia: A Bermuda triangle in partners in the research enterprise: A National Conference on University-Corporate Relations in Science and Technology, University of Pennsylvania, December 14–16, 1982. Philadelphia: University of Pennsylvania Press.

Zientek, D. M. (2003). Physician entrepreneurs, self-referral and conflicts of interest: an overview. *HEC Forum*, 15, 111–133.

TWELVE

Commentary

Financial Conflicts of Interest and the Identity of Academic Medicine

Scott Y. H. Kim

University of Michigan Medical School

Andrew Stark sees intractable polarization in the conflicts of interest debates in biomedicine and wants to move them forward by clarifying one of the underlying causes. The key to his argument is a distinction between internal versus external conflicts of interest. Stark's thesis is immensely useful, even if some of his empirical assumptions are somewhat questionable.[1] But to focus on these details would be to miss the meat of Stark's argument. Rather, I want to burrow deeper into the internal/external distinction. The two goals of this commentary will therefore be to, first, briefly clarify the distinction between internal and external conflicts, and two, draw out in broad strokes its key implications.

In what follows, the reader can assume that the main set of conflicts of interest that I am referring to are those that arise for academic physicians, in the realm of creation and dissemination of clinical knowledge. In my view, the academic physician clearly sits on the moral fulcrum of this debate.

---

[1] For example, conflicts of interest in biomedicine might be similar to those in fields such as environmental, nutrition, agricultural, engineering, or education sciences, and therefore not so unique. I also doubt that all four of the selected cases of conflict of interest are as central and intractable as Stark states. For instance, I do not see the issue of conflict of interest in peer review in biomedical journals a source of intractable debate. And, at least in principle, self-referral by physicians is presumed to be unethical by the medical profession (Council on Ethical and Judicial Affairs of the American Medical Association, 2000). Other factual details are also problematic. Contrary to Stark's claim, samples actually are of personal and professional value to many physicians. Also, clinical laboratories are not usually considered "part of the medical profession," as Stark states. Nevertheless, the importance of Stark's internal/external distinction holds.

INTERNAL AND EXTERNAL CONFLICTS OF INTEREST

Although the distinction between internal and external conflicts of interest has intuitive appeal, Stark's discussion of it can sometimes be confusing. An uncharitable reader might argue that the "blurring" of the internal/external distinction that Stark sees in medical conflicts of interest may actually be due to an instability in his description (rather than in the relatively unique features of the medical profession). Because this is the central idea of his essay, it deserves some attention.

Stark seems to use a variety of definitions to distinguish between internal and external conflicts of interest. At various points, we read the following possibilities for setting the boundary between internal and external: boundaries set by the fiduciary relationship with the principal, by one's professional role, by any aspect of professional conduct that we value, by the profession itself, or by a professional's office/organization.

These definitions create different boundaries. The boundary between internal and external conflict of interest cannot be set by the fiduciary relationship with the patient because then it is hard to see how a conflict would arise (an interest internal to that relationship would not be in conflict with the relationship). Of course, it is all too easy to see that certain professional roles, interests of one's practice site, or interests of the profession itself can come into conflict with one's fiduciary obligations to one's patients. For example: a thriving professional society serving a particular medical specialty might be good for the specialty but not for patients, as when the American College of Cardiology changed its recommendation of "discontinue" to "reassess" for a drug – marketed by Pfizer who happened to be a major donor to the ACC – conclusively shown to be inferior to a generic drug (Lenzer, 2003).

Stark also relies on the relationship between origins, functionality, and remediability of a conflicting interest to elaborate the internal/external distinction, but this does not always help. It is not clear why a researcher who starts a biotech company (an example close to the one Stark dismisses as clearly external conflict of interest) has created a (solely) external interest, in relation to a study she is designing. The researcher may create the company because she sees it as a mechanism to rapidly advance a scientific product, and she reasonably expects to get remunerated for doing what is essentially scientific work. To paraphrase Stark, do not we want scientists to rapidly bring safe and effective products to market, even if they get to be millionaires in the process?

For the purposes of understanding the distinction (between internal and external conflicts of interest) and its implications, an intuitive, normative idea of a "professional role" is probably the best working definition. Stark's claim is then that the most contentious conflicts of interest in medicine tend to involve the interests of the physician (or researcher) that can be seen as both inside and outside the professional role of that physician or researcher. It seems in general true that internal conflicts will appear more difficult to remedy than external ones, because policies to eliminate internal interests will run the risk of disrupting seemingly essential components of the profession's identity.

THE INTERNAL–EXTERNAL DISTINCTION AND THE IDENTITY OF THE PROFESSION

Stark's argument shows that what underlies the key debates about conflicts of interest in medicine is a disagreement about the normative boundaries of the profession, or, to put it in more dramatic terms, a battle over the identity of the profession. This makes more understandable why there are powerful emotions involved in the debates over conflicts of interest. (True, blurred distinctions can cause confusion, but that does not explain the extreme polarization and heated emotions.) In my view, this conflict is primarily between the "internalists" and the "externalists." The internalists see extensive involvement as internal to the profession's identity and feel entitled to the accompanying remunerative benefits. The externalists, by contrast, see such involvement as external factors that threaten the moral fabric of the profession.

This battle over the normative boundaries of the profession is the essence of the conflict of interest debate in medicine. Let me illustrate this by looking at a recent editorial that defends precisely and head-on what Dr. Kassirer elsewhere in this volume finds very alarming. (Although it is not easy to find academic researchers publicly defending the status quo in writing; usually drug companies or their lawyers tend to do that [Relman, 2003]. It is more common to find physicians supporting industry largesse in letters to the editor, but these are short bursts of annoyance rather than sustained arguments.)

In a recent article entitled "Is academic psychiatry for sale?" in the *British Journal of Psychiatry* (Thase, 2003), a respected psychiatrist-researcher defends the status quo of extensive involvement between academic psychiatrists and the pharmaceutical industry.

First, he notes that extensive involvement with industry is not illegal and not immoral (defined as no fraud or dishonesty), nor does it seem to increase the risk of scientific misconduct (p. 389). Second, he notes that involvement with industry is not only permissible but also essential to what an academic psychiatrist does. He believes that "it would be difficult to develop and maintain expertise" without relationships with industry. Specifically addressing the issue of treatment guidelines being written by experts with financial ties to industry, he notes, "Is this a shocking revelation? No – academics are selected to work on guideline panels precisely because of their expertise, which typically includes experience conducting industry-sponsored clinical research" (p. 389). Third, he notes that "the labours of psychiatrists, like those of barristers, stone masons, and plumbers or engineers are exchanged for money every day, everywhere" (p. 389). Finally, he believes disclosure plus relying on the integrity of academics is the best solution.

In other words, academic psychiatrists who have extensive financial ties to industry are moral (not doing anything illegal or dishonest), competent (part of what makes them experts), and deserving (a worker deserves his wages). It is interesting to note that this kind of defense is precisely what one might expect if the concept of "bounded ethicality" is true (see Chugh, Bazerman, & Banaji, this volume).

The externalists – those who view the financial encumbrances of modern academic physicians as external to the profession – are essentially bemoaning the disintegration of a profession. These are impassioned pleas to uphold a certain ideal for the profession. Writings that represent this perspective are not difficult to find. For instance, Marcia Angell (2000) writes, "[t]he incentives of the marketplace should not become woven into the fabric of academic medicine. We need to remember that for-profit businesses are pledged to increase the value of their investors' stock. That is a very different goal from the mission of medical schools". On this view, the very mission – and, by implication, identity – of academic medicine is at stake.

CAN POINTING OUT THE ESSENCE OF THE DISAGREEMENT BE THE FIRST STEP TOWARD A CURE?

The boundaries of the medical profession are actually fairly plastic. For instance, doctors being trained today are more comfortable with incorporating cost concerns into clinical decision making than their elders were (an older generation would have dismissed it as "bedside rationing").

Closer to the topic at hand, the *New England Journal of Medicine* recently changed its conflict of interest policy for authors of reviews and editorials (Drazen, 2002). Until 2002, the *Journal* required that "authors of such articles will not have any financial interest in a company (or its competitor) that makes a product discussed in the article." The new policy bars "any significant financial interest," with significant interest defined as annual remuneration of greater than $10,000 or any equity or patent ownership in a company. The *Journal* altered an important normative boundary: what was once external, intolerable conflict is now accepted as "internal," tolerable conflict.

But how plastic is the boundary? The internal–external distinction is more than descriptive. The normative component derives from a traditionally valued, but perhaps not clearly articulated, social function of medicine and medical science: viz., it must serve as the society's arbiter of what constitutes safe and effective treatment when the source of those proposed treatments come with commercial or other interests.

What is the social value of an independent profession? The more the profession's identity incorporates industry interests as part of its internal interests, the more it loses one of its traditional social functions as an independent profession. Whether this is acceptable to society is a political question in a liberal democracy. After all, there may be other, more important social values that we would rather not give up. If a transparent tradeoff of these social values can be accomplished, we should be willing to live with that.

The problem, of course, is that this societal debate will not be transparent. Part of the battle for our "externalist" reformers is convincing the profession and the public that there is such a social tradeoff to be faced at all. This will be difficult to do. The very basis for pharmaceutical industry influence is maintaining the illusion that because doctors and medical researchers are by and large smart, honest, and well-meaning, they can be trusted to function as independent arbiters despite their financial ties to industry (Spilker, 2002). The industry's marketing success hinges on making us believe that we can have our cake and eat it, too. This illusion is even easier to sell to doctors (Munro, 2002) than selling drugs, for all the reasons discussed in this volume.

References

Angell, M. (2000). Is academic medicine for sale? *New England Journal of Medicine*, 342, 146–151.

Council on Ethical and Judicial Affairs of the American Medical Association. (2000). *Code of medical ethics: Current opinions with annotations.* Chicago: AMA Press.

Drazen, J. M. (2002). Financial associations of authors. *New England Journal of Medicine,* 346, 1901–1902.

Healy, D., & Thase, M. E. (2003). Is academic psychiatry for sale? *British Journal of Psychiatry,* 182, 388–390.

Lenzer, J. (2003). Spin doctors soft pedal data on antihypertensives. *British Medical Journal,* 326, 170.

Munro, Neil. (2002, November). Doctor who? *Washington Monthly.* http://www. washingtonmonthly.com/features/2001/02 11.murno.html.

Relman, A. S. (2003). Defending professional independence: ACCME's proposed new guidelines for commercial support of CME. *Journal of the American Medical Association,* 289, 2418–2421.

Spilker, B. (2002). The benefits and risks of a pack of M&Ms. *Health Affairs,* 21, 243–244.

PART THREE

LAW

THIRTEEN

Legal Responses to Conflicts of Interest

Samuel Issacharoff*

Columbia Law School

Conflicts of interest abound in the law. The core attorney–client relation-ship is a classic example of a principal–agent relationship, with all the attendant and endemic tensions and risks of opportunistic behavior. The basic legal definition of attorney, as set forth in the standard law reference, "denotes an agent or substitute, or one who is appointed and authorized to act in the place or stead of another" (Black, 1951). The ability to act on behalf of another of itself creates conflicts that are "intrinsic to the ex-ercise of trust" (Shapiro, 2003). Much of legal regulation, including that directed at attorney–client relations, attempts to mediate the conflicts inherent in a world where dependence on agents is the norm.

This chapter will assess distinct legal responses to conflicts of interest. The aim will not be to catalogue the range of conflicts that the law rec-ognizes or to identify all of the various regulatory responses that may be tried. Rather, the object will be to use a couple of examples of significant conflicts of interest, whether labeled as such or not, to map the types of regulatory methodologies that may be employed. By mapping different responses to conflicts of interest onto certain regulatory patterns, the costs and benefits of different approaches can be assessed. In particular, iden-tifying the range of regulatory responses may help clarify the competing tensions that exist in principal–agent relations, such as that between attor-ney and client. The primary risk is that of agent misbehavior in terms of misappropriation of goods or gains that properly belong to the principal. At the same time, however, there is a corresponding risk in burdening principal–agent relations with more direct legal oversight than they may

---

* Harold R. Medina Professor of Procedural Jurisprudence, Columbia Law School.

bear, particularly if the costs of compliance exceed the gains to be had in representing a principal.

The area that concerns me most is one in which it is unlikely that market mechanisms alone can protect the principals. This may be for a variety of reasons. Most significantly, there are undertakings in which the interest of the principals is both diffuse and of low overall value, but where the interest of the agent is highly concentrated and of great value. Another obstacle to parties protecting themselves through ordinary market mechanisms is high information costs that make effective monitoring difficult. This can result from either the difficulty of acquiring the information or the inability for a diffuse group to monitor at all. The latter may be partially moderated by the use of intermediaries, or "super-agents" as I refer to them in a paper with Daniel Ortiz, but this then moves the monitoring problem up one level to the issue of who monitors the monitors of the agents (Issacharoff & Ortiz, 1999). The third obstacle is high barriers to entry for rivals to agents who may seek to win over the representation of the principals and, in so doing, provide assistance in scaling back agency costs. The higher the barriers to entry, the less effective market challenge becomes.

The next question is how the law responds to such conflicts of interest. Here I would categorize three different mechanisms. The first is substantive regulation. By this, I mean specific prohibitions on certain substantive decisions of the agent. The classic examples include such obvious ones as rule of attorney professional conduct stating that client funds must be held in segregated accounts and may not be invested in the attorneys' home, business, or other private undertakings. This approach turns on *ex ante* rules of prohibition on defined acts. Alternatively, there may be rules of prohibition applied *ex post*, what generally falls under the rubric of liability rules. Thus, we find liability regimes that create a risk of fine or even incarceration if a fiduciary bond is broken and there is resulting harm. Much of the "gatekeeper" system in the corporate and securities world turns on this sort of fiduciary liability and the prospect that gatekeepers will sufficiently internalize the prospective costs of a breach of their duties as a deterrent to misconduct. Finally, there is the prospect of what I shall term procedural regulations. Here, the examples are prohibitions not on substantive outcomes, but on the participation in decision making by conflicted agents. Examples here would include the prohibition on government officials negotiating contracts with firms in which they have or have had a financial involvement. At issue is not whether the contract was in the public interest or not, or whether it was subject to self-serving manipulation, but the appearance of corruption of the agent. What is significant here is that the emphasis is on process barriers that do not turn on a substantive assessment of the outcome of the transaction.

I will conclude that, as a general matter, procedural regulation is the single most effective strategy for dealing with conflicts of interest. Substantive regulation is difficult to apply and suffers from the same information deficits as exist generally in the principal–agent relationship. Liability regimes suffer from a dependence on the proper ability of agents to internalize the cost calculus, something that may be compromised by heuristic biases that tend toward seeing desired short-term objectives free of the full liability consequences. Procedural regulation is effective in that it cuts straight to the heart of the matter, by attempting to remove the conflict of interest altogether.

SUBSTANTIVE REGULATION OF LEGAL CONFLICT

Discussions of conflicts of interest tend to get bogged down in semantic difficulties over what exactly constitutes a conflict. At a certain level of abstraction, all decisions subject to multiple objectives may be described as conflicted, in the sense of arising "in situations in which a decision maker's desire – or duty – to serve conflicting interests might undermine the decision maker's neutrality or objectivity" (Orentlicher, 2002). Pitched so broadly, the more difficult enterprise may be identifying nonconflicted settings. Rather than pursue this definitional search, perhaps it is more useful to ground the concept of a legally significant conflict of interest in those settings in which principal–agent problems are most likely to arise and in which the risk of agent opportunism is most acute. Focusing on agency cost, rather than on competing objectives, narrows the scope of conflicted decisions to those that are of most consequence to the law. It necessarily excludes the triage decisions made by an emergency room or a wartime hospital, but those arise from conditions of choice under scarcity rather than choice infected by self-interest.

One approach to the problem of conflicts of interest defined to focus on the temptations of agent self-interest is to regulate the substantive range of choices available to an agent. For example, it is well-understood that having client funds accessible to private use by lawyers is an invitation to trouble. It is far too easy to rationalize dipping into such funds to cover attorney shortfalls or treating it as part of the investment capital of the firm. Accordingly, the rules of professional conduct prohibit the intermingling of funds and require that client funds be held in specially designated escrow accounts. In this fashion, a substantive choice, temporary or permanent use of client assets, is removed from consideration – at least in theory. This is an example of what I will term substantive regulation. Its defining characteristic is the focus on decisional outputs and its policing of the substance of the decisions.

Although substantive regulation is premised on clear *ex ante* rules of prohibition, the contours of the prohibition and the punishment of its transgression cannot be determined ahead of time. Generally, these restrictions operate by means of *ex post* judicial oversight – a reviewing court must assess a given situation after the fact to determine whether an agent's actions conformed with the relevant legal standard.

By way of illustration, let me turn to the concern over corporate financial misdealings. The problem of corporate accounting scandals and the failure of what my colleague Jack Coffee focuses on as gatekeeper responsibility by lawyers, investment bankers, and accountants brings new urgency to the study of legal regulation of conflicts of interest. The repeated failings of agents to protect the interests of shareholders and other vulnerable constituents of these corporate entities create a tremendous pressure for regulation to ensure that those with responsibility for the health of corporate America behave properly. Unfortunately, it proves exceedingly difficult to write rules of substantive regulation that are both sufficiently precise to compel specific conduct and yet are of sufficient generality to prove adaptable to a broad array of settings. To take an example from a completely unrelated area of law, consider the problem of workplace safety. It is easy to require overhead guards on a forklift to protect against workplace injuries. The use of forklifts is sufficiently widespread and uniform as to allow a simple rule to be applied across the entirety of workplace use. It is far more difficult to write a rule for safe conduct in nonstandard settings or for the use of workplace tools that come in a variety of shapes, sizes, and configurations.

The same problem occurs in the world of complex financial transactions. Outside very broad definitions of fraud and insider payoffs, it becomes more and more difficult to write rules of prohibition in a constantly mutating world of financial instruments and investment strategies. To the extent that prohibitions have force, they are likely overinclusive and risk deterring innovation. To the degree they are flexible, they risk losing their prohibitory value and invite only a difficult effort to police improper transactions after the fact. Most often, the transactions will be sufficiently idiosyncratic as to defeat easy generalization from case to case. Moreover, the best proof of impropriety may well be the fact that the transaction failed or that the firm went under. A rule of substantive prohibition that admitted as evidence such proof would risk becoming an invitation to second-guessing the transaction through the prism of hindsight bias. For this reason, the law generally imposes the shield of the business judgment rule to avoid any temptation to ascribe liability to the fact of failure, lest entrepreneurialism be curtailed and risk-taking dampened (Rachlinski, 1998). Attempting to regulate substantively not only bears the general burden of imprecision and after-the-fact second-guessing, but it also risks creating regulatory barriers to initiative. By their nature, *ex ante* rules of prohibition work best when the commands are as precise as possible; the precision is what in turn defeats the flexibility necessary for complex entrepreneurial activity.

As a result, the more complex and multifactored the endeavor, whether redistricting or complex financial transactions, the more difficult it will be to regulate through substantive limitations of outcomes.

LIABILITY REGULATION

A related legal response to conflicts of interest is to impose civil or criminal liability on agents for violating a fiduciary duty. Liability regimes share with substantive prohibitions the desire both to define specific forbidden conduct and to police transgressions here after the fact. The primary difference is that the range of prohibitions in liability regulations is considerably broader than in express prohibitions, with the expectation that the risk of punishment will deter improper agent behavior. This type of deterrence theory has a long pedigree in criminal and tort law, a result being that agent liability is the response most often applied to conflicts entailing tangible harm. The primary attraction of liability regimes is that they provide the greatest appearance of responsive regulation with the least investment of time or effort. Passing new liability laws, be they criminal or civil, and increasing penalties make for the appearance of concern and allows plenty of "get-tough" press conferences. Unlike the third category of process regulation, which requires careful assessment of the structures that are likely to give rise to compromised decision making, or even substantive regulation, which requires some clear definition of desireable and undesirable outcomes, liability rules can be written with relatively little investigation of the actual institutional settings in which conflicted decisions are likely to arise. Moreover, as Jack Coffee has noted, many new liability rules are surplusage – there is precious little evidence that there were not a myriad of criminal and civil penalties already potentially in place during the last wave of corporate accounting scandals (Coffee, 2002).

Not surprisingly, liability regimes have their limitations. First, agent liability is subject to the same problems of *ex ante* legal uncertainty and *ex post* application difficulties as is substantive regulation. In order to overcome the narrow range of expressly targeted prohibitions, liability rules have to be formulated at a fairly high level of generality, limited by the due process constraints that individuals must have notice of potential areas of proscribed conduct. This leads to the second problem, that of liability regimes depending on the ability of conflicted agents to accurately internalize the risk of future costs against the near-certainty of present benefits. In a typical conflict-of-interest situation, agents may tend to overdiscount the likelihood of eventual punishment, thus undermining the deterrent function of the prescribed penalty. Third and finally, the imposition of liability on certain kinds of actors can have the perverse effect of exacerbating conflicts of interest, as the primary interest of the agent becomes avoiding liability rather than representing his or her principals. The potential for the first two of these problems can be seen in the criminal provisions of the Public Company Accounting Reform and Investor Protection Act, generally known by the name of its sponsors as the Sarbanes-Oxley Act, which I discuss below as a representative example of a deterrence-oriented liability regime. The third problem is raised by recent movements toward holding lawyers liable for the unlawful activities of their corporate clients.

We can begin with the liability regime of Sarbanes-Oxley. By contrast to the procedural regulation of accounting set out in Title II of the Act, Titles VIII, IX, and XI deal with corporate fraud by enhancing the penalties of existing civil and criminal offenses, and creating new criminal offenses. For example, §802 increases the penalties for destruction of documents to impair a federal investigation to twenty years in prison, §804 extends the statute of limitations for prosecution of fraud, §807 increases the penalty for securities fraud to twenty-five years in prison, §903 increases the maximum terms for mail and wire fraud, and so forth. One would think that prosecutors were already obtaining the maximum prison terms already on the books and finding that those were insufficient to deter. Far from it. Most federal statutes already carry massive potential incarceration, at levels rarely meted out even in homicide cases.

Although it may be premature to criticize these latter provisions before their long-term effects can be judged by the empirical record, one can predict that they will encounter the same systemic problems as the preexisting liability regime on which they are based. Keeping in mind the limitations of agent liability identified earlier – particularly the potential for short-term bias on the part of agents to undermine deterrence, and the subsequent costs of application once deterrence fails – there is little obvious reason that the increase in penalties standing alone is likely to significantly increase deterrence. The premise must be that by raising the stakes for agents personally, these sections will provide a powerful disincentive against committing corporate fraud. One also can see, however, the dependence of these sections on corporate agents accurately weighing the costs of future punishment against the benefits of present gain. If the analyses of agents are biased toward the short term, then the deterrent effect of the liability regime breaks down. Moreover, considering the administrative burdens and necessary procedural constraints of the criminal justice system, many agents may well be correct in thinking that they will "get away with it."

Ultimately, the criminal provisions of the Sarbanes-Oxley Act surely constitute more of a political reaction to corporate scandal than a carefully considered regulatory response. By "getting tough" on corporate fraud, Sarbanes-Oxley sends a symbolic message (to a variety of audiences) that white-collar crime is deserving of real punishment. This is not to say that altering liability rules will have no impact on agent behavior. Although no cases against individuals have yet been brought under Sarbanes-Oxley's criminal provisions, the Act has doubtless changed how many corporate leaders consider their responsibilities to investors. The real question, though, is whether liability rules without process reforms can achieve their intended purpose. Ten years from now, will the conflicts of interest involved in corporate governance be less intense than they are today? By merely ratcheting up liability consequences without addressing the underlying conflicts, Sarbanes-Oxley may have missed an opportunity for more meaningful corporate reform.

Let me shift focus and turn from Sarbanes-Oxley to the question of attorney liability and privilege in corporate law. Increasingly, liability rules are being crafted to obligate "gatekeepers" to assume liability to their parties as a way of compelling them to police the behavior of their clients. Examples include the "noisy withdrawal" from representation if improprieties are suspected. By requiring corporate lawyers, under threat of legal penalty, to remove themselves from improper client behavior and in many cases to report that behavior to organizational authorities, the hope is that (1) lawyers will not aid clients in committing fraud, and (2) clients will be less likely to commit fraud in the first place, for fear that if they do so their lawyers will reveal it (Coffee, 2003).

There is reason to be cautious in not considering the secondary, and unintended, effects of a regime of liability to third parties. As noted at the beginning of this chapter, every attorney–client relationship bears the fragility of principal–agent relations. The key insight from the economic studies of principal–agent relations is that the agency costs are likely to increase as the incentives operating on the agent increasingly depart from the bonds holding the agent to the aims of the principal. This is no less true in legal representation. To the extent that lawyers are held accountable to the world writ large for the conduct of their clients, the lawyers will predictably protect themselves by compromising the duty of loyalty to the client. Although this may break the bonds of silence that accompanied some of the more notorious corporate scandals, it also is possible that such requirements will simply encourage corporate actors to withhold potentially damaging information from their lawyers, thus undermining the compliance-enhancing function of legal counsel. Under this scenario, the original conflict of interest problem is only worsened. Actions that might have been in the interest of principals, such as seeking legal advice concerning activities of questionable legality, would now be precluded by the agent's pressing interest in avoiding punishment.

Moves toward broadening attorney liability have come from a variety of different institutional angles. Until recently, the governing standard for attorney liability to nonclients was the decision of the Supreme Court in *Central Bank of Denver v. First Interstate Bank of Denver*, which took a very restrictive view under which private liability would only run to those who had a direct contractual expectation of a duty of loyalty. In the *In re Enron*, litigation, however, this rule was effectively called into question by the district court in Texas in allowing Enron's primary law firm, Vinson & Elkins, to be sued by Enron Corp. investors for its role in the corporation's fraudulent business practices. If such decisions signal an emerging trend in federal case law, the effect will be a significant expansion of the extent to which lawyers can be held liable for the malfeasance of their clients. This parallels the decision of the SEC, acting under the authority of Sarbanes-Oxley, to require "up-the-ladder" reporting by attorneys wishing to practice before the SEC. Perhaps most significant, the ABA, long the protector of the practicing bar, joined in with a proposed alteration that would mirror the Sarbanes-Oxley reporting requirements for lawyers who become aware of unlawful conduct by a client.

This section is not intended as a plea for immunity for lawyers who actively abet fraudulent or criminal conduct by their clients. Rather, in the context of imprecise liability rules and the failure to engage in serious process regulation to get at the heart of conflicted behavior, the rules extending further liability to lawyers may further erode the role of lawyers as counselors *against* misconduct. The preceding legal standards together represent a trend toward placing greater responsibility on lawyers for the improprieties of their corporate clients. This may seem a natural means of responding to current legal problems in corporate governance (Coffee, 2003). Lawyers have, after all (and let us be frank), played strong supporting roles in many recent dramas of corporate malfeasance. Before diving headlong into a curtailment of traditional attorney privilege, however, courts and regulators should consider the full consequences of their decisions. It is possible that expanding attorney liability will chill attorney–client communications that are important to promoting legal compliance.

PROCESS REGULATION

Substantive regulation addresses its concern to the outcomes of a decision-making process. Liability rules similarly focus on the consequences of the wrong decision having been made. As discussed earlier, each of these approaches requires an after-the-fact assessment of the decision itself and the conditions under which it was selected. By contrast, it is possible to think of decisions implicating conflicts of interest in terms not of the substance of the decisions, but the process by which the decisions are made. Most central to this approach is to ask the question whether the proper decision maker is acting, or whether the decision maker is overly subject to conflicted incentives to be allowed to decide alone – or at all. The key to this form of regulation is that it is capable of being enforced ex ante rather than ex post and focuses on the screens that are in place to mitigate conflict. The aim of such process rules is to isolate conflicted agents from a particular decision-making position.

To take but one example, a recent study of how law firms handle conflicts of interest in client representation found that in firms of any size it has become almost standard practice to have a standing conflict committee that must independently review any new clients or new representation for potential conflicts with other firm clients or matters (Shapiro, 2003) – as opposed to leaving such matters either to the discretion of the lawyers who have generated the new business or awaiting a claim that a conflicted decision emerged. Another example is the common bar on government officials negotiating contracts with companies in which they are financially involved. In this situation, although it is possible that an official would not allow a relationship with a firm to bias his or her judgment in allocating government business, the procedural bar removes the obvious conflict-of-interest risk altogether. It should be noted that procedural regulation pays no formal attention to the substantive outcome of a regulated transaction. The enforcement mechanism does not inquire whether the actual transaction was a good deal for the firm or the governmental entity. Instead, the transaction itself is structured so as to get at the underlying conflict.

In that it focuses on set rules rather than substantive decision making, procedural regulation lies on the other side from substantive regulation across the theoretical distinction between rules and standards. Rules tend to be a fixed form of regulation in which great specifics are applied to the definition of permissible and prohibited conduct, but in which little discretion is left to their application or enforcement. Standards, by contrast, tend to be more sweeping and rely on more after-the-fact examination of the context of their application. In simple terms, a red light at an intersection is a rule; a yield sign or an instruction to proceed with caution, more of a standard. Like legal rules generally, procedural regulation has the advantages of being predictable *ex ante* and cheap to apply *ex post*. Moreover, the main weakness of legal rules, their inflexibility in the face of unknown future circumstances, is less of a problem when responding to recognized conflicts of interest where the conflicted agents have already shown themselves liable to engage in opportunistic behavior.

A worthwhile example of process regulation emerges in parts of the Sarbanes-Oxley response to the spate of recent corporate accounting scandals. The Sarbanes-Oxley Act's numerous provisions address an array of observed conflicts of interest in corporate gate keeping, placing particular emphasis on those involved in independent accounting and corporate governance. Most relevant here are the sections dealing specifically with accounting, in that they function by erecting process barriers between the auditing work of accounting firms and the business interests of their clients. These barriers, meant to ensure the objectivity of corporate auditing, provide a useful example of how procedural regulation can feasibly be structured.

The sections of the Sarbanes-Oxley Act affecting accounting and auditing practices are found primarily within Title II of the Act, under the heading of Auditor Independence. The main effect of this section is to prohibit accounting firms engaged in auditing a client from contemporaneously performing for that client any of a list of nonaudit financial services, including accounting, consulting, and legal services. Section 201 also requires that for an accounting firm to perform any other permissible nonaudit financial services contemporaneous with an audit, such services must be preapproved by the client's auditing committee. These rules are intended to prevent the conflict of interest problems that can arise when an accounting firm is engaged to serve as a client's putatively independent auditor, while at the same time providing lucrative consulting services. In such circumstances, an auditor may be tempted to overlook a client's improper accounting, or even to provide aid in structuring that accounting, in order to secure the income accruing from a profitable consulting contract. This was exactly the scenario that led to the most catastrophic corporate scandal of them all, ending in the bankruptcy of Enron Corporation and the utter destruction of Arthur Andersen. After §201 of the Sarbanes-Oxley Act, this particular conflict-inducing relationship is precluded by law.

Other sections of Title II provide further, more specific restrictions on the relations permissible between accountants and their clients. For instance, §203 requires that an accounting firm rotate the auditing partner assigned to a particular client at least once every five years. Section 206 prohibits an accounting firm from performing auditing work for a client if an officer of the client was formerly employed by the accounting firm and participated in an audit of the client within the previous year. Together, these sections attempt to address situations where individual partners of an accounting firm may be induced by personal ties to compromise the level of outside detachment deemed necessary for the independent auditor function. Of significance for this chapter is not whether these rules are either necessary or sufficient for auditor independence, but the form of regulation. Rather than requiring any substantive judgment of an accountant's behavior, these rules instead operate by structuring institutional relationships so as to obviate potential conflicts of interest before they have a chance to arise.

This form of process regulation is more difficult to enact and requires a more careful assessment of specific conditions likely to give rise to conflicts of interest. Where feasible, however, there is every reason to suspect that addressing the decision-making role of conflicted agents is a superior approach rather than trying to police complicated outcomes after the fact – particularly when the manifestation of the conflict may make the harm irreparable. It is likely to be superior not only in providing clear direction to potentially conflicted agents, but also in effectiveness. The evidence so far is that Sarbanes-Oxley has already prompted broad compliance in the form of significant policy changes at affected accounting firms. Contemporaneous with the enactment of Sarbanes-Oxley, the "big four" accounting firms, and many other, smaller firms, stated that they would no longer perform nonaudit financial services for companies with which they were engaged to audit. The accounting firms have since lived up to their promises – in fact, three of the big four have gone so far as to spin their consulting businesses off as separate companies. The result is that in just over the last year, the once-common practice of performing both auditing and nonaudit services for the same client has largely disappeared from corporate accounting. Although this phenomenon can be attributed partly to the intense efforts of postscandal accounting firms to rebuild public credibility, it is also evidence of Title II's regulatory effectiveness. By clearly establishing *ex ante* which accounting practices are and are not permissible, Title II appears to be yielding high legal compliance at effectively zero enforcement cost.

The example of procedural regulation through Title II of the Sarbanes-Oxley Act should illustrate the following basic principles. First, unlike substantive regulation and individual liability regimes, which demand that agents simply not succumb to recognized conflicts of interest, procedural regulation structures interactions so as to prevent conflicts from arising in the first place. Also, as compared to substantive standards, clear procedural rules can provide for greater *ex ante* compliance by agents and cheaper *ex post* application by officials. Together, these principles explain the particular effectiveness of procedural regulation as a legal response to conflicts of interest.

CONCLUSION

Conflicts of interest are endemic in the law in two senses. First, the nature of legal representation itself is an example of a principal–agent relation that is by its nature a source of conflict for the agent. Second, much of legal regulation is directed at either the processes or the consequences of conflicted decision making, not just in the narrow setting of the attorney–client relation. In presenting a taxonomy of regulation of conflict, I clearly showed my preference for ex ante checks on the scope of action by conflicted agents. I find that attempts to check compromised decision making before the fact to be preferable both to after-the-fact substantive review and general liability regimes that risk overdeterrence of desired risk taking. Unfortunately, effective process regulation requires an initial investment in information about the nature of the conflict and how to cabin the undesired behaviors of actors facing conflicted incentives. It is far easier to generalize vaguer substantive regulations or just create a sweeping liability regime. There is something distinct, I would suggest, about conflicts of interest that make them relatively immune to substantive or liability based regimes. The combination of self-serving belief about the propriety of conduct combined with the clear incentives running to the here and now limit the effectiveness of regulatory responses that do not remove conflicted actors from decision making. Unfortunately, figuring that out takes work.

References

Black, Henry C. (1951). *Black's law dictionary, 4th ed*. St. Paul, MN: West Publishing Company.

Central Bank of Denver v. First Inter-state Bank of Denver, 511 U.S. 164 (1994).

Coffee, Jr., John C. (2002). Are we really getting tough on white collar crime? 15 Federal Sentencing Reporter 245 (2002).

Coffee, Jr., John C. (2002). *The attorney as gate keeper: An agenda for the securities and Exchange Commission*, 103 Columbia Law Review 1293, 1302 (2003).

In re Exxon, 235 F.Supp.2d 549 (S.D. Tex. 2002).

Issacharoff, Samuel, & Ortiz, Daniel R. (1999). *Governing through Intermediaries*, 85 Virginia Law Review 1627.

Orentlicher, David. (2002). *Conflicts of interest and the constitution*, 59 Washington and Lee Law Review 713, 718.

Rachlinski, Jeffrey. (1998). *A positive psychological theory of judging in hindsight*, 65 University of Chicago Law Review 571.

Shapiro, Susan P. (2003). *Bushwhacking the ethical high road: conflict of interest in the practice of law and real life*, 28 Law & Social Inquiry 87, 93.

FOURTEEN

Commentary

Conflicts of Interest Begin Where Principal–Agent Problems End[1]

George Loewenstein
Carnegie Mellon University

Sam Issacharoff argues that conflicts of interest can be dealt with as a classic case of a principal–agent problem in which the agent's interests differ from those of the principal. After articulating this general perspective and illustrating it with the case of law, Issacharoff then proposes a tripartite classification of legal responses to conflicts of interest, each of which, he argues, has the goal of bringing the agent's behavior more closely in line with the interests of the principal. The main thrust of this commentary is a question of whether, in fact, conflicts of interest are well dealt with as a principal–agent problem.[2]

---

[1] Title from a comment by Ashish Nanda during discussion of the paper.

[2] As a subsidiary issue, I have some questions about the usefulness of Sam's tripartite categorization of mechanisms through which the law responds to conflicts of interest – substantive regulation, process-based regulation, and liability regimes. Ideally, we would like the partitioning of mechanisms defined by the categorization rule to be *complete*: it should be possible to classify any mechanism that is proposed into one of the three categories, and there should be widespread agreement about which category such a mechanism belongs in. Knowing a tiny bit about conflicts of interest in medicine, I decided to see how well it could classify some of the most basic remedies for conflicts of interest in this domain. A commonplace conflict of interest in medicine occurs when pharmaceutical companies present gifts to "high-volume prescribers" of their medications. Jason Dana and I have argued, in a recent issue of *JAMA*, that the obvious and logical response to the conflict of interest that results is to simply ban such gifts. I am not sure whether this is best classified as a regulation or a procedure. At first blush, it would seem to be a substantive regulation, because it involves a specific prohibition on behavior, but a close reading of Sam's piece made me wonder. He writes: "First, unlike substantive regulation and individual liability regimes, which demand that agents simply not succumb to recognized conflicts of interest, procedural regulation structures interactions so as to prevent conflicts from arising in the first place." Banning gifts, it seems to me, does not demand that agents not succumb to conflicts of interest; it prevents them from arising in the first place (which

The conflicts of interest that were the focus of this conference all take a common form: a clash between individuals' self-interest, on the one hand, and their professional duties, on the other. Principal–agent formulations, I would argue, are well-suited to modeling the self-interest side of this equation, but they have almost nothing to say about the other side of the equation: professionalism.

When professionals are confronted with charges of bias resulting from conflicts of interest, inevitably their first reaction is that they are not vulnerable to bias as a result of their professional training. Thus, for example, Don Moore, in his commentary on Mark Nelson's paper, cites Gary Shamis, Chairman of the Management of an Accounting Practice Committee at the American Institute of Certified Public Accountants, to the effect that, "We are professionals that follow our code of ethics and practice by the highest moral standards. We would never be influenced by our own personal financial well being." However, contrary to this oft-espoused view, in Issacharoff's presentation, as well as in other presentations at the conference (including Moore's commentary on Nelson), professionalism is viewed with a high degree of cynicism. Indeed, my own past work[3,4] has taken a dim view of the protections provided by professionalism.

But can professionalism be dismissed so easily? Is it naive to think that professionalism can counteract conflicts of interest? In fact, it could be argued that professionalism is the first, and primary, bulwark against bias, and that the types of incentive-based solutions discussed by Issacharoff are mere fixes.

In most professions, such as medicine, law, and academia, it is virtually impossible to monitor the "micro" behavior of individuals. As a result,

seems to classify it as a procedural regulation). But perhaps this logic is wrong. Given that pharmaceutical companies would still have the option of giving gifts (even though it would involve breaking the law) and physicians would have the option of accepting them, perhaps they still would confront a conflict of interest. But, by this logic, would not most remedies have to be classified as substantive regulation? Or, consider another common solution to the problem – to give centralized "formularies" the power to determine what drugs can be prescribed. Superficially, this seems to be a case of process-based regulation, but ultimately, the formulary is going to be specifying what drugs can and cannot be prescribed, which sounds more like substantive regulation (albeit implemented by a formulary).

[3] Bazerman, Max H., Loewenstein, George, & Moore, Don A. (2002). Why good accountants do bad audits: The real problem isn't conscious corruption. It's unconscious bias. *Harvard Business Review*, (November), 96–103.

[4] Dana, J., and Loewenstein, G. (2003). A psychological perspective on the influence of gifts to physicians from industry. *Journal of the American Medical Association, 290*(2), 252–5.

one simply has to rely on the integrity of the individual. In academia, for example, opportunities for fraud abound, and the individual incentives to commit fraud are monumental. Professionalism is the main thing that is preventing us from fudging our data – for example, deleting inconvenient subjects – even when it could make the difference between publishing or "perishing." If professional ethics were to collapse in academia, it would spell the demise of the profession. No kind of substantive regulation, process-based regulation, or liability regime could possibly take the place of professionalism in such a situation.

The same is true in medicine. Monitoring physicians effectively is costly, if not impossible. Indeed, there have been a number of documented cases in which physicians have gone about systematically killing hundreds of their patients, and in each case it took years to discover the problem and even longer to prosecute. With the increasing commercialization of medical care and the resultant increase in opportunities for self-advancement at the expense of patients, professionalism has, if anything, become more *necessary* (whether or not it has actually become more prevalent) in medicine.

If professionalism is as important as this argument suggests, then any policies designed to deal with conflicts of interest need to take into account not only economic incentives – that is, of principal–agent issues – but also of the other side of the equation – their impact on professionalism. Consider, for example, liability regimes. Although outlawing bias is unlikely to deter fraud, laws can influence behavior indirectly, through their influence on professionalism. On the one hand, laws serve a symbolic function, defining certain behaviors as "beyond the pale." As Issacharoff notes,

> This is not to say that altering liability rules will have no impact on agent behavior. Although no cases against individuals have yet been brought under Sarbanes-Oxley's criminal provisions, the Act has doubtless changed how many corporate leaders consider their responsibilities to investors.

On the other hand, laws can have a perverse effect by shifting patterns of behavior that would otherwise fall into the moral realm into the legal realm of costs and benefits. Such an effect is beautifully illustrated by a study conducted by Gneezy and Rustichini[5] in which a fine was introduced at a day care center for picking up children after the closing hour. Surprisingly, late pickups actually increased after the fine was introduced.

---

[5] Gneezy, Uri, & Rustichini, Aldo. (2000). A fine is a price. *Journal of Legal Studies, 29*, 1–17.

One possible explanation for the effect is that picking up one's child on time was seen as a socially desirable action; introducing the fine converted it into a market transaction, at which point people started to ask themselves whether the inconvenience of picking their children up on time was worth the cost of the fine. The same principal applies with equal force to substantive rules and changes in process. Such rules and procedures may circumvent conflicts of interest in the specific domains they cover, but can, perversely, lead people to believe that anything not covered by the rules must be ethically permissible.

The notion of professionalism, and its interactions with the types of economic issues highlighted by principal–agent problems, may help to address the riddle of why diverse conflicts of interest have seemingly grown so much more severe, and their effects so much more pernicious, in the recent past.

Part of the answer seems to involve a widespread deterioration in professionalism. Professionalism involves more than a series of rules; it refers to the whole way that people construe what their job is all about. And, in profession after profession – for example, banking, auditing, and medicine – there seems to have been a change in the way professionals mentally construe what their job is about. For example, in earlier times, auditors saw their task as that of a detective – to ferret out errors and inconsistencies in the client's accounts. When a client asked him to certify an inaccurate financial report, Arthur Andersen, in his early days as an auditor, is famously said to have replied that he would not do so for all the money in the city of Chicago. Current auditors, however, are being imbued with the very different view of auditing as one of many services offered to earn profits from client companies. Many doctors, similarly, complain that an increasing fraction of their time is spent on recordkeeping and accounting – on the business side of their job.

The self-interest side of conflicts of interest – the side better described by principal–agent models – is the easy part to deal with. Professionalism is much trickier. Developing and fostering a code of ethics and behavior in a profession is a slow, painstaking process. But, professionalism can deteriorate with frightening rapidity, as we have seen in recent decades. And, once the egg of professionalism has been cracked, all of the legal regulations in the world may not be able to put Humpty back together again.

FIFTEEN

Conflicts of Interest and Strategic Ignorance of Harm

Jason Dana*

Carnegie Mellon University

Professionals with conflicts of interest face a choice between acting in accord with their self-interest or their professional responsibility. As this choice nearly always has consequences for others, an understanding of these conflicts necessarily entails a discussion of social preferences. In this discussion, I defend the notion that altruistic behavior often results from a desire not to violate rules of ethical conduct, rather than, as current economic theories suggest, a taste for altruistic outcomes per se. Whereas some situations compel people to sacrifice personal gains in favor of social concerns, these same individuals may prefer to avoid such situations in order to be selfish. For example, one may forgo even costless information about the consequences for others of a desired action, as discovering that the action is harmful could compel one not to take it. As described later, such an agent would be engaging in "strategic ignorance of harm."

Rather than an intentional violation of ethical or moral rules, professional misconduct is often best described as a circumvention of them. Although this distinction might appear pedantic, it suggests challenges and opportunities for how we deal with the problem. In particular, our tendency to give the benefit of doubt in determining whether one has violated a moral rule provides incentives for strategic ignorance of harm, as ignorance raises a question of intent. I will discuss how conflicts can thus remain problematic even where extensive oversight and punishment

* I am grateful to Cristina Bicchieri, Daylian Cain, Robyn Dawes, George Loewenstein, and Gabe Silverman for helpful comments and conversations.

are possible. To the extent that this account of altruistic behavior is accurate, we should refine our ethical training as well as take action to correct incentive structures that reward ignorance of social harm.

THE NATURE OF SOCIAL PREFERENCES

People quite often exhibit nonselfish concerns. They may give to charity or bear a cost to ensure that someone who has behaved unfairly is punished. Economics experiments have demonstrated nonselfish behavior in an environment in which fewer confounding explanations exist. In dictator games, subjects often share some positive amount of their experimental endowment with an anonymous other, even though they are not obliged to do so. In ultimatum bargaining games, responders may reject highly inequitable offers and leave both parties with nothing, a punishment costly to themselves. (For a thorough review of experimental findings in these games, see Camerer, 2003.)

To reconcile fair behavior with the traditional economic assumption of rational self-interest, many theories assume a selfish concern for social outcomes. These theories, which I will henceforth refer to as theories of *outcome preference*, postulate that the utility guiding an agent's choice is functional in some way on one's own and others' monetary payoffs. The utility functions may include terms representing others' wealth (e.g., Andreoni, 1990; Andreoni & Miller, 2002), concern for relative wealth between self and others (Fehr & Fischbacher, 1999; Bolton & Ockenfels, 2000), or concern for relative wealth and overall welfare (Charness & Rabin, 2000). Viewed from this perspective, a personal sacrifice of money that benefits another person maximizes self-interest because it brings about the outcome that is desired. That is, altruistic behavior reflects a selfish taste to help others.

Theories of outcome preference are a tractable and effective way to explain many simple demonstrations of other-regarding behavior, especially those we see in economic experiments. Where contracts are incomplete, we must rely on the agent having concern for the principal's welfare to prevent discretionary behavior. Should these theories, then, enlighten our efforts to curb professional misconduct? I question whether they could.

My main objection to using theories of outcome preference as a policy guide is that the body of experimental literature that drives these theories is too homogeneous. Consider again the example of the dictator game. In the standard paradigm, the subject in the role of sender is placed in a rare situation: she is asked to make an unambiguous decision to give or not to give. The consequences of her actions are clear to her, as well as to the receiver with whom she is matched. Although the receiver is anonymous, she knows that he is one of the people in the room and she has probably even looked at his face. Furthermore, she can likely infer a great deal about him. He is a student who, like her, signed up for the experiment to make some extra money, but due to some random assignment (though there are several variations on this) was placed in a disadvantaged role.

All of these stipulations, which typically are not present in the ecology of a financial conflict of interest, are chronic in the laboratory and potentially determine the experimental altruism we observe. Generalizing theories of outcome preference to the domain of conflict of interest is thus risky. It could be that the features of the typical economic experiment make subjects with no specific taste for augmenting others' wealth feel compelled to give. In fact, the experimental economic literature does not rule this possibility out.

Recent experiments (Dana, Weber, & Kuang, 2003) provide a test of this possibility. In a variant of the dictator game, experimental participants were randomly assigned the roles of either "sender" or "receiver." Senders chose one of two actions with monetary consequences for themselves and an anonymously matched receiver, who made no choice. The payoffs reflected conflicting interests among the players; action **A** yielded the sender the best payoff of $6 and the receiver the worst payoff of $1, while action **B** yielded $5 to both parties. This is depicted in Figure 15.1. This particular payoff structure was chosen to encourage generosity – **B** provides more overall welfare, whereas **A** costs the receiver $4 at a benefit of only $1 to the sender. Any situational manipulations leading to selfish choice must thus be all the more effective. Although senders made their choices, receivers also chose hypothetically as if in the role of sender, in part to make everyone appear equally busy so as to maintain the anonymity of the roles.

Perhaps not surprisingly, 74 percent of senders chose the equitable option. This might be thought of as an experimental demonstration of altruism, since the parties were anonymous to each other and no punishment option was available to the receiver. Typical explanations of such behavior involve a preference for kind outcomes. All of the receivers hypothetically chose **B**. Because this choice was inconsequential, one might argue that the responses reflected a bias toward providing the socially desirable response. The fact that *every* receiver knew which answer was desirable, however, is informative. It suggests that people have a shared knowledge

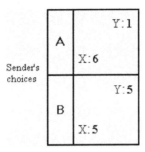

Figure 15.1. Sender (X) and receiver (Y).

of the rule of conduct in this situation. Senders and receivers are surely aware of what ideal behavior is, and if the sender did choose **A**, the receiver might think she has behaved badly.

Additional sessions employed a modification of this game that left the payoffs to the receiver unrevealed to all subjects. These payoffs were either as in the known condition described earlier or "flipped" so that the interests of both parties were mutual ($6, $5 vs. $5, $1). The true payoff state was determined by the flip of a fair coin, and all subjects were informed of this. Senders could, if they wanted, privately reveal the receiver's true payoff before making their choices by simply clicking a button on their computer interface. This situation is depicted in Figure 15.2.

If the outcome preference interpretation of the above results is correct, then 74 percent of senders in this version should reveal the payoffs and choose the mutual interest option. The intuition is simple: revealing is a win–win proposition. If the true payoffs reflect conflicting interests, a beneficent sender can choose the favored **B**, giving each party $5. If the payoffs are mutual interest, it is all the better as the sender can choose **A** and receive $6 while still doing the most good for the receiver. The authors' intuition, however, was that there would be significantly less revelation and more selfishness. By revealing, senders only risk finding that the true state of the world is matrix 1 in figure 15.2, where there is a strong feeling that one should choose **B**. Without revealing, **A** yields a better payoff and is no more likely to harm the receiver than is **B**. Revealing could thus place the sender in a position to feel empathy, costing her $1.

The proportion of senders who revealed and chose the mutual interest option was just under half, indeed significantly less than the 74 percent that chose **B** in the earlier version. Of the choices made when the true payoffs turned out to reflect conflicting interests (matrix 1), only 37 percent chose **B**. Thus, it seems that many senders who would be beneficent avoided

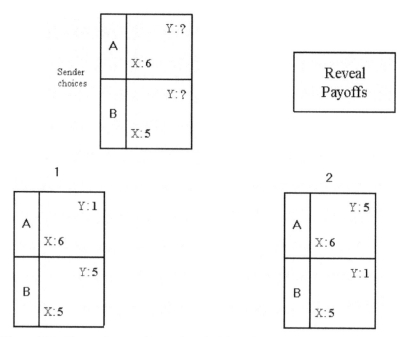

Figure 15.2. The sender can choose A or B without knowing the receiver's payoffs. If she wants, she can privately reveal the payoffs by clicking "reveal game." The true state is known to be either matrix 1 or matrix 2, as determined prior to the experiment by a coin flip.

the situation, ultimately benefiting themselves and harming receivers.[1] Variance in the receivers' choices reflected how the shared notion of ideal conduct breaks down when information is incomplete – although no receivers claimed they would choose **A** in the earlier version, 41 percent indicated they would do so in the unrevealed condition.

These experiments demonstrate both that subjects do not prefer the even split ($5, $5) in the sense that outcome preferences postulate and that they choose it when there is no uncertainty about outcomes. How can these findings be reconciled? It seems that the choice of **A** bears an additional cost only when it is known that it is harmful. Furthermore, the subjects' choices, particularly the receivers (none of which hypothetically chose A), seem to indicate that **A** is not the action one would ideally take only when it is known that it is harmful. The authors interpreted this

---

[1] These senders were quizzed thoroughly about their understanding of the choice and its consequences. Unintended or unconscious bias is therefore an inappropriate interpretation for the allocators' ignorance. In this case, it is more properly thought of as strategic.

behavior as evidence of concern for a moral rule because the anonymous dictator game precludes concerns of punishment or reputation. Senders apparently want to maximize their own payoffs but do not want to be seen or see themselves as bad. To that end, they seek "smoke and no mirrors" to allow themselves a selfish choice. The authors' intuitions were that allowing the selfish choice to be made uncertain, though knowable, consequences for the receiver would suffice. Why and whether it is sensible that people do not perceive uncertain, though knowable harm as a moral violation will be addressed later.

Further experimental work (Dana, Cain, & Dawes, 2004) demonstrates that people will pay a premium to avoid social binds that oblige them to give. An unannounced $10 dictator game was administered immediately following another experimental task. Again, roles of sender or receiver were randomly assigned. Senders first made their allocation choices, and then receivers were informed that a dictator game was being played and given whatever the sender allocated for them. Before the choice was executed, senders were surprised with a new option of taking $9, dubbed by the authors as an "exit" option. If they accepted this $9, the receiver would not be informed that a dictator game was being played and would receive no payment.[2]

Even though exiting reduces overall welfare, yields a lower payoff to senders than they could have ensured themselves, and requires in some sense that senders countermand their original decision, 30 percent of senders chose to exit. Those exiting typically profited, however, relative to their intended division of the endowment. As the exit option was a surprise, this intention can be considered sincere. Apparently, these senders felt compelled to give away more than $1 to the receiver before they knew of the exit option. By exiting, the receiver was kept ignorant of the situation, and thus had no expectations regarding the sender's behavior. Selfishness was thus victimless – a receiver who does not know there is a game is not upset that surprise money has not come his way. Note again that outcome preferences cannot explain this behavior, as ($9, $0) was chosen when both ($10, $0) and ($9, $1) were available.

The sender's concern with what the receiver knows is again interesting, since the receiver is anonymous and cannot punish the sender. It is as if the sender gauges whether a desired action is bad, and thus should not

---

[2] By not announcing the game, it was possible to have the sender simply leave after the prior experimental task without suspicion that they were denied an opportunity to play the dictator game.

be taken, by whether it can be justified to an internalized public. To this end, the evaluation of behavior by even anonymous receivers is salient, as is common knowledge of the game structure. This prompted the authors to conclude that the behavior of their subjects was consistent with the principle "what you don't know won't hurt me."

A recent theoretical literature complements these findings. In laying out his theory of the origins and nature of altruism, Field (2001) argues that "failure-to-harm" is the canonical form of human altruism. When positive assistance is given, he notes, we applaud it, because it is unusual. But most altruism comes in the form of not harming others, even though we often have the opportunity to do so. This is consistent with the notion of harm-avoidant preferences. The altruism that we observe when people are equitable arises mainly from their desire not to upset others by violating their expectations. However, we should not expect many to voluntarily put themselves in situations where fairness is expected.

Rabin (1995) formally modeled an idea quite similar to the theme of this chapter: the difference between what he called "moral preferences" and "moral constraints." In the former case, people prefer not to cause socially harmful outcomes. In the latter, they prefer to maximize self-interest subject to the constraint that they not cause socially harmful outcomes. What he shows is that decision makers with moral constraints will sometimes forgo costless learning. His conclusions regarding knowledge acquisition are qualitatively similar to those assumed in the present discussion. In his example of boycotting certain grapes because they exploit farm labor, a consumer may not want to know if farm labor was exploited so that she can enjoy grapes. He summarizes, "When her beliefs tell her it is morally okay to engage in an enjoyable activity, an agent will avoid gathering further information that might jeopardize her moral green light." In choosing what information to gather, Rabin's agents were manipulating their own beliefs so that they could take a desired action, prompting him to call his model one of self-serving biases.

It is informative to differentiate the present thesis from Rabin's theory and, more generally, self-serving bias in the perception of fairness (e.g., Loewenstein et al., 1992; Messick & Sentis, 1979, 1983). Self-serving bias describes an unconscious altering of beliefs about what is fair to bring them in line with one's self-interest. Agents who strategically ignore harm, however, remain consistent in that they abide by principles of fair conduct, yet they prefer to avoid situations in which they know these principles will apply. In the Dana, Weber, and Kuang experiments, it is hard to interpret not revealing and choosing **A** as reflecting anything but conscious strategy.

Furthermore, the perception by senders that such behavior is acceptable is apparently shared by a number of the receivers, so that we could hardly call it a bias in favor of one's self-interest.

This point, however subtle, is where the present formulation diverges from Rabin's model: willingness to take a potentially harmful action does not require any belief manipulation. Indeed, Rabin comments (1995, p. 28): "We do not consciously and openly think such thoughts as 'I merely need to turn over this paper to find out the social consequences of an action I plan, but I choose to remain ignorant so that I feel justified in taking the action.'" Yet, this seems an appropriate description of what the experimental subjects did.

A "TEXTBOOK" EXAMPLE OF IGNORANCE OF HARM

The experiments described earlier bear features analogous to those in real principal–agent relationships. Consider the sender and receiver as the parties in the fiduciary relationship, with the sender being an agent for the receiver, who is the principal. The choices of **A** and **B** represent a professional conflict between the agent's personal interests and duty to behave altruistically toward the principal. The receiver's inability to punish represents information asymmetries that prevent the principal from monitoring the agent. Assume that this agent subscribes, as do the principals, to the ethical principle of nonmaleficence. This agent will not take an action that is much more costly to his principals than it is beneficial to himself. Yet, we can imagine that when faced with the prospect of taking a personally beneficial action, he does not wonder "is this action in the best interest of the principals?" nor is he anxious to find out that it is a harmful action and that he cannot take it.[3] The following example will help to illustrate.

An instructor has to assign a textbook for an introductory course with five hundred students. A publishing company representative offers him course materials including lecture outlines and homework assignments for use with her company's book. These materials are time-saving, and so he assigns the book. As the book is marketed in this fashion and the supporting materials are costly, the book's price is $20 higher than a

---

[3] Of course, I do not believe that the motivation to not want to know about harm is completely insensitive to the amount of harm possible. For instance, in the Dana, Weber, and Kuang experiment, subjects would surely reveal if A yielded either $6, $5 or $6, -$10,000. In cases in which the harm is potentially large, a principle of disaster avoidance takes over.

worthy competitor, but the instructor did not know this when he assigned the book, nor did he ever ask what the book cost. Although he has made small personal gains, his choice has transferred an extra $10,000 from the students he serves to a party outside of the fiduciary relationship, a trade-off he wouldn't have made had he known the relevant price information.[4]

A couple of years ago, one professor scoffed when hearing this example. He claimed that no such problem existed because prices were pretty similar for all of the textbooks and lecturers chose the book with which they were most comfortable. To see if he was right, I went online looking for posted syllabi for introductory psychology courses to see what book was required. Quickly, I was able to identify twenty different books (from only twenty-four different classes!), some in as high as their eighth edition. I then checked the prices of those books at an online bookseller and found that their prices ranged from $53 to $100. Interestingly, perhaps the most highly regarded text in the group, an edition of Gleitman's book, was the second cheapest at $56. So, contrary to what the professor insisted, costs imposed on the students varied a great deal.

I can only speculate as to why someone would be so resistant to the notion that members of the profession might be choosing books that are not in the students' best interests. That such a mistaken claim could be made about textbook prices when that claim is so easily tested seems to reflect a motivation not to know. Furthermore, I would suggest such a condition is chronic, as the variance in textbooks assigned makes it doubtful that quality is the only consideration in choosing a book. Yet, I doubt that many instructors would knowingly choose an overly expensive book just to save themselves a little time.

Before discussing the implications of the experimental work for problems of professional misconduct, an objection should be addressed. It is impermissible for a professional to knowingly shirk her duty to the principals. However, the same cannot be said for the selfish behavior of experimental subjects. Allocating $6 to oneself while leaving the passive receiver $1 is self-interested, but senders who do this are acting within their rights; they are under no obligation to choose equitably. Therefore,

---

[4] Another good example is pharmaceutical companies trying to influence physicians' prescription choices with gifts. A thought exercise: I speculate that if we eliminated all largesse from industry and then taxed prescriptions to pay doctors the loss in gifts, prescriptions would still be much cheaper, as their current price reflects both costly marketing and the driving out of price competition for the ultimate consumers. If the only relevant parties are those in the fiduciary relationship, as the professional oath holds, then the current situation is Pareto inefficient.

it could be the case that the strategic ignorance of harm we see in the experiments, for example, not having to choose **B** because one has not revealed the consequences, would not occur in real-world situations in which a failure to help represents a more serious offense.

Although there may be no impermissible actions in the experiments, they do seem to represent what Driver (1992) refers to as "morally charged situations." That is, there is a conflict between an ideal of behavior and a right the sender has to behave otherwise. If a sender chooses the equal split, then she has been more generous than she had to be; her deed is more than required, it is supererogatory. If she chooses ($6, $1), although she has behaved within her rights, there is a sense that her behavior was poor (but not forbidden), what Driver calls suberogatory. Adding the option not to reveal outcomes provides senders with a more neutral option out of this dilemma. The experiments are thus informative in that they suggest that an agent's ignorance is mitigating in the perception of whether the agent has behaved badly. If ignorance of consequences makes a bad less bad, it is quite plausibly a factor that facilitates transgressions. The real-world examples considered later in this chapter bear similarities with the experimental games, and it appears in these cases that there is benefit in remaining ignorant to potential harms.

NONMALEFICENCE AND STRATEGIC IGNORANCE

"First, do no harm" has been variously referred to as the doctor's edict, the Hippocratic ideal, and the fundamental principle of medicine. The quote, attributed to Hippocrates, has been embraced in many other branches of human service, such as social work and psychology. Countless commentaries on professional misconduct have invoked the phrase. Pundits have suggested that it should guide practice in disciplines like law, education, and public policy.

Thus, it may surprise many that the exact phrase "first, do no harm" appears neither in the modern nor the original version of the Hippocratic Oath. The phrase does appear in a Latin [mis]translation of Hippocrates' *The Epidemics*: "primum non nocere." The original Greek, however, is translated: "As to diseases, make a habit of two things – to help, or at least do no harm." Hippocrates clearly meant to make primary positive acts of assistance, while implying that not doing harm is the least one can do if helping is impossible. That do no harm has been distilled as an ideal is symptomatic of a shortcoming in our ethical thinking. Non-harm is an obligation, not an ideal. Moreover, it seems unnecessary to train young initiates not to harm. Most of us are inclined not to harm, at least wittingly.

The "wittingly" proviso, however, is more interesting and causes concern as to whether this principle accomplishes what so many hope it will: Does "do no harm" prevent as much harm from occurring as possible? Consider again the experiment described earlier in which senders could choose whether or not to reveal payoffs. Did senders violate the principle by choosing self-interestedly without revealing the receivers' payoffs? Of course, their actions ultimately lead to harm (or something harmlike), but the principle would be nonsensical if it told us not to cause harms of which we are unaware. Nature at least jointly determined the fate of receivers when it chose heads or tails (conditional on the sender's choice, it completely determined fate), leaving it equally possible that the sender's action helped. Even if the action did cause harm, senders would be blissfully unaware of it. By choosing not to reveal, senders ensured that they would not know what the receiver was paid. Furthermore, some of the receivers in the experiment seem to acknowledge that this act is not so clearly bad, as evidenced by their willingness to hypothetically choose the self-interested "A" option (when payoffs to others were not revealed), a choice that, if anything, should elicit a bias toward social desirability. Yet, if we accept that subjects who are randomly assigned to treatments are interchangeable, it seems that most of these same people believe in the principle, since a majority will pay a cost to ensure equity.

The problem, then, is that an agent who subscribes to a principle of nonmaleficence may cause unwitting harm without feeling that the principle was violated, even if the agent chose not to investigate possible harms. This excuse of ignorance strikes many as mitigating. That is, many of us feel more willing to punish someone who knew of harm but acted anyway than someone who knew that harm was possible but acted without exploring this possibility and ultimately caused harm. Yet, this excuse also smacks of flimsiness. After all, the agent chose ignorance.

Consequentially speaking, this behavior is logically inconsistent; preferences which dictate that my choice would change depending on others' outcomes but I do not want to know those outcomes cannot be reconciled with rational choice theories. Yet, educated and seemingly moral people seem to reflect this behavior. It feels as if we must somehow give the benefit of doubt to an agent who truly did not know her action was harmful, as if there were a question of intent to do harm. This is the case even if she knew harm was possible and did not take measures to detect it. The nonmaleficence principle can thus fall short, in practice, of what we want.

But is this a case of the principle being faulty, the principle not applying to this case, or of our intuitions about the principle being faulty? As Frank points out elsewhere in this volume, when our intuitions disagree with the standard, sometimes it is our intuitions that must be called into question rather than the standard. I submit that this is such a case. This feeling of benefit of doubt is neither useful nor informative in cases where there is willing ignorance of harm. Ethical training should stress this, if for no other than pragmatic reasons; it will help curtail professional misconduct. I do not wish to make the radical claim that any unwitting harm should be judged as harshly as a knowing harm. Yet, not holding agents culpable for harm when they "didn't know" they were harming can reward the psychological lengths the agents took to remain ignorant. In taking such lengths, the agent has in a sense answered whether there is intent, as ignorance is valuable only in preventing future incantations from behaving in accord with the principle and/or preventing others from enforcing the principle.

Put another way, the unwittingly harmful actions that we should hold in violation of nonmaleficence are those in which the ignorance can be thought of as strategic.[5] In order for ignorance of harm to be thought of as strategic, three necessary conditions should be met.

1. It is recognizable to a reasonable person that a possible result of the action is harm. We could not hold an agent responsible for dreaming up every exotic set of circumstances that possibly caused social harm, or else they would hardly be able to act.
2. Reasonable measures were available to the agent to detect harm, but were not exercised. That is, the agent, without undue cost to self, could potentially have learned that the action was harmful by performing some check (as in the case of the "reveal" button) but did not.
3. The agent had private incentives to take the action that caused harm. Although possibly incompetent, we should not assume an agent strategic by causing harm to both himself and others. For example, imagine a sender choosing **B** in the game in Figure 15.2

[5] My use of the phrase "strategic ignorance" should be distinguished from its use in economic theory as avoiding information so that one will not have a self-control problem (e.g., Carrillo & Mariotti, 2000). Here, the term "strategic" implies a best response to others who will punish conditional on intent to harm or future selves who will abide by the principle. The latter case could be argued to be strategic ignorance in the self-control sense of the word if one is willing to argue that choosing fairly, while indulgently self-maximizing for a given incarnation, is regrettable over the life span.

without revealing the true payoff state, which in this example will be matrix 1. This choice is "harmful" to the receiver, but most would infer that the sender did not understand the game, as she also lost as a result of her choice.

When society does not hold strategic ignorance of harm in violation of ethical principles, we are providing incentives which will ensure that harm happens. We must close any epistemic loopholes by punishing those who cause harm regardless of strategic ignorance. Examples of such problems are provided in the following section.

CREATING DISINCENTIVES FOR IGNORANCE OF HARM

Writing to managers, business ethicist Marianne Jennings (1996) suggested principles for ensuring "ethical lapses that lead to resignation of the CEO or a precipitous drop in your company's stock." Among them: send a clear message that you expect results at any cost. Within organizations, one's incentives often depend on the output of others, especially those who they supervise or employ. Although they may not be able to order others to lie, cheat, or steal to satisfy their personal incentives, supervisors can promote environments which encourage malfeasance by setting high rewards for unrealistic goals. If the goals are met, there is little motivation to want to know *how* they were met. Punishing the individual transgressor rather than those who create these problematic incentives will be of little deterrence.

Drug Use in Collegiate Football
Collegiate football programs are responsible for the development of their young athletes, but also face tremendous financial incentives to remain competitive. They may implicitly or explicitly put pressure on their players to become bigger and stronger than they are naturally capable, without telling the players how to accomplish this or wanting to know how they did. Although this could help the team, the player's health could be jeopardized and NCAA rules violated if the player takes performance-enhancing drugs. By promoting a competitive environment that could encourage steroid use, and then turning a blind eye, coaches and institutions can reap the rewards of strategic ignorance of harm.

The following exchange from a panel discussion (Outside the lines: bigger, stronger, faster; 2000) between an athletic director, his assistant in charge of compliance, and a sports correspondent, speaks volumes:

Athletic Dir. – Quite frankly, in our business, we're much more concerned with alcohol abuse, marijuana, cocaine. That to us is much more prevalent.
Correspondent – And that opinion is reflected in [institution removed]'s in-house drug testing program, which is distinct from the NCAA's testing program.
Asst. Athletic Dir. – We test the kids four times a year, two times a semester. And we test them for street drugs.
Correspondent – Not steroids?
Asst. Athletic Dir. – No, we do not test for steroids. We have good kids here. And we know that they're not using steroids.

Apparently, good kids are only prone to using drugs that could interfere with, rather than enhance, their football performance. Even though these testing practices are suspect, I believe that coaches and athletic directors subscribe to the principle of nonmaleficence and see themselves as ethical people. During the same panel discussion, a coach said: "I don't know of any coach who would ever in any [way] do anything that would hurt a youngster. That's the reason most coaches are in this business." I take this statement at its word; few of the professionals with a stake in the outcomes could bring themselves to order players to take steroids. More importantly, the rest of us find this knowing violation of nonmaleficence so reprehensible that severe punishments would be likely.

At the same time, I would suggest that coaches, athletic directors, and even fans turn a blind eye to the problem. Major college programs trot out entire offensive lines with average weights of over three hundred pounds, while as recently as 1980, *no one* in professional football, let alone collegiate football, weighed three hundred pounds. Can even the casual fan claim not to notice this trend? In the unlikely case that this incredible bulk up involves no illegal substances, still it must be harmful.[6] With players collapsing and even dying during summer workouts, it is clear that even in the short term such weight gain is dangerous. Yet, college football remains popular. How many fans, when watching their favorite team, think "that nineteen-year old will likely die early because of the things he's doing to his body?" An objective consideration of the evidence suggests harm has likely been caused, yet most fans are not morally outraged. I suggest that this results in part from our faulty intuitions about nonmaleficence.

Could collegiate football programs be strategically ignorant of harm, if their players use performance-enhancing drugs, and thus culpable?

---

[6] One professional player disclosed that a teammate used to consume eight thousand calories per day to try to reach three hundred pounds.

Following the above argument, it is clear that conditions 1 and 3 are met; it is clearly possible that players are being harmed and the programs stand to gain from this so long as they can deny knowing of that harm. What about condition 2; what constitutes a program failing to take reasonable measures to detect? The NCAA as a body has limited oversight capabilities, and players may only get tested by the NCAA once or twice in a four-year career as well as at any championship games. Even if some players are caught, punishing them is unlikely to stem the tide of weight gain, since there will be others willing to do almost anything to have a shot at being a millionaire playing professional football. On the other hand, the institutions and coaches have significantly more oversight capacity, as is evident when an institution can test four times a year for street drugs. If the NCAA, then, detects drug use with its limited oversight capacity, we should take it as prima facie evidence that condition 2 is met. If we are serious about curtailing the use of performance-enhancing drugs among collegiate athletes, we must align incentives by punishing the athletic programs.

The Conduct of Drug Trials Research

Drug trials have become increasingly commercial, often being conducted by the drug's manufacturer or a firm they hire (Bodenheimer, 2000).[7] This shift has been prompted by a need to conduct trials more quickly than academic medical centers have traditionally conducted them. As the exclusive right to market a product is protected by a time-limited patent, quick trials mean more profit. To obtain subjects, companies typically pay large amounts on a per-patient basis for community physicians to enroll their patients. Tremendous bonus incentives may be given if physicians can meet the company's recruiting goal, which is often hardly possible. Physicians who cannot meet enrollment deadlines usually are not rehired. Successful recruiters can earn up to $1 million in a year (Eichenwald & Kolata, 1999a). This could tempt physicians to enroll subjects who are not appropriate for studies, take on studies outside of their expertise, and in extreme cases to invent clinical data (e.g., Eichenwald & Kolata, 1999b).

Much of the accounting of the recruiters' work is also done by the hiring company, which has interest in the speed with which the research is

---

[7] This involves a myriad of conflicts not addressed here, including ownership of results, "authorship" of ghostwritten articles in exchange for honoraria, and for-profit ethics reviews of clinical trials.

conducted (as well as the results). The FDA also oversees these trials but has limited resources to monitor a growing and diffuse network of commercial research. We are sold costly and potentially dangerous medications on the assumption that the research demonstrating their effectiveness is valid. That research is conducted in such a diffuse manner is a choice endogenous to pharmaceutical companies, who profit by completing their studies in a timely manner while the patent clock ticks. Inventing data is not a new problem in science, nor is incompetence in data collection, and it seems that such a system is more vulnerable to both. Yet, we are assured by the pharmaceutical industry that oversight is sufficient to preserve research integrity.

Although I make no specific claims of impropriety on the part of these companies, it should be noted that there is incentive for them to engage in strategic ignorance when overseeing their own trials, at least while recruiting goals are met and trials are moving forward. By not knowing how recruiting goals are met and results obtained, trials can continue unfettered and sanction is of little concern. A recruiter found engaging in any impropriety will be culpable, but not the hiring company unless that company knew of the impropriety. The Food and Drug Administration's Office of Human Research Protection has a rather limited capacity to oversee the thousands of ongoing clinical trials. If they detect impropriety using public dollars before the researching company does, it should again be taken as prima facie evidence that reasonable measures to detect harm were not taken.

The incentive structure in this example is clearly perverse in that it would reward strategic ignorance of harm by the researching companies. If we were serious about protecting the integrity of clinical trials, we would assume that pharmaceutical companies were negligent in overseeing research if public dollars were required to uncover any impropriety. Levying harsh penalties to such companies would help the incentives of the researching company to detect harm with those of the general public.

CONCLUSION

Strategic ignorance of harm provides an insight into dealing with difficult conflict-of-interest problems. In cases of professional misconduct, it may not be profitable to assume a lack of ethics or concern for others. Rather, ethical rules may have been circumvented, even if those guilty of misconduct subscribe to them. Deterrence through punishing individual transgressors may have limited effectiveness if those creating the incentives for malfeasance are protected by their strategic ignorance. Ethical training should emphasize that one is violating the principle of nonmaleficence when choosing to remain ignorant of possible harms. This principle should be applied in structuring incentives such that strategic ignorance of harm is not rewarded. This means that we must rethink our willingness to punish agents who caused harm unwittingly.

References

Andreoni, J. (1990). Impure altruism and donations to public goods: A theory of warm glow giving. *The Economic Journal*, 100, 464–477.
Andreoni, J., Miller, J. (2002). Giving according to GARP: an experimental test of the consistency of preferences for altruism. *Econometrica*, 70, 737–753.
Bodenheimer, T. (2000). Uneasy alliance: Clinical investigators and the pharmaceutical industry. *New England Journal of Medicine*, 342, 1539–1543.
Bolton, G. E., Ockenfels, A. (2000). A theory of equity, reciprocity and competition. *American Economic Review*, 100, 166–193.
Camerer, C. (2003). *Behavioral Game Theory: Experiments on Strategic Interaction*. Princeton, NJ: Princeton University Press.
Carrillo, J. D., & Mariotti, T. (2000). Strategic ignorance as a self-disciplining device. *Review of Economic Studies*, 67, 529–544.
Charness, G., & Rabin, M. (2000). Understanding social preferences with simple tests. *Quarterly Journal of Economics*, 117, 817–869.
Dana, J., Weber, R., & Kuang, J. X. (2003). Exploiting moral wriggle room: Behavior inconsistent with a preference for fair outcomes. Accessible online: <http://ssrn.com/abstract = 400900.>
Dana, J., Cain, D., & Dawes, R. (2003). What you don't know won't hurt me: Costly (but quiet) exit in a dictator game. Accessible online: <http://ssrn.com/abstract = 494422.>
Driver, J. (1992). The suberogatory. *Australasian Journal of Philosophy*, 70(3), 286–295.
Eichenwald, K., & Kolata, G. (1999a). Drug trials hide conflicts for doctors. *New York Times*, May 17.
Eichenwald, K., & Kolata, G. (1999b). A doctor's drug studies turn into fraud. *New York Times*, May 17.
Fehr, E., & Schmidt, K. M. (1999). A theory of fairness, competition and cooperation. *Quarterly Journal of Economics*, 114, 817–868.
Field, A. J. (2002). *Altruistically inclined? The behavioral sciences, evolutionary theory, and the origins of reciprocity*. Ann Arbor: University of Michigan Press.
Jennings, M. (1996). Manager's journal: Five warning signs of ethical collapse. *Wall Street Journal*, November 4.
Ley, B. (Host). (12/10/00). Bigger, stronger, faster. [Television series episode]. In B. Leonard (Producer), Outside the lines. Bristol, Conn.: ESPN studios. Transcript available online: http://sports.espn.go.com/page2/tvlistings/show37transcript.html.

Loewenstein, G., Issacharoff, S., Camerer, C., & Babcock, L. (1992). Self-serving assessments of fairness and pretrial bargaining. *Journal of Legal Studies*, 12, 135–159.

Messick, D. M., & Sentis, K. P. (1979). Fairness and preference. *Journal of Experimental Social Psychology*, 15, 418–434.

Messick, D. M., & Sentis, K. (1983). Fairness, preference, and fairness biases. In D. M. Messick & K. S. Cook (Eds.), *Equity theory: Psychological and sociological perspectives* (pp. 61–94). New York: Praeger.

Rabin, M. (1995). Moral preferences, moral constraints, and self-serving biases. Berkeley Department of Economics Working Paper No. 95–241, August.

SIXTEEN

Commentary

Strategic Ignorance of Harm

Daylian M. Cain

Carnegie Mellon University

Anthropologist Colin Turnbull's classic book *The Mountain People* (1972) describes the unfortunate tale of the Ik (pronounced "eek"). The Ik are a small group of hunters who live in the mountains separating Kenya, the Sudan, and Uganda. Uprooted by Uganda's formation of the Kidepo National Park, the Ik were forced from their traditional hunting grounds and had to turn to farming unproductive land, resulting in rampant starvation. As Turnbull describes it, in less than three generations, the once proud Ik deteriorated into a brutal people whose only goal was individual survival. The Ik have forsaken bonds of friendship and even family, abandoning the weak and letting their own children fend for themselves. The Ik, Turnbull tells us, have come to think that altruism is foolish and literally laughable.

There are several parallels to draw from the Ik to the behavior that Dana describes, wherein a substantial portion of experimental subjects would act altruistically "in broad daylight" but would act in distasteful and selfish ways so long as their actions were somewhat out of sight. First, many participants in lab experiments – especially those with formal training in economics – are like the Ik in that they often see altruism as foolish and literally laughable. I disagree: Not being altruistic is one thing, but thinking that altruism is foolish is quite another. Despite how often we are asked to *momentarily* assume that we have entirely selfish preferences (e.g., "Assume that all you care about is maximizing your own financial wealth . . . ") for the sake of clarifying some lab or classroom exercise, we are not irrational for displaying more social concerns in the real world. Most economic theories tell us to maximize on our preferences without making any claim over the *content* of these same preferences. In theory, I could care very much about your well-being. So, in giving you a portion of my newly found riches – especially when an experimenter seems to give me money in order to see if I will share it – I might be acting perfectly rationally.[1]

Many economists have taken altruistic giving in their experiments as evidence for what Dana has called "*selfish* preferences for altruistic outcomes" (emphasis added), but these alleged outcome preferences need not be selfish. When I ensure that my younger sister is financially secure in my Living Will, I might be doing so for selfish reasons (e.g., it makes me feel good, it gets my sister off of my back, etc.) or I might be doing so purely out of my concern for her – this trading on the notion that my *selfish* concerns may be a proper subset of all concerns that are *mine* (for more on this, see the *Stanford Encyclopedia of Philosophy*: Egoism[2]). But this point aside, as I will argue, Dana is right to point out that altruistic behavior might not imply any real preference for altruistic outcomes, selfish or not.

My own research (including that done with Dana) suggests that a substantial portion of altruism seen in economic games might more properly be explained by norms, and a desire to follow norms for their own sake, rather than being explained by what is typically thought of as an outcome preference.[3] Sometimes we share with others merely because we are following norms of sharing, or because we care about what others think of us (even if only anonymously), not because we care about the others *per se*. I may not even care about "seeing myself as a giving person," because I might take actions which lead to no giving whatsoever, so long as doing

---

[1] In fact, while Adam Smith himself thought that the overall social good was maximized when we each sought our own interests (via the "invisible hand"), this was built on assumptions that people are concerned with more that just money, and indeed more than just themselves – not even Hobbes was a psychological egoist (for more on egoism, see the next footnote). Whereas Smith's most famous book is *Wealth of Nations* (1776), Smith was first and foremost a moral philosopher whose favorite of his own books was *Theory of Moral Sentiments* (1759), which spelled out what sort of people made a market work: It turns out that ours is not a market for Iks. For more on this reading of Smith's work, see Werhane (1999).

[2] <http://plato.stanford.edu/entries/egoism/#1>: "Say a soldier throws himself on a grenade to prevent others from being killed. It does not seem that the soldier is pursuing his perceived self-interest. It is plausible that, if asked, the soldier would have said that he threw himself on the grenade because he wanted to save the lives of others or because it was his duty. He would deny as ridiculous the claim that he acted in his self-interest."

[3] For more on norms, see Elster (1989); Bicchieri (2000); and Bicchieri (forthcoming).

so does not violate the norm.[4] For example, imagine giving money to
a beggar on the street. Such charity might be interpreted as a display
of a preference for altruistic outcomes, i.e., preferring that the beggar
have more money. But consider those occasions where we feel tempted
to cross the street to avoid the same beggar; and note that we rarely seek
beggars out. Perhaps we cross the street when the beggar is not looking
because we want to hold onto our money without hurting his feelings. But
perhaps we do not really care about the beggar's wealth or the beggar's
feelings at all (even if we give him money on several occasions). Granted,
in crossing the street, perhaps we want to avoid *coming to care* for the
beggar. But often, we simply want to avoid the situation and the decision
altogether, only giving money when we feel that "we have to." If confronted by the beggar, we might give money to him, but *we prefer not to
be confronted* and thus we do not prefer an altruistic outcome. One might
insist that we prefer an altruistic outcome *when confronted*, but this preference for altruistic outcomes seems fragile at best, because it is so easily
circumvented.[5]

It is here that I see the most interesting parallel between us and the
Ik. The Ik are often cited as an example of massive breakdown of society
and cultural norms. But, I contend (and Dana agrees) that many norms
remained with the Ik and that the Ik remained a highly socialized – albeit
brutal – people. For example, Turnbull observed that the Ik would take
great pains to eat far away from their homes in order to avoid having
to share what little food they had. As I shall argue, it is not a concern
of threat or robbery that causes the Ik to keep their goods out of view;
rather, it is a self-defense mechanism against expectations to share these
goods. This phenomenon is what we find in the lab: People feel the pull
of norms of altruism, cooperation, reciprocity, and the like, but these
same people are prone to seek every excuse to circumvent such feelings.
As Dana suggests, it is easy to imagine cases in which the same coach
who would never explicitly encourage teenage athletes to take steroids
(because he "cares about his athletes") is willing to turn a blind eye to
steroid abuse and might even support social structures which encourage

---

[4] When, how, or why *circumventing* a norm is somehow more permissible (at least psychologically) than violating the norm is a question that I have been thinking about recently,
but one that I shy away from here.

[5] I am here reminded of discussions about the distinction between acts and omissions: It is
not merely outcomes that we care about, but how they come about that matter, at least
descriptively (e.g., killing vs. letting die; see Steinbock, 1980). We may not particularly care
if the beggar is refused all help, but we do not want to do the refusing ourselves.

steroid abuse. And most readers can imagine that the same fellow who would give money to a beggar *if confronted* might sometimes cross the street to avoid that homeless person altogether. Likewise, the Ik who will share his food with someone who intentionally "stumbles" on him roasting a meal, will expend precious energy to conceal any food that might come up for grabs.

In Dana, Cain, and Dawes (2004), we see how socially costly such behavior can be: A significant portion of subjects would rather take $9 in secret instead of executing their prior allocation of a $10 dictator game in which they could have openly (but anonymously) refused to give anything and kept all $10 (10,0) instead. Keeping all the money for oneself (10,0) is better for the dyad than the (9,0) exit. The receiver would likely be upset if she knew that a Dictator sent no money (10,0), but perhaps she can learn to get over this; for, finding this out might be no worse than (9,0) "never finding out" that someone could-have-but-did-not give her any money. The latter is something that all of us, as potential recipients of others' charity, can assume happens all the time anyway, since, right now, there is someone who is not giving us anything. Likewise, consider that the Ik are all wasting precious energy to eat alone and often become ill because they eat things that are barely cooked – fire is avoided because fire means smoke, and where there is visible smoke, there come uninvited dinner guests. Most importantly, by Turnbull's account, the Ik all seem to know that each other is doing this. It would be a Pareto improvement if everyone just said, "Hey, we're all sneaking off not to share anyway (9,0), and this is putting us all in further danger, so let's just stop sharing altogether and eat at peace in our own homes (10,0)." But the norms of sharing are too deeply ingrained for this to come about with the Ik. Perhaps the Ik would benefit from a visit by those lab participants who do espouse open selfishness (10,0). But perhaps such a visitor is likely to be attacked.

Another gem from the Ik: Turnbull gave a gift of tobacco to a tribal leader with villagers in plain sight. To understand the significance of this, consider that one of the main greetings of the Ik means "give me tobacco." The leader turns his back, *obviously* to pocket some tobacco, and then turns around to face everyone and share what tobacco is left, pronouncing that as leader, it was his duty to divide all gifts among his people and keep nothing for himself. Although Turnbull discusses how the leader might have at least attempted some sleight of hand, the Ik would view such sleight of hand as both dishonest and unnecessary. The Ik expect self-interest. What was not seen by the others did not belong to them, and (at least in this case) they will not request it or take it by force. Merely knowing that you have tobacco is somehow different than actually "seeing it on you."

But what are the boundary conditions for the "pull" of norms of altruism? Dana's research and the tales of the Ik suggest some intriguing possibilities. Dana suggests that many people use "strategic ignorance" to feel licensed to be entirely unhelpful (if not "harmful") to another person.[6] So long as one is not shown or reminded of the implications of one's own acts, many people feel that they have somehow escaped (but not violated) the norm of altruism. I am reminded of even an "animal lover's" tendency to purchase factory-farmed meat, and the accompanying tendency to want to remain ignorant (or at least not reminded) of how that meat got on to the dinner plate.

Even if one is clear about the ramifications of one's actions and can see perfectly what one is doing, it will be important that no one else sees one do the questionable deed (especially those affected by our deeds). And this is maintained even when one remains an anonymous (but known) other to the audience. On this latter point, Elster (1989) makes the insight that we tend to avoid picking our noses in public, even say, when on a once-in-a-lifetime visit to Tokyo, where for all intents and purposes we are anonymous to our audience. But if we were truly invisible, and not merely anonymous, we might do all sorts of nasty deeds.

It is illuminating that Plato's infamous Ring of Gyges – with but a twist on the finger – turned the wearer "invisible," not "invincible." Recall that the challenge the ring posed to ethics is that so-called good people would, if invisible, gladly get away with murder. As did Plato's ring-bearer, you might feel free to take the King's wife, jewels, and kingdom from him if the King does not know that (or at least how) this is all happening. But the invisibility is key: Just as in Dictator experiments, you will feel less free to engage in such selfish abandon if your victim sees you even when your victim can do nothing about it. Anonymity is not secretive enough: It is restraining if your victim knows that you are there even if they cannot identify you.[7] If our actions are totally invisible to others however,

---

[6] For example, see Dana's comments on allocations of (6,1) versus (5,5), in which people will choose the fair outcome (5,5) unless they can be greedy in ignorance of the other's outcome: (6,?) is preferred to (5,5) even where "?" is known to equal either 1 or 5 and where the true value can be freely revealed. (6,1) can be given, but only in "ignorance."

[7] In Plato's tale, the ring-bearer could activate the ring in a room full of people such that the people would not even notice his vanishing and would continue talking as if he were not ever there. Now *that* is an *exit*.

most – if not all – bets are off. As Dana and his collaborators succinctly point out, this total invisibility has crucially been lacking in the standard economic experiments wherein the "sender" is anonymous but known to be lurking about.

Although Hume, Smith, Schopenhauer, and others all declared human sympathy to be the "inborn and indestructible instinct," Dana's research suggests that such instincts can be strategically avoided. Indeed, some things need not be *destroyed* to be rendered impotent. In making this clear, Dana's research gives pause to, say, managers who think that they can leave as unsupervised employees who "seem to care about the firm." People's social and organizational concerns might be surprisingly conditional and, behind closed doors, employees might even take pains to keep these conditions from being met. I have found (e.g., Cain, Loewenstein, & Moore, 2004; forthcoming; Cain, forthcoming) that, when it comes to organizational rules, people will follow the "letter of the law," but will seek ingenious ways of circumventing the "spirit of the law." Perhaps, with the proper moral upbringing, we will come to realize that such circumventions are, for all intents and purposes, costly violations of broader norms of good organizational behavior. At the very least, society needs to examine our willingness to invisibly turn our backs on (or stab in the back) those who we might otherwise show concern for.

References

Bicchieri, C. (2000). Words and deeds: A focus theory of norms, in J. Nida-Rumelin and W. Spohn (Eds.), *Practical rationality, rules, and structure.* Theory and Decision Library. New York: Kluwer.

Bicchieri, C. (forthcoming) *The grammar of society: The nature and dynamics of social norms.* Cambridge, UK: Cambridge University Press.

Cain, D. M. (forthcoming). Covering their ears, but yelling louder: "Low-Quality Compliance" with disclosure regulation. In Mannix, B., Neale, M., and Tenbrunsel, A. (eds.), *Research on Managing Groups and Teams: Ethics and Groups* (volume 8), JAI Press.

Cain, D. M., Loewenstein, G., & Moore, D. A. (2004). Honesty and its discontent. Working paper, Tepper School of Business at Carnegie Mellon University.

Cain, D. M., Loewenstein, G., & Moore, D. A. (forthcoming). The dirt on coming clean: Perverse effects of disclosing conflicts of interest. *Journal of Legal Studies.*

Dana, J., Cain, D. M., & Dawes, R. (2003). What you don't know won't hurt me: Costly (but quiet) exit in a dictator game. Online Access: <*http://papers. ssrn.com/sol3/papers.cfm?abstract_id = 494422*>.

Elster, J. (1989). Social norms and economic theory. *Journal of Economic Perspectives*, 3(4); 99–117.

Smith, A. (1759). The Theory of Moral Sentiments. London: A. Millar; Edinburgh: A. Kincaid & J. Bell.

Smith, A. (1776). *An inquiry into the nature and causes of the wealth of nations*, volume 2. London: W. Strahan & T. Cadell.

Steinbock, B. (Ed.). (1980). *Killing and letting die*. Englewood Cliffs, NJ: Prentice Hall.

Werhane, P. (1999). Business ethics and the origins of contemporary capitalism: Economics and ethics in the work of Adam Smith and Herbert Spencer, in R. E. Frederick (Ed.) *A companion to business ethics* (pp. 243–256). Malden, MA, and Oxford: Blackwell Publishers.

PART FOUR

PUBLIC POLICY

SEVENTEEN

Conflicts of Interest in Public Policy Research

Robert J. MacCoun*

University of California at Berkeley

ABSTRACT

In this chapter, I discuss the difficulty of sustaining an inquisitorial system of policy research and analysis when it is embedded in a broader adversarial political setting. Conflicts of interest in public policy research exist on a continuum from blatant pecuniary bias to more subtle ideological bias. Because these biases are only partially susceptible to correction through individual effort and existing institutional practices (peer review, replication), I consider whether a more explicitly adversarial system might be preferable to the awkward hybrid that exists today. But there are important disanalogies between policy-relevant empirical debates and the kinds of conflicts we address with our adversarial legal system. If we are stuck with a muddled inquisitorial–adversarial hybrid, we need to encourage a more heterogeneous form of inquisitorialism, in which investigators strive for within-study hypothesis competition and greater clarity about roles, facts, and values.

THE VARIETIES OF CONFLICTS OF INTEREST

In public policy research, as in other domains of professional life, conflicts of interest (henceforth, COIs) are legion. Most policy researchers can readily provide many personal war stories from their professional

* Professor, Goldman School of Public Policy and Boalt Hall School of Law, University of California at Berkeley. Please send comments to <maccoun@socrates.berkeley.edu>.

experience. Generically, the most blatant cases tend to fall into four categories:

1. Investigators with a commercial or proprietary interest in the research outcome, or the use of funding from sources with a commercial or proprietary interest in the research outcome (e.g., Hilts, 2000; also see the June 5, 2002, special issue of *JAMA*).
2. The use of funding from sources with a political agenda that would benefit from particular research outcomes (e.g., Revkin, 2003).
3. Paid expert testimony in an adversarial legal proceeding (see Faigman, 1999).
4. The use of proprietary data sources unavailable to other investigators (Metcalf, 1998).

To varying degrees, these four categories involve pecuniary motives and interests. But even if we could eliminate pecuniary motives in policy research, we would not eliminate conflicts of interest, because there is a fifth, subtler category:

5. The influence, whether conscious or unconscious, of an investigator's allegiance to extrapolitical or ideological values and attitudes.

Even if pecuniary biases and ideological biases differ in their origins, they can have similar effects on research conduct and evidence interpretation.

Pecuniary biases are perhaps more troublesome in domains like medicine and engineering than in public policy, simply because there are few opportunities for researchers to reap financial reward for their research (patents, commercial applications). By contrast, ideological biases may be less pervasive in domains like medicine and engineering, because disputes are more likely to center on means (the best techniques, author credit for innovations, etc.) than on ends (whether we should improve health, safety, or performance). In the public policy arena, the ends (income equality, reproductive rights, welfare entitlements, environmental preservation, a "drug-free society") are often as contested as the means that would achieve them.

Merriam-Webster's Collegiate Dictionary defines a conflict of interest as "a conflict between the private interests and the official responsibilities of a person in a position of trust." In the domain of public policy research, we can construe both "private interests" and "a position of trust" either narrowly or broadly. Narrowly defined, "private interest" would involve the potential attainment of money, prestige, or other resources for oneself or one's organization. A broader definition would include the researcher's personal values and political views. Narrowly defined, "a position of trust" would involve particular professional offices with explicit rules proscribing bias or the pursuit of personal gain. A broader definition might invoke Robert Merton's (1973) articulation of the norms of science that are widely shared in our culture:

- Scientific accomplishments should be judged by impersonal criteria ("universalism") rather than the personal attributes of the investigator.
- Scientific information should be publicly shared ("communalism").
- Investigators should proceed objectively, putting aside personal biases and prejudices ("disinterestedness").
- And the scientific community should hold new findings to strict levels of scrutiny, through peer review, replication, and the testing of rival hypotheses ("organized skepticism").[1]

There are now a good many published case studies documenting conflict of interest in this broader sense in many research domains, including HIV/AIDS (Epstein, 1996), tobacco (Cummings, Sciandra, Gingrass, & Davis, 1991; Glantz, 1996), sexual orientation (LeVay, 1996), intelligence testing (e.g., Fraser, 1995), drug prevention (Gorman, 2003; Moskowitz, 1993), risk prevention (Fischhoff, 1990), marijuana policy (MacCoun, 1997), and global warming (Gelbspan, 1997).

"Conflict of interest" also can be defined intrapersonally or interpersonally. In the traditional sense, the "conflict" is *intrapersonal* – a conflict between her role obligations and her behavior. But the term "conflict of interest" also has been used in a very different sense in the social psychology literature, one that defines the conflict *interpersonally*, between people or factions of people. For example, in the small group literature, McGrath's (1984) group task circumplex defines "conflicts of interest" in terms of mixed-motive payoff structures. Of greater relevance to this essay, John Thibaut (a psychologist) and Laurens Walker (a lawyer) (1978) distinguish "cognitive conflicts," where the parties have a joint interest in solving a problem, from "conflicts of interest," where "a particular solution will maximize the outcome of one of the parties only at the expense

---

[1] Koehler (1993) presents evidence that scientists endorse such norms.

of the other." The intrapersonal definition is more conventional, but most real-world examples meet the interpersonal definition as well.

Identifying the Right Normative System

Thibaut and Walker (1978; also see Lind & Tyler, 1988) identify the goal of cognitive conflicts as "truth," and the goal of conflicts of interest as "justice." These are lofty claims, but then, the authors had the lofty goal of defining the proper domains for inquisitorial versus adversarial procedures of conflict resolution. In an adversarial process, as exemplified by the Anglo-American trial system, disputants retain "process control" by selectively presenting the facts most favorable to their position to a third-party decision maker. In an inquisitorial process, evidence is assembled by the third-party decision maker, or by a neutral investigator who reports to that decision maker. Some continental European legal systems are inquisitorial in this sense, but more relevant for present purposes, Merton's norms of scientific practice are inherently inquisitorial.

Thibaut and Walker make two normative claims. First, "an autocratic system delegating both process and decision control to a disinterested third party is most likely to produce truth," and hence cognitive conflicts should be resolved through the inquisitorial method. Second, "a procedural system designed to achieve distributive justice . . . will function best if process control is assigned to the disputants," as exemplified by "the Anglo-American adversary model."

Thibaut and Walker's normative theory has been much less influential than their empirical program, and although their treatment is more sophisticated and nuanced than this brief sketch, I do not find it entirely persuasive. Although it is useful to examine ideal types in the laboratory, few real-world problems seem to fit neatly into these cognitive-conflict and conflict-of-interest bins. Thibaut and Walker allow for the possibility of "mixed conflicts," but for this category – arguably the largest one – they call for a mix of inquisitorial and adversarial procedures.

Hence, I call attention to their theory because of the question they pose rather than the answers they offer. I believe that the central problem of conflicts of interest in public policy research is the *blurring of adversarial and inquisitorial norms and roles*. Public policy research and its utilization routinely falls far short of Merton's inquisitorial ideals. Yet, our allegiance to those norms, and our pretense to be operating under those norms, also keeps us from realizing some benefits of a more explicitly adversarial approach. We largely seem to muddle in the middle. In the abstract, a purely inquisitorial model might well be best, but we are unlikely to achieve one. An explicit, robust adversarial research process might be more attainable, and it might even have some advantages over a muddled mixed model, in which some investigators play by one set of rules, some play by another, and some vacillate back and forth either strategically or unwittingly. But the adversarial model, whatever its merits in legal settings (and those are decidely mixed), has serious drawbacks outside the trial context. What are needed are clearer norms defining a realistically heterogeneous inquisitorialism – an "honest broker" role that explicitly engages competing views rather than tacitly promoting a single view.

What Is Not in this Section

The topic of bias in politically relevant research is an old one, and it has been examined many times before from other angles. There is enormous literature on the details of bias in research methodology, including biased research designs, biased statistical analyses, biased data presentation, and experimenter expectancy effects (e.g., Rosenthal, 1994). Note that the kinds of investigator biases examined here may express themselves through these methodological problems, but bad methodology may instead reflect ignorance or real-world data constraints rather than bias on the part of the investigator.

There is extensive sociology literature on the effects of institutional factors, professional incentives, social networks, and demographic stratification on the scientific research process (see Cole, 1992; Zuckerman, 1988). And, of course, the troubled relationship between facts and values was a preoccupation of twentieth-century philosophy of science (see Gholson & Barker, 1985; Laudan, 1990; Shadish, 1995). I also sidestep the postmodernist literatures on social constructivism, deconstructionism, hermeneutics, and the like, for reasons explained elsewhere (MacCoun, 1998, 2003; also see Gross & Levitt, 1994).

ATTRIBUTING BIAS TO OTHERS

It is very easy to attribute bias to researchers, and observers readily do so. But how are we to know whether the bias resides in the attributor, rather than (or in addition to) the investigator? The same forces that can produce bias in researchers can produce bias in consumers of that research. A case in point is the cottage industry in books denouncing "junk science." These books are quick to criticize particular experts for sloppy and careless thinking – especially an overreliance on unsystematic and unrepresentative clinical case evidence and an underreliance on rigorous multivariate analysis and controlled experimentation. And what evidence do the authors offer for their indictment of junk science? Anecdotes about particular cases and particular experts, selected by an unspecified but surely nonrandom sampling process, with no correction for hindsight bias (the use of later science unavailable to the experts at the time in question), and no consideration of alternative motives for the expert testimony (MacCoun, 1995). I am not questioning whether sloppy or biased expert testimony occurs – it surely does – but simply arguing that we are often willing to attribute bias based on the "junkiest" of evidence.

Obviously, some attributions of bias are self-serving; if an investigator presents findings you do not like, the quickest way to discredit her – much quicker and more reliable than conducting your own study – is to question her motives or her integrity. But there also are some more subtle cognitive phenomena that complicate the attribution process.

In a classic experiment by Jones and Harris (1967), students were enlisted to conduct an in-class debate on the topic of whether mid-1960s America ought to adopt a friendlier stance toward Fidel Castro. Half the participants were told that the debate positions were assigned by the debating coach; half were not told anything about how the debating roles were determined. After the debate, audience members estimated speakers' actual attitudes toward Castro. The audience overwhelming assumed the "pro-Castro" debater was indeed pro-Castro. This was true not only in the control condition but also among audience members who knew that the debating position was situationally determined (by the coach). Subsequent research using this "attitude attribution" paradigm has shown that this "shoot the messenger" tendency is quite robust (see Ross & Nisbett, 1991), exemplifying what Ross calls "the fundamental attribution error" – the tendency to give disproportionate weight to dispositional explanations (those internal to the actor, like traits and desires) for others' behavior, while discounting or overlooking situational influences.

The problem is a familiar one for policy analysts; audiences often assume that we favor (and, presumably, always favored) whichever political viewpoint our findings most readily benefit. In a recent statewide telephone survey of 1,050 California adults (MacCoun & Paletz, 2004), we found that for controversial research topics over half of all respondents were willing to speculate on a researcher's ideological beliefs knowing nothing other than whether a hypothetical study found that the intervention worked. For gun control and medical marijuana, positive findings led them to infer that the researcher was a liberal; for capital punishment, positive findings implied that the researcher was a conservative. Rather than viewing social science as an attempt to reveal facts about the world (the "discovery" model of research), many citizens construe social science as a process of political exhortation, and social scientists are seen as advocates who find what they want to find.

Naive Realism

Ross and his colleagues (Pronin, Lin, & Ross, 2002; Robinson et al., 1995) have argued that humans are predisposed to assume that our views of the world are objective and veridical, and to neglect the ways in which our perceptions might be filtered by our biases and distorted by the evidence available to us. Because of this "naive realist" stance, we tend to assume that those who disagree with us must be plagued by subjectivity, blinded by desire, or just plain confused. Thus, Pronin et al. (2002) have demonstrated that most people believe that they themselves are much less susceptible to judgmental biases than the average person in their peer group. And partisans on both sides of a dispute tend to see the exact same media coverage as favoring their opponents' position (the "hostile media phenomenon"; Vallone, Ross, & Lepper, 1985). A corollary is that people are likely to genuinely believe that research that coincides with their own beliefs must be less biased and more objective than research that favors other positions (Lord, Ross, & Lepper, 1979; MacCoun & Paletz, 2004).

Adjusting for Perceived Bias

There is evidence that observers try to adjust their interpretation of new evidence based on their perceptions of bias in the source (Wegener et al., 2000). Thus, the results of a study by an ostensibly liberal researcher are assumed to be somewhat less favorable to a liberal position than was actually reported. This kind of adjustment process sounds like good news, but the catch is that the adjustment is based not on actual bias but on "individuals' naïve theories of the biasing factor(s) at hand" (Wegener et al., 2000). So bias correction will introduce distortions when these lay theories are inaccurate.

In research on communications between university officials and their seismic engineering consultants, we found anecdotal evidence for this distortion process (DeVries et al., 2001). Each side assumed that the other was biased, and adjusted their interpretations accordingly. Making matters worse, the more experienced actors on each side assumed the other side was making such adjustments, and *adjusted for the adjustments* so that their "adjusted positions" would match their true positions. It would be desirable to "hit the reset button" so that all parties could see exactly where everyone else stood, but how to accomplish this was not obvious to us.

One might hope that a source's open disclosure of COI would help observers to correctly adjust for the source's bias. Distressingly, Cain, Loewenstein, and Moore (Chapter Seven in this volume) present new evidence suggesting that audiences fail to fully discount such biases. Moreover, they show that sources who disclosed COI actually behaved in a more biased fashion. Cain and colleagues used a task that was explicitly inquisitorial rather than adversarial; it remains to be seen whether observers fare better in more blatantly adversarial settings.[2]

THE VARIETIES OF INVESTIGATOR BIAS

Documenting Bias

The biases I describe have been variously operationalized using one of the four methodological strategies discussed by Hastie and Rasinski (1988; Kerr et al., 1996; MacCoun, 1998, 2002): (a) documenting differences between observers (weak because it does not show who is biased), (b) documenting a difference between a judgment and a normatively defined true value, (c) documenting the use of a normatively proscribed cue, or (d) documenting the failure to use a normatively prescribed cue. (The normative system in question can be Bayes theorem, classical statistics, decision theory, the legal rules of evidence, or Merton's aforementioned norms of science).

It is easier to establish bias in the laboratory than in field studies. "Researcher allegiance" effects have been reported in meta-analyses of the research literatures on psychotherapy (Gaffan et al., 1995; Robinson

---

[2] Also, Cain and colleagues obtained these effects in studies in which the source provided quantitative information, leading to anchoring effects. Arguably, it might be easier to discount biased sources in domains where their information is qualitative or categorical ("vouchers worked," "right-to-carry gun laws prevent crimes," and so on).

et al., 1990; Shadish et al., 1993) and drug treatment (Prendergast et al., 2002). These analyses suggest that investigators with identifiable allegiances with a treatment program report significantly larger treatment effects than other, more disinterested investigators. For example, Gaffan, Tsaousis, and Kemp-Wheeler (1995) meta-analyzed outcome data from clinical trials of treatments for depression. They estimated that about half of the relative superiority for cognitive therapy reported in previous meta-analyses was attributable to researcher allegiance.

On its face, this is a stunning claim, but the researchers used a very broad conceptualization of allegiance. Among the study features that, in their view, constituted strong allegiance were: "reference to previous published research showing the superiority of X to some other treatment," "specific hypothesis or rationale as to why X should be superior to other treatments in this study," "X was devised or first introduced by one of the authors," and "X is the only treatment included in the study, and the authors regard it as superior to other available treatments." Another problem is that indicators of allegiance are confounded with other factors and may disappear when such factors are controlled (Shadish et al., 1993).

Still, more detailed case studies of program evaluation practices leave little doubt that such allegiance effects do occur. In a series of papers, Gorman (1998, 2002, 2003) has documented numerous highly misleading statistical practices deployed by prevention program designers evaluating their own programs. Reported outcomes effects are frequently based on only a carefully chosen subset of the study population and the dependent variables. Gorman's own "intention-to-treat" reanalyses suggest that these programs are far less successful than reported. Still, when pressed, program advocates will claim such practices are meaningful in helping to provide "fair tests" of what the programs are capable of when "implemented with high fidelity."

Perhaps the most unequivocal evidence for biased evidence evaluation comes from controlled laboratory demonstrations. Mahoney (1977) and Lord, Ross, and Lepper (1979) developed the basic experimental paradigm that is now used to study biased interpretation of research data. Participants – usually practicing scientists or graduate students with professional training in methodology – are asked to assess research studies. Unbeknownst to them, they have been randomly assigned to receive one of several experimental variants of a research manuscript, with the obstensible methods and results systematically varied. The participants are more persuaded by findings that support their own (previously assessed) political views, even when the methodology is identical. A given

Table 17.1. *Five prototypical forms of investigator bias*

	Intentional?	Motivated?	Justifiable?
Fraud	Yes	Yes	No
Advocacy	Yes	Yes	Maybe
Hot bias	No	Yes	No
Cold bias	No	No	No
Skepticism	Maybe	Yes	Yes

methodology is viewed favorably when it produces congenial results, and critically when it does not.[3] These "biased assimilation" results (Lord et al., 1979) have been widely replicated, although there are boundary conditions (see MacCoun, 1998, for a review). For example, biased assimilation effects are robust among judges with extreme attitudes, but more difficult to replicate among those with moderate views (Edwards & Smith, 1996; McHoskey, 1995; Miller et al., 1993).

Prototypical Forms of Bias

On its face, biased assimilation seems like a corruption of Merton's ideals of scientific reasoning. But a fair assessment – and a search for solutions – requires an inquiry into the causes of the bias. Elsewhere (MacCoun, 1998), I have sketched five prototypes of biased evidence processing (see Table 17.1). The prototypes vary with respect to intentionality, motivation, and normative justifiability. By *intentionality*, I refer to the combination of consciousness and controllability; a bias is intentional when the judge is aware of a bias, yet chooses to express it when she could do otherwise (see Fiske, 1989). *Motivation* is shorthand for the degree to which the bias has its origins in the judge's preferences, goals, or values; intentional bias is motivated, but not all motivated biases are intentional. Finally, *normative justification* distinguishes appropriate or defensible biases from inappropriate or indefensible biases, relative to some normative system (e.g., Bayesian decision theory, the rules of evidence in law).

FRAUD. The first prototype is *fraud* – intentional, conscious efforts to fabricate, conceal, or distort evidence, for whatever reason – material gain, enhancing one's professional reputation, protecting one's theories, or influencing a political debate (see Fuchs & Westervelt, 1996; Murray,

---

[3] Lord et al. also argued that such situations actually produce *attitude polarization*, such that respondents became *more* extreme in the direction of their initial views. Happily, this truly perverse finding has not been replicated (see MacCoun, 1998).

2002; Woodward & Goodstein, 1996). At a macro level, they are often explicable from sociological, economic, or historical perspectives
(Cole, 1992; Zuckerman, 1988). At a micro level, they are sometimes
explicable in terms of individual psychopathology. These cases are extremely serious, but again, I am interested here in less blatant, subtler
problems.

Absent from direct evidence of intent, it can be difficult to distinguish
fraud from ignorance or incompetence. For example, a study reporting
a 1 to 2 percent average difference in various comparisons of marijuana
prevalence between Dutch versus U.S. youth (MacCoun & Reuter, 1997)
was widely cited as finding a 32 percent difference (see MacCoun, 2001).
This was done by selectively quoting estimates from different parts of
a table providing fair year-by-age range comparisons. This could have
been a simple misunderstanding of the study, but the estimates chosen
were those most likely to make marijuana look more popular in the
Netherlands (eighteen-year-olds in 1996) than the United States (twelve-
to seventeen-year-olds in 1992).

ADVOCACY. A second prototype is *advocacy* – the selective use and emphasis of evidence to promote a hypothesis, without outright concealment
or fabrication. As I discuss below, advocacy is normatively defensible provided that it occurs within an explicitly advocacy-based organization or
an explicitly adversarial system of disputing. Trouble arises when there
is no shared agreement that such an adversarial normative system is in
effect. When we speak of an investigator as being ideologically driven
or biased, we imply that his or her attitudes or values have influenced
his or her interpretations of the evidence. This is clearly a violation of
the impartial inquisitorial model. But, of course, the temporal and causal
sequence is often reversed. Is it truly desirable, much less feasible, for an
investigator's attitudes and beliefs to be "kept in a lockbox," hermetically
sealed from his or her research findings? I return to this quandary in a
later discussion of inquisitorial versus adversarial role conflicts.

HOT AND COLD BIASES. Contemporary psychology recognizes that most
biased evidence processing can occur quite unintentionally through some
combination of "hot" (i.e., motivated or affectively charged) and "cold"
cognitive mechanisms. The prototypical *hot bias* is unintentional and perhaps unconscious, but it is directionally motivated – the judge wants a
certain outcome to prevail. I suspect this is what most people have in
mind when they speak of "biased" researchers.

But in professional psychology for the past several decades, the focus has been on "cold" unmotivated biases. The prototypical *cold bias* is

unintentional, unconscious, and it occurs even when the judge is earnestly striving for accuracy. Numerous mechanisms have been identified in basic cognitive psychological research on memory storage and retrieval, inductive inference, and deductive inference that can produce biased evidence processing even when the judge is motivated to be accurate and is indifferent to the outcome.[4] Arkes (1991) and Wilson and Brekke (1994) have offered taxonomies for organizing these different sources of judgmental bias or error, and offer detailed reviews of the relevant research. These cold biases are an important source of bias in research (MacCoun, 1998), but because they are nonmotivational they seem less relevant to conflicts of interest than the other prototypes.

Tetlock and Levi (1982) made a persuasive case for the difficulty of definitively establishing whether an observed bias is because of hot versus cold cognition; the recent trend has been toward integrative "warm" theories (Cohen, Aronson, & Steele, 2000; Kruglanski & Webster, 1996; Kunda, 1990; Liberman & Chaiken, 1992; Pyszcynski & Greenberg, 1987). Most "hot" and "warm" accounts examine *directional* biases favoring a particular conclusion – what Kruglanski (1989) calls a "need for specific cognitive closure." But another form of bias is the motivation to "find something" rather than finding nothing – what Kruglanski (1989) calls a "need for nonspecific cognitive closure." The most obvious source of such a bias is a professional reward system that rewards studies that "reject the null hypothesis" (statistical jargon for "finding something") – that find an effect of an intervention or a significant association rather than a lack of effect or a lack of association.[5] But professional policy analysts often feel enormous pressure to "find something" to justify their efforts. And many a professional policy briefer has been on the receiving end of an angry policy maker's tirade: "Don't tell me you need more research! Don't say 'it depends'! Tell me right now, yes or no, what should I do?"[6]

---

[4] As an example, the availability heuristic (Kahneman, Slovic, & Tversky, 1982) is our tendency to give disproportionate weight to those items of evidence that come most readily to mind (because they are vivid, were encountered recently, or have received lots of media coverage).

[5] The difficulty of publishing null results is well-known, but it is defensible when studies are plagued by noisy measurement and/or inadequate sample sizes.

[6] The briefer may rightfully respond "wait a second, that's your job, this is my job," but I have learned that this will make the briefing end very badly. The question seems to reflect a mix of alpha-dog posturing, genuine frustration, and some magical thinking about the possibility that the public will forgive a bad decision if the policy maker was poorly advised.

SKEPTICISM.[7] Research on biased processing of scientific evidence has given somewhat less attention to the final prototype, which might be called *skeptical* processing. In skeptical processing, the judge interprets the evidence in an unbiased manner, but her conclusions may differ from those of other judges because of her prior probability estimate, her asymmetric standard of proof, or both. This is arguably normative on decision theoretic grounds, but those grounds are controversial.

In a highly simplified decision theoretic analysis of scientific evidence evaluation, the judge assesses $p(H|D)$, the conditional probability of the hypothesis (H) given the data (D). Most of the research reviewed thus far has focused on this judgment process. Of course, in a simplified Bayesian model, $p(H|D)$ equals the diagnosticity of the evidence, $p(D|H)/p(D)$, weighted (multiplied) by the judge's *prior probability* (or "prior"), $p(H)$. (More complex models appear in Howson & Urbach, 1993; Schum & Martin, 1982.)

For a Bayesian, the prior probability component is an open door to personal bias; so long as diagnosticity is estimated in a sound manner and integrated coherently with one's "priors," the updated judgment is normatively defensible (see Koehler, 1993). Of course, the normative status of this framework is a source of continuing controversy among philosophers and statisticians (see Mayo, 1996), especially the notion of subjective priors. Moreover, challenges to the theory's descriptive status (Arkes, 1991; Kahneman, Slovic, & Tversky, 1982; Pennington & Hastie, 1993) leave its normative applicability in doubt. And much of the evidence reviewed here implies that the diagnosticity component is itself a major locus of bias, irrespective of the judge's prior.

But decision theory also identifies a second, less controversial locus of potentially defensible "bias." Our probabilistic assessment of the hypothesis yields a continuous judgment on a 0–1 metric, yet circumstances often demand that we reach a *categorical* verdict: Will we accept or reject the hypothesis? This conversion process requires a *standard of proof.* Statistical decision theory, signal detection theory, and formal theories of jurisprudence share a notion that this standard should reflect a tradeoff among potential decision errors. A simple decision theoretic threshold for minimizing one's regret is $p^* = u(FP)/[u(FN) + u(FP)]$, where $u(FP)$ equals one's aversion to false positive errors, and $u(FN)$ denotes one's aversion to false negative errors (see DeKay, 1996; MacCoun, 1989). The standard of proof, p^*, cleaves the assessment continuum into rejection

---

[7] This section is a slight revision of a similar section in MacCoun (1998).

and acceptance regions. Thus, the standard of proof reflects one's evaluation of potential errors, and this evaluation is extrascientific, arguably even in the case of the conventional 0.05 alpha level.

When one error is deemed more serious than the other, the standard of proof becomes asymmetrical and can easily produce greater scrutiny of arguments favoring one position over another. Thus, even for most non-Bayesians, there is a plausible normative basis for "bias" in assessments of scientific research (see Hammond, Harvey, & Hastie, 1992). Note, however, that this form of bias is limited to qualitative, categorical decisions ("it's true"; "he's wrong"); it cannot justify discrepancies across judges (or across experimental manipulations of normatively irrelevant factors) in their quantitative interpretations of the diagnosticity of evidence.

Are These Biases Controllable?

Of the five prototypes, fraud and advocacy are arguably under the conscious control of the actor, but the other three often operate in an unconscious and automatic fashion (see Wegner & Bargh, 1998). Judgmental biases are remarkably resistant to eradication efforts; they tend to persist in the face of education (Arkes, 1991; Wilson & Brekke, 1994), incentives for accuracy (Camerer & Hogarth, 1999), and many forms of public accountability (Lerner & Tetlock, 1999). Three strategies that are at least somewhat successful at reducing bias are the so-called "consider the opposite strategy" (Lord, Lepper, & Preston, 1985), "devil's advocacy" role-playing (Schwenk, 1990), and accountability to audiences of unknown or mixed viewpoints (Lerner & Tetlock, 1999). The mechanism may be the same in each case – getting the actor to actively consider alternative, competing points of view. This raises the question: Even without formal debiasing interventions, will the rough and tumble of collective adversarial debate correct these individual judgmental biases?

COMPARING THE ADVERSARIAL AND INQUISITORIAL MODELS

In her splendid book *The Argument Culture*, Deborah Tannen (1998) describes "a pervasive warlike atmosphere that makes us approach public dialogue, and just about anything we need to accomplish, as if it were a fight.... [This] argument culture urges us to approach the world – and the People in it – in an adversarial frame of mind." This adversarial mind-set is a self-fulfilling prophecy. Keltner and Robinson (1996) review evidence that the gap between partisans' perceptions in a variety of attitudinal disputes are objectively much smaller than each side believes. Careful public surveys rarely show stark bimodal distributions of opinion; rather, there often is a continuum of viewpoints that gets bifurcated by the way journalists summarize the results. But journalists, political parties, civil litigation, and our brain's own categorization processes dichotomize important policy problems, encouraging us to take sides.

In the Anglo-American adversarial legal system, advocates actively seek and selectively report the most favorable evidence for their clients. This approach is defended as a means of finding the facts; the traditional claim is that the "truth will *win* out." Surprisingly few studies have directly compared the relative ability of adversarial and inquisitorial methods for accurately determining facts.[8] It appears (see Lind & Tyler, 1988) that adversary proceedings may work well for legal discovery; mock attorneys playing an adversarial role seek out as much evidence or more evidence as neutral inquisitors. But this is offset by systematic distortions in fact presentation (Lind & Tyler, 1988). But when evidence strongly favors one party, evidence presented at trials is misleadingly symmetrical, exaggerating the facts in support of the other party. And in adversarial proceedings, witnesses slant their testimony in a direction that favors whichever party called them to testify.

Because of such problems, Thibaut and Walker (1978) argued that the inquisitorial method is to be preferred for "truth conflicts," purely cognitive disagreements in which the parties are disinterested (or have shared interests) and simply want to discover the correct answer. But they asserted that the adversarial approach is to be preferred for conflicts of interest in which the parties face a zero-sum (or constant sum) distribution of outcomes.

Even if legal disputes were to fit this dichotomy (and I do not believe they do), public policy disputes surely do not. There are purely technical policy analysis problems (queuing, optimization, and the like), but anything that merits the label "dispute" involves a messy blend of truth conflicts and conflicts of interest, making it difficult to separate factual disputes from value disputes (see Hammond, 1996; Tetlock et al., 1996).

Making matters worse, features of the legal system that may promote good adversarial fact-finding are lacking in public policy research disputes (MacCoun, 1998; also see Burk, 1993). Five of these features are highlighted in Table 17.2.

---

[8] There are lots of studies of accuracy *within* the adversarial context (eyewitnesses, jury comprehension, and so on).

Table 17.2. *Features that Distinguish Legal and Scientific Fact-Finding*

	Legal Fact-Finding	Scientific Fact-Finding
Explicit adversarial role?	Yes	No
At least 2 sides represented?	Yes	Not always
Explicit standard of proof?	Yes	Yes/No
Explicit 3rd party decision maker?	Yes	No
Positions bound the truth?	Usually	Rarely

ROLE CLARITY. In legal disputes, the adversarial roles of the participants are quite explicit; no one mistakes an American trial lawyer for a dispassionate inquisitor. Despite the popularity of lawyer jokes, surveys show that Americans (and Europeans) actually like the notion of a fierce adversary; as President Lyndon Johnson said in another context, "he may be a son of a bitch, but at least he's *my* son of bitch."

As expressed by Merton's (1973) norms, citizens in our culture have very clear role expectations for scientists; if one claims the authority of that role, one is bound to abide by its norms or risk misleading the public. This surely does not preclude advocacy activities on the part of scientists, but it does mean that we must be quite explicit about which hat we are wearing when we speak out, and whether we are asserting our facts (e.g., the death penalty has no marginal deterrent effect) or asserting our values (e.g., the death penalty degrades human life).

Graduate training in schools of public policy analysis is much more explicit about managing these conflicting roles. For example, Weimer and Vining's (1992) textbook provides a neutral discussion of three different professional models: the *objective technician* who maintains a distance from clients but lets the data "speak for itself," avoiding recommendations; the *client's advocate* who exploits ambiguity in the data to strike a balance between loyalty to the facts and loyalty to a client's interests; and the *issue advocate* who explicitly draws on research opportunistically in order to promote broader values or policy objectives.

WHO DECIDES, AND WHO HOLDS THE BURDEN OF PROOF? In legal disputes, there is explicit agreement about the standard of proof, burden of proof (who wins in a tie?), and ultimate decision maker (i.e., the judge or jury). Disputes over scientific findings typically lack an explicit standard of proof and an explicit final decision maker. This contributes to the seeming intractability of many debates; when each observer is free to establish her own p^*, there are no grounds for consensus on who "won." Expert

panels assembled by the National Academy of Sciences and other organizations attempt to circumvent this problem, with mixed success. This
is not entirely a bad thing. Research findings are rarely a direct deter-
minant of policy decisions, and social scientists are sometimes strikingly
naive about the gaps between our research findings and the inputs needed
for sound policy formation (see Weimer & Vining, 1992).

Trials are actually unusual in having a single burden of proof. Indeed,
in policy disputes (and social argumentation more generally; Rips et al,
1999), there are multiple burdens in play. Participants and political factions have their own notions of where the burden lies – almost always
with the other side. But political power (incumbency and/or public opinion) often creates an overarching burden that is greater for one side than
for the other. For example, MacCoun and Reuter (2001) argue that the
drug legalization debate involves three standards of proof – a philosophical burden on prohibiters to explain why liberty should be curtailed, a
policy-analytic burden to prove that the benefits of legal change would
outweigh the costs, and a political burden on legalizers to provide overwhelming evidence that drug use would not rise.

Policy-analytic standards of proof have been justified by principles of
logic, statistics, and epistemology, but the result is not always politically
neutral. A clear example is null hypothesis testing, where the .05 conven-
tion for statistical significance puts much greater emphasis on avoiding
false positive findings (saying an intervention works when it does not)
than on avoiding false negative findings (failing to recognize a truly beneficial intervention). Increasingly rigorous econometric standards and the
traditional emphasis on internal validity over external validity can have
a similarly conservative effect. I recently publicly defended a National
Academy of Science critique of drug treatment research before an audience of angry treatment experts (see Horowitz, MacCoun, & Manski,
2001). Not one of them directly challenged our argument that treatment
estimates were vulnerable to selection biases and regression to the mean;
instead, they decried the patent unfairness of holding treatment to such
a high standard when drug law enforcement is more generously funded
without any evaluation.

IS ANYONE RIGHT? Finally, in many (though not all) legal disputes, the
opposing positions "bound" the truth, either because one of the positions is in fact true or because the truth lies somewhere between the
two positions. But the history of science (e.g., Gholson & Barker, 1985;
Thagard, 1992) reveals little basis for assuming that the truth is represented among those factual positions under dispute at any given moment

(also see Klayman & Ha, 1987). This underscores the inherent ambiguity of using discrepancies among judges to locate and measure bias (Kerr et al., 1996) – all of us might be completely off target.

WILL COLLECTIVE JUDGMENT CORRECT INDIVIDUAL BIASES?

Will "Truth Win" Via Collective Rationality?[9]

Institutional practices like peer review, expert panels (e.g., National Academy of Sciences, Institute of Medicine), and expert surveys (e.g., Kassin, Ellsworth, & Smith, 1989) are premised on a belief that collective judgment can overcome individual error, a principle familiar to small-group psychologists as the *Lorge-Solomon Model A* (Lorge & Solomon, 1955). (Model B having long since been forgotten.) In this model, if p is the probability that any given individual will find the "correct" answer, then the predicted probability that a collectivity of size r will find the answer is $P = 1 - (1 - p)^r$. Implicit in this equation is the assumption that if at least one member finds the answer, it will be accepted as the collectivity's solution – the so-called *Truth Wins* assumption (e.g., Laughlin, 1996). This can only occur to the extent that group members share a normative framework that establishes the "correctness" of the solution. That framework might be acknowledged by most academicians (the predicate calculus, Bayes Theorem, organic chemistry), or it might not (e.g., astrology, numerology, the I Ching).

For almost half a century, social psychologists have tested the "truth wins" assumption for a variety of decision tasks (see Kerr et al., 1996; Laughlin, 1996). Even in purely intellective tasks, "truth" rarely wins, in the strict sense that a solution will be adopted if a single member identifies or proposes it. At best, "truth supported wins" – at least some social support is needed for a solution to gain momentum, indicating that truth seeking is a social as well as intellective process (see Laughlin, 1996). But even that only occurs in limited settings. When members lack a shared conceptual scheme for identifying and verifying solutions – what Laughlin calls "judgmental" as opposed to "intellective" tasks – the typical influence pattern is *majority amplification*, in which a majority faction's influence is disproportionate to their size, irrespective of the truth value of their position (see Kerr et al., 1996).

---

[9] This discussion is adapted from MacCoun (1998).

In theory, collective decision making (or statistical aggregation of individual judgments) is well-suited for reducing *random error* in individual judgments. (Indeed, this is a major rationale for meta-analysis, discussed later.) What about bias? A common assertion is that group decision making will correct individual biases, but whether in fact this actually occurs depends on many factors, including the strength of the individual bias, its prevalence across group members, heterogeneity because of countervailing biases, and the degree to which a normative framework for recognizing and correcting the bias is shared among group members (see Kerr et al., 1996). Elsewhere, my colleagues and I (Kerr et al., 1996; MacCoun, 2001) have demonstrated that under a wide variety of circumstances, collective decision making will *amplify* individual bias, rather than attenuating it. The collective will be *less* biased than its individuals when:

1. The correct answer is obvious to almost everyone, or
2. there is "strength in arguments," such that a shared conceptual scheme allows participants to recognize a "correct" (relative to that scheme) result and endorse it. (This is the aforementioned Lorge-Solomon rule.)

The collective will tend to *amplify* individual bias when:

3. There is "strength in numbers," such that large factions have influence disproportionate to their size, as will occur explicitly in a "majority rules" system and implicitly in any "majority amplification" process.
4. The case at hand is "close" rather than lopsided.

Our analysis focused on small groups reaching collective decisions. Collective research interpretation is of course quite different – aside from the occasional blue-ribbon panel or NAS/NRC/IOM committee, there is rarely any explicit group sitting in one place to determine what the evidence says. Rather, collective research interpretation is diffuse, spread over multiple audiences and decision makers over an indeterminate period of time.

Nevertheless, the mathematical framework used by Kerr et al. (1996) is sufficiently abstract that the conclusions summarized above are probably generally true. If there is a collective process that favors faction strength (where strength could refer to economic power rather than faction size), and the case is close, the collective may well amplify bias. If there is a collective process that favors argument strength (such that an argument once voiced is highly persuasive), the collective will tend to be less biased than the individuals in it.

"Strength in arguments" sometimes prevails in adversarial systems; for example, there are legal defenses or evidentiary problems that will lead most lawyers to reject a case. And, of course, "strength in numbers" effects are well documented in the sociology of science (Cole, 1992), where trendiness, networking, and social stratification can privilege some hypotheses and findings irrespective of their validity. But, by its very nature, an inquisitorial system seems more likely than an adversarial system to favor "strength in arguments" over raw factional strength or resources.

DOES ACCUMULATING EVIDENCE DRIVE OUT BIAS?

In our analyses of collective bias (Kerr et al., 1996; MacCoun, 2001), groups were more likely to correct individual biases when strong evidence favored one position. This is observed, for example, in mock jury experiments using strongly slanted trial evidence; an occasional juror will endorse the less popular position, but he or she will quickly yield to overwhelming majority argumentation (and, sometimes, ridicule or disdain).

Kalven and Zeisel's (1966) "liberation hypothesis" contends that jurors are most likely to allow personal sentiments to influence their verdicts when the trial evidence is ambiguous. Similarly, physicist and science fiction author Gregory Benford (1980) proposes a "law of controversy": "Passion is inversely proportional to the amount of real information available." In support, MacCoun (1990; Kerr et al., 1996) cites several lines of individual- and group-level research demonstrating enhanced extraevidentiary bias when evidence is equivocal.

Pyszcynski and Greenberg (1987) argue that although motivation influences hypothesis testing, most of us feel constrained by the desire to maintain an "illusion of objectivity." Similarly, Kunda (1990, p. 482) argues that directional biases "are not unconstrained: People do not seem to be at liberty to conclude whatever they want to conclude merely because they want to. Rather . . . people motivated to arrive at a particular conclusion attempt to be rational and to construct a justification of their desired conclusion that would persuade a dispassionate observer." But we should be wary of overstating the case for an "objectivity constraint." Even when evidence is strong and unidirectional, we may have difficulty recognizing it. "Cumulative meta-analyses," in which a running (weighted) average effect size is updated over time, show that research communities are often slow to realize that the accumulated evidence decisively favors a proposition (see Ioannidis & Lau, 2001; Mullen et al., 2001). And in real-world

Table 17.3. *"Close cases" and their prospects for resolution*

What makes the case "close"?	Will more and better evidence resolve the dispute?
Indifference on the part of the participants.	Probably, if they are motivated and able to process the evidence.
Lack of preexisting evidence, such that individual choices "could go either way."	Probably, if they are motivated and able to process the evidence.
Opposing factions with the same interpretation of facts, but different Bayesian priors.	Yes, if they are Bayesian updaters, but people tend to "anchor and adjust" instead.
Opposing factions with the same interpretation of facts, but different standard-of-proof thresholds.	One side will be persuaded long before the other, and the evidence may never be sufficient to cross very stringent thresholds.
Directly conflicting evidence regarding the same proposition.	The discrepancies will be viewed with suspicion on both sides, and until they are satisfactorily explained, each side will have grounds for holding firm.
Clear evidence for each of two or more propositions that evoke conflicting values.	The conflict will persist, but rather than reframing the debate as a value conflict, each side may cite its preferred "facts."

policy conflicts, the evidence is often too weak to constrain partisan judgment. Moreover, there is often evidence in support of each faction.

What Makes a Case "Close"?

Partisans operating in good faith can disagree on the facts for a variety of reasons (see Table 17.3). Normatively, any of the deadlocks in Table 17.3 might be expected to "give way" in the face of a sufficient accumulation of evidence favoring a given proposition. In reality, whether this will happen seems increasingly less plausible as one moves down the list.

In cases of indifference or of genuinely equivocal evidence, people may quickly accept a proposition once the available evidence in its favor is overwhelming (or unopposed), provided they have the motivation and ability to comprehend it (Petty & Cacioppo, 1986).

To the extent that people are Bayesian updaters, the effects of differing "priors" should be attenuated, but several decades of research suggests that people often fail to update in a Bayesian fashion, although this is a matter of some controversy (see Gilovich, Griffin, & Kahneman, 2002). In many settings, inductive updating is better described by a weighting-averaging rule. If people anchor on their priors and adjust insufficiently, they may well fail to converge on a consensus viewpoint.

Differing standards of proof will also discourage consensus on the evidence. For example, several studies indicate that the kind of biased assimilation effect documented by Lord et al. (1985) is largely mediated by more stringent processing of evidence supporting views contrary to one's own. Ditto and Lopez (1992) found that students were significantly more likely to scrutinize a medical test when they tested positive for a potentially dangerous (fictitious) enzyme; they also were more than twice as likely to retest themselves. These reactions might appear to be normatively reasonable, but Ditto and Lopez also found that relative to students testing negative, students testing positive perceived the disease as less serious and more common. Similarly, Edwards and Smith (1996) find support for a "disconfirmation bias," in which evidence inconsistent with the judge's prior beliefs was scrutinized more extensively.

There are many literatures where evidence continues to accumulate on *both* sides of an empirical question. For example, evidence continues to accumulate on the question of whether marijuana is a "gateway" to hard drug use; almost every year some new studies present evidence that the association is causal, whereas other new studies suggest it is spurious (MacCoun & Reuter, 2001). Even putting aside the blatant partisanship and dubious logic that characterizes much of the debate, the truth fails to come into focus because strong inferential methods (like randomized experiments) are ethically precluded. In other cases, facts that appear contradictory from an adversarial perspective are not. For example, the Dutch decision to stop penalizing marijuana possession appears to have no effect on levels of marijuana prevalence, but their decision to allow coffeeshops to sell marijuana has probably increased its use (MacCoun & Reuter, 1997). These statements only seem contradictory when one bifurcates the debate into "Dutch policy is good" versus "Dutch policy is bad."

Finally, accumulating evidence sometimes shifts the terms of debate without bringing about resolution or consensus. This happens when ostensibly factual disagreements are a smokescreen for deeper differences in values. Specific deterrence was once the major argument of capital punishment supporters. As evidence accumulated questioning any marginal deterrent effect, the rationale shifted to retribution. Most recently, a new rationale is cited – "closure" for victims' families (see Zimring, 2001). There has been a similar evolution of stated rationales for the ban on gay and lesbian military service (MacCoun, 1996). First, gays were too effeminate to be soldiers, then they were a "security risk," and in the 1990s, they were a threat to "unit cohesion."

PROMOTING "HONEST BROKER" PRACTICES

Our system for introducing science and empiricism into policy discourse is clearly an awkward muddle of inquisitorial and adversarial methods. It would be quixotic to simply call for a return to a pure inquisitorialism that probably never has and never will exist. Indeed, some forms of bias are defensible. There are ample normative grounds for accepting differing opinions about imperfect and limited research on complex, multifaceted issues. There is nothing inherently wrong with differing standards of proof and nothing shameful about taking an advocacy role – provided that we are self-conscious about our standards and our stance and make them explicit. Fostering hypothesis competition and a heterogeneity of views and methods can simultaneously serve the search for the truth and the search for the good.

At the same time, a shift toward a more explicit, robust adversarialism could make things worse instead of better. Instead, perhaps we need to better articulate the boundary between adversarialism and what might be called "heterogeneous inquisitorialism" – a partnership of rigorous methodological standards, a willingness to tolerate uncertainty, and the encouragement of a diversity of hypotheses and perspectives (MacCoun, 1998).

In principle, this should happen through the traditional scientific quality control procedures: peer review and replication. Unfortunately, the evidence for the effectiveness of these institutional safeguards is pretty depressing (see MacCoun, 1998). Cicchetti (1991) and Cole (1992) report dismally low interreferee reliabilities in psychology journals (in the .19 to .54 range), medical journals (.31 to .37), and the NSF grant reviewing process (.25 in economics, .32 in physics). But with Internet technologies, it is surely feasible to improve peer-reviewing practices. NSF and other funders are now using Web-based peer-review portals. It is now logistically feasible to ask reviewers to review the theory section of a paper before receiving the method section, and the method section before they receive the results.

Exact replications are fairly rare (Bornstein, 1990), in part because editors and reviewers are biased against publishing replications (Neuliep & Crandall, 1990, 1993). An important development in this respect has been the dramatic growth of meta-analysis, the statistical aggregation of results across studies (e.g., Cooper & Hedges, 1994; Schmidt, 1992).

Meta-analyses also have the benefit of being fairly explicit and transparent, and they have led to new standards for literature reviewing that
seem likely to attenuate the citation biases that plague traditional reviews
(Greenwald & Schuh, 1994).

Government agencies and private foundations need to actively promote and encourage greater use of randomized experiments, especially
those conducted by independent investigators. A particularly encouraging development in this regard is the Campbell Collaboration, which is
modeled on the influential Cochrane Collaboration for the dissemination
of clinical trial evidence in medicine.[10]

But we also need to take institutional steps to promote and encourage
analytic methods that promote debiasing.[11] The key here is to discourage
what might be called hypothesis *promotion* (testing single hypotheses and
putting forth evidence on their behalf) and encourage investigators to engage in within-study hypothesis *competition*. Recall that devil's advocacy
and the "consider the opposite" technique are among the few effective
debiasing methods in the laboratory. A methodological stance that is similar in spirit was advocated by Platt (1964), who suggested that rapidly
advancing research programs tend to employ a *strong inference* strategy,
in which the researcher designs tests of an array of plausible competitors
rather than a single favored hypothesis. Greenwald, Pratkanis, Leippe,
and Baumgardner (1986) applaud Platt's intent but suggest that his strategy is rooted in a naive faith in falsificationism. Instead, they recommend
a strategy of *condition seeking*, in which a researcher deliberately attempts to "discover which, of the many conditions that were confounded
together in procedures that have obtained a finding, are indeed necessary
or sufficient" (p. 223). For example, in Anderson and Anderson's (1996)
destructive testing approach, the investigator tests alternative model spec-
ifications to identify what it takes to make an effect go away.

---

[10] "The international Campbell Collaboration (C2) is a nonprofit organization that aims
to help people make well-informed decisions about the effects of interventions in the
social, behavioral and educational arenas. C2's objectives are to prepare, maintain, and
disseminate systematic reviews of studies of interventions. We acquire and promote access to information about trials of interventions. C2 builds summaries and electronic
brochures of reviews and reports of trials for policy makers, practitioners, researchers
and the public." See <http://www.campbellcollaboration.org/>.

[11] Glanz (2000) reports that particular physicists have developed a new procedure for reducing bias by blinding their analyses; a computer algorithm adds an unknown "offset"
constant to their data, which is only removed when the analysis is complete. This might
work well when competing theories make strong point predictions, but such is rarely the
case in policy analysis. For us, the equivalent might be to add unknown "offsets" to each
entry in our covariance matrices prior to multivariate analysis.

Discouraging bias does not necessarily invariably mean making our methods more stringent. In at least one sense, we might discourage mischief by being *less* stringent. One of the most common expressions of investigator bias involves attempts to "cross the .05 threshold" of statistical significance via analytic "fishing expeditions," dropping outliers, and so on. But as Cohen (1994) and others have pointed out, almost any comparison will be statistically significant given a large enough sample, yet levels of statistical power are scandalously low in the social sciences – a problem further compounded by the inherent noisiness of social science measurement. This is particularly a problem in field research, where logistical, economic, ethical, and political obstacles make it difficult to increase sample sizes. Thus, whereas we obsess about false positives (Type I statistical errors), we arguably have a more serious problem with false negatives (Type II statistical errors; Cohen, 1994). But the growing influence of meta-analysis ought to diminish the value of null hypothesis testing. Meta-analysis helps solve the power problem, provided enough studies are found. It encourages lots of small studies (improving the heterogeneity and robustness of our research basis) rather than a handful of mega-studies. It does not solve the false-positive problem so much as make it moot – it provides robust estimation of the actual effect size across studies. Attention shifts to the magnitude of effects, their moderating conditions, and their *substantive* significance.

Finally, a more heterogeneous inquisitorialism would welcome investigators from the full spectrum of social categories and political beliefs (Redding, 2001; Tetlock, 1994), while at the same time encouraging greater clarity and candor about the values that motivate us, the facts that run counter to our views, and the role we are playing in any given setting (scientist vs. expert advocate). It may well be impossible, as philosophers and postmodernists insist, to separate facts from values, but we should not accept this as a license for unfettered bias cloaked as "expertise."

References

Anderson, C. A., & Anderson, K. B. (1996). Violent crime rate studies in philosophical context: A destructive kesting approach to heat and southern culture of violence effects. *Journal of Personality and Social Psychology*, 70, 740–756.

Arkes, H. R. (1991). Costs and benefits of judgment errors: Implications for debiasing. *Psychological Review*, 110, 486–498.

Benford, G. (1980). *Timescape.*

Camerer, C., and Hogarth, R. (1999). The effects of financial incentives in experiments: A review and capital-labor-production framework. *Journal of Risk and Uncertainty*, 19, 7–42.

Cicchetti, D. V. (1991). The reliability of peer review for manuscript and grant submissions: A cross-disciplinary investigation. *Behavioral and Brain Sciences,* 14, 119–186.

Cohen, J. (1994). The earth is round (p < .05). *American Psychologist,* 49, 997–1003.

Cohen, G. L., Aronson, J., & Steele, C. M. (2000). When beliefs yield to evidence: Reducing biased evaluation by affirming the self. *Personality and Social Psychology Bulletin,* 26, 1151–1164.

Cole S. (1992). *Making science: Between nature and society.* Cambridge, MA: Harvard University Press.

Cummings, K. M., Russell, S., Gingrass, A., and Davis, R. (1991). What scientists funded by the tobacco industry believe about the hazards of cigarette smoking. *American Journal of Public Health,* 81, 894–896.

DeVries, F., Mannen, K., Comerio, M., Ellwood, J., & MacCoun, R. (2001, 7 February). *Design faultlines: A study of seismic decisionmaking in universities.* Presented at the Annual meeting of the Earthquake Engineering Research Institute, Monterey, California.

Ditto, P. H., Lopez, D. F. (1992). Motivated skepticism: Use of differential decision criteria for preferred and nonpreferred conclusions. *J. Pers. Soc. Psychol.,* 63, 568–584.

Edwards, K., & Smith, E. E. (1996). A disconfirmation bias in the evaluation of arguments. *Journal of Personality and Social Psychology,* 71, 5–24.

Epstein, S. (1996). *Impure science: AIDS, activism, and the politics of knowledge.* Berkeley: University of California Press.

Faigman, D. L. (1999). *Legal alchemy: The use and misuse of science in the law.* Freeman.

Fischhoff, B. (1990). Psychology and public policy: Tool or toolmaker? *Am. Psychol.,* 45, 647–653.

Fischhoff, B., & Beyth-Marom, R. (1983). Hypothesis evaluation from a Bayesian perspective. *Psychol. Rev.,* 90, 239–260.

Fiske, S. T. (1989). Examining the role of intent: Toward understanding its role in stereotyping and prejudice. In J. S. Uleman and J. A. Bargh (Eds.), *Unintended thought* (pp. 253–283). New York: Guilford Press.

Fraser, S., (Ed.), (1995). *The Bell Curve wars: Race, intelligence, and the future of America.* New York: Basic Books.

Fuchs, S., and Westervelt, S. D. (1996). Fraud and trust in science. *Perspectives in Biology and Medicine,* 39, 248–270.

Gaffan, E. A., Tsaousis, J., & Kemp-Wheeler, S. M. (1995). Researcher allegiance and meta-analysis: The case of cognitive therapy for depression. *Journal of Consulting & Clinical Psychology,* 63(6), 966–998.

Gelbspan, R. (1997). *The heat is on: The high stakes battle over earth's threatened climate.* New York: Addison Wesley.

Gilovich, T., Griffin, D. W., & Kahneman, D. (2002). *Heuristics and biases: The psychology of intuitive judgment.* New York: Cambridge University Press.

Gholson, B., and Barker, P. (1985). Kuhn, Lakatos, and Laudan: Applications in the history of physics and psychology. *Am. Psychol.,* 40, 755–769.

Glantz, S. A. (1996). *The cigarette papers*. Berkeley: University of California Press.

Glanz, J. (2000, 8 August). New tactic in physics: Hiding the answer. *New York Times*, D1, D4.

Gorman, D. M. (1998). The irrelevance of evidence in the development of school-based drug prevention policy, 1986–1996. *Evaluation Review*, 22, 118– 146.

Gorman, D. M. (2002). The "science" of drug and alcohol prevention: The case of the randomized trial of the Life Skills Training program. *International Journal of Drug Policy*, 13, 21–26.

Gorman, D. M. (2003). Prevention programs and scientific nonsense. *Policy Review*, February and March, 65–75.

Greenwald, A. G., Pratkanis, A. R., Leippe, M. R., & Baumgardner, M. H. (1986). Under what conditions does theory obstruct research progress? *Psychol. Rev.*, 93, 216–229.

Gross, P. R., & Levitt, N. (1994). Higher superstition: *The academic left and its quarrels with science*. Baltimore: Johns Hopkins University Press.

Hammond, K. R. (1996). *Human judgement and social policy: Irreducible uncertainty, inevitable error, unavoidable injustice*. New York: Oxford University Press.

Hammond, K. R., Harvey, L. O., & Hastie, R. (1992). Making better use of scientific knowledge: Separating truth from justice. *Psychol. Sci.*, 3, 80–87.

Hilts, P. J. (2000, September 1). Company tried to bar report that HIV vaccine failed. *The New York Times*.

Horowitz, J. L., MacCoun, R. J., & Manski, C. F. (2002). Response to comments regarding the National Research Council report. *Addiction*, 97, 663– 665.

Howson, C., & Urbach, P. (1993). *Scientific reasoning: The Bayesian approach* (2nd ed.). Chicago: Open Court.

Ioannidis, J. P., & Lau, J. (2001). Evolution of treatment effects over time: Empirical insight from recursive cumulative metaanalyses. *Proceedings of the National Academy of Sciences*, 98, 831–836.

Jones, E. E., & Harris, V. A. (1967). The attribution of attitudes. *Journal of Experimental Social Psychology*, 3, 1–24.

Kahneman, D., Slovic, P., & Tversky, A. (Eds.). (1982). *Judgment under uncertainty: Heuristics and biases*. New York: Cambridge University Press.

Kalven, H., & Zeisel, H. (1966). *The American jury*. Boston: Little, Brown.

Keltner, D., & Robinson, R. J. (1996). Extremism, power, and the imagined basis of social conflict. *Current Directions in Psychol. Sci.*, 5, 101– 105.

Kerr, N., MacCoun, R. J., & Kramer, G. (1996). Bias in judgment: Comparing individuals and groups. *Psychological Review*, 103, 687–719.

Klayman, J., & Ha, Y. W. (1987). Confirmation, disconfirmation, and information in hypothesis testing. *Psychol. Rev.*, 94, 211–228.

Koehler, J. J. (1993). The influence of prior beliefs on scientific judgments of evidence quality. *Org. Behav. & Human Dec. Proc.*, 56, 28–55.

Kruglanski, A. W. (1989). *Lay epistemics and human knowledge: cognitive and motivational bases*. New York: Plenum.

Kruglanski, A. W., & Webster, D. M. (1996). Motivated closing of the mind: "Seizing" and "freezing." *Psychol. Rev.*, 103, 263–283.

Kunda, Z. (1990). The case for motivated reasoning. *Psychol. Bul.*, 108, 480–498. Kruglanski.

Laudan, L. (1990). *Science and relativism: Controversies in the philosophy of science*. Chicago: University of Chicago Press.

Laughlin, P. R. (1996). Group decision making and collective induction. In E. Witte and J. H. Davis (Eds.), *Understanding group behavior: Volume 1: Consensual action by small groups* (pp. 61–80). Matwah, NJ: Erlbaum.

Lerner, J. S., & Tetlock, P. E. (1999). Accounting for the effects of accountability. *Psychological Bulletin*, 125, 255–275.

LeVay, S. (1996). *Queer science: The use and abuse of research into homosexuality*. Cambridge, MA: MIT Press.

Liberman, A., & Chaiken, S. (1992). Defensive processing of personally relevant health messages. *Pers. Soc. Psychol. Bul.*, 18, 669–679.

Lord, C. G., Lepper, M. R., & Preston, E. (1985). Considering the opposite: A corrective strategy for social judgment. *J. Pers. Soc. Psychol.*, 47, 1231–1243.

Lord, C. G., Ross, L., & Lepper, M. R. (1979). Biased assimiliation and attitude polarization: The effects of prior theories on subsequently considered evidence. *J. Pers. Soc. Psychol.*, 37, 2098–2109.

Lorge, I., & Solomon H. (1955). Two models of group behavior in the solution of Eureka-type problems. *Psychometrika*, 20, 139–148.

MacCoun, R. J. (1989). Experimental research on jury decision making. *Science*, 244, 1046–1050.

MacCoun, R. J. (1990). The emergence of extralegal bias during jury deliberation. *Criminal Justice and Behavior*, 17, 303–314.

MacCoun, R. J. (1995). Review of K. R. Foster, D. E. Bernstein, and P. W. Huber (Eds.), *Phantom risk: Scientific inference and the law* (MIT Press, 1993). *Journal of Policy Analysis and Management*, 14, 168–171.

MacCoun, R. J. (1996). Sexual orientation and military cohesion: A critical review of the evidence. In G. M. Herek, J. B. Jobe, and R. Carney (Eds.), *Out in force: Sexual orientation and the military*. Chicago: University of Chicago Press.

MacCoun, R. J. (1998). Biases in the interpretation and use of research results, *Annual Review of Psychology*, 49, 259–287.

MacCoun, R. J. (2001). American distortion of Dutch drug statistics. *Society*, 38, 23–26.

MacCoun, R. J. (2002). Comparing micro and macro rationality. In M. V. Rajeev Gowda and Jeffrey Fox (Eds.), *Judgments, decisions, and public policy* (pp. 116–137). Cambridge University Press.

MacCoun, R. (2003). Review of Shadish, Cook, and Campbell's *Experimental and quasi-experimental designs for generalized causal inference* (book review). *Journal of Policy Analysis and Management*, 22, 330–332.

MacCoun, R. J., & Paletz, S. (2004). California survey of perceived bias in public policy research findings (manuscript in preparation). University of California at Berkeley.

MacCoun, R. J., & Reuter, P. (1997). Interpreting Dutch cannabis policy: Reasoning by analogy in the legalization debate. *Science*, 278, 47–52.

MacCoun, R. J., & Reuter, P. (2001). *Drug war heresies: Learning from other vices, times, and places*. Cambridge University Press. [Details and reviews at socrates.berkeley.edu/~maccoun/DWH.html]

Mayo, D. G. (1996). *Error and the growth of experimental knowledge.* Chicago: University of Chicago Press.

McGrath, J. E. (1984). *Groups: Interaction and performance.* Englewood Cliffs, NJ: Prentice Hall.

McGuire, W. J. (1983). A contextualist theory of knowledge: Its implications for innovation and reform in psychological research. *Adv. Exp. Soc. Psychol.,* 16, 1–47.

Merton, R. K. (1973). *The sociology of science.* Chicago: University of Chicago Press.

Metcalf, C. E. (1998). Research ownership, communication of results, and threats to objectivity in client-driven research. *Journal of Policy Analysis and Management,* 17, 153–163.

Moskowitz, J. M. (1993). Why reports of outcome evaluations are often biased or uninterpretable: Examples from evaluations of drug abuse prevention programs. *Eval. & Planning,* 16, 1–9.

Mullen, B., Muellerleile, P., & Bryant, B. (2001). Cumulative meta-analysis: A consideration of indicators of sufficiency and stability. *Personality and Social Psychology Bulletin,* 27, 1450–1462.

Munro, G. D., & Ditto, P. H. (1997). Biased assimilation, attitude polarization, and affect in reactions to stereotype-relevant scientific information. *Pers. Soc. Psychol. Bul.,* 23, 636–653.

Murray, B. (2002, February). Research fraud needn't happen at all. *APA Monitor,* 27–28.

Neuliep, J. W, & Crandall, R. (1990). Editorial bias against replication research. *J. Soc. Behav. & Pers.,* 5, 85–90.

Neuliep, J. W., & Crandall, R. (1993). Reviewer bias against replication research. *J. Soc. Behav. & Pers.,* 8, 21–29.

Pennington, N., & Hastie, R. (1993). The story model for juror decision making. In R. Hastie (Ed.), *Inside the juror: The psychology of juror decision making,* (pp. 192–221). New York: Cambridge University Press.

Platt, J. R. (1964). Strong inference. *Science,* 146, 347–353.

Pronin, E., Lin, D. Y., & Ross, L. (2002). The bias blind spot: Perceptions of bias in self versus others. *Personality and Social Psychology Bulletin,* 28, 369–381.

Pyszczynski, T., & Greenberg, J. (1987). Toward an integration of cognitive and motivational perspectives on social inference: A biased hypothesis-testing model. *Adv. in Exp. Soc. Psych.,* 20, 297–340.

Redding, R. E. (2001). Sociopolitical diversity in psychology. *American Psychologist,* 56, 205–215.

Revkin, A. C. (2003, August 5). Politics reasserts itself in the debate over climate change and its hazards. *The New York Times,* D2.

Rips, L. J., Brem, S. K., & Bailenson, J. (1999). Reasoning dialogues. Current Directions in *Psychological Science,* 8, 172–177.

Robinson, L. A., Berman, J. S., & Neimeyer, R. A. (1990). Psychotherapy for the treatment of depression: A comprehensive review of controlled outcome research. *Psychological Bulletin,* 108, 30–49.

Robinson, R. J., Keltner, D., Ward, A., & Ross, L. (1995). Actual versus assumed differences in construal: "Naïve realism" in intergroup perception and conflict. *Journal of Personality and Social Psychology,* 68, 404–417.

Rosenthal, R. (1994). Science and ethics in conducting, analyzing, and reporting psychological research. *Psychol. Sci.*, 5, 127–134.

Ross, L., & Nisbett, R. E. (1991). *The person and the situation.* New York: McGraw-Hill.

Schwenk, C. R. (1990). Effects of devil's advocacy and dialectical inquiry on decision making: A meta-analysis. *Org. Behav. & Hum. Dec. Proc.*, 47, 161–176.

Shadish, W. R., Montgomery, L. M., Wilson, P., Wilson, M. R., et al. (1993). Effects of family and marital psychotherapies: A meta-analysis. *Journal of Consulting & Clinical Psychology*, 61(6), 992–1002.

Schum, D. A., & Martin, A. W. (1982). Formal and empirical research on cascaded inference. *Law & Soc. Rev.*, 17, 105–151.

Shadish, W. R. (1995). Philosophy of science and the quantitative-qualitative debates: Thirteen common errors. *Evaluation & Program Planning*, 18, 63–75.

Tetlock, P. E. (1994). Political psychology or politicized psychology: Is the road to scientific hell paved with good moral intentions? *Poli. Psychol.*, 15, 509–529.

Tetlock, P. E, & Levi, A. (1982). Attribution bias: On the inconclusiveness of the cognition-motivation debate. *J. Exp. Soc. Psychol.*, 18, 68–88.

Tetlock, P. E., Peterson, R. & Lerner, J. (1996). Revising the value pluralism model: Incorporating social content and context postulates. In C. Seligman, J. Olson, and M. Zanna (Eds.), *Ontario symposium on social and personality psychology: Values.* Hillsdale, NJ: Erlbaum.

Thagard, P. (1992). *Conceptual revolutions.* Princeton, NJ: Princeton University Press.

Thibaut, J., & Walker, L. (1978). A theory of procedure. *Calif. Law Rev.*, 26, 1271–1289.

Vallone, R. P., Ross, L., & Lepper, M. R. (1985). The hostile media phenomenon: Biased perception and perceptions of media bias in coverage of the Beirut massacre. *J. Pers. Soc. Psychol.*, 49, 577–585.

Wegener, D. T., Kerr, N. L., Fleming, M. A., & Petty, R. E. (2000). Flexible corrections of juror judgments: Implications for jury instructions. *Psychology, Public Policy, and Law*, 6, 629–654.

Wegner, D. M., & Bargh, J. A. (1998). Control and automaticity in social life. In D. Gilbert, S. Fiske, and G. Lindzey (Eds.), *Handbook of social psychology* (4th ed.). Boston: McGraw-Hill.

Weimer, D. L, & Vining, A. R. (1992). *Policy analysis: Concepts and practice* (2nd ed.). Englewood Cliffs, NJ: Prentice Hall.

Wilson, T. D., & Brekke, N. (1994). Mental contamination and mental correction: Unwanted influences on judgments and evaulations. *Psychol. Bull.*, 116, 117–142.

Woodward, J., & Goodstein, D. (1996). Conduct, misconduct and the structure of science. *Am. Scientist*, 84, 479–490.

Zimring, F. (2003). *The contradictions of American capital punishment.* Oxford University Press.

Zuckerman, H. (1988). The sociology of science. In N. J. Smelser (Ed.), *Handbook of sociology* (pp. 511–574). Beverly Hills, CA: Sage.

EIGHTEEN

Commentary

Conflicts of Interest in Policy Analysis

Compliant Pawns in Their Game?

Baruch Fischhoff

Carnegie Mellon University

BEHAVIORAL RESEARCH SHOWS NEED FOR POLICY RESEARCH AND ITS LIMITS

MacCoun (2004) insightfully uses a Bayesian framework to character-
ize debates regarding the relative validity of competing policies and the
theories underlying them. That framework allows a thoughtful sorting
and integration of empirical, analytical, and philosophical evidence. It reveals cognitive and motivational barriers to fulfilling the Bayesian vision
of explicit, coherent hypothesis evaluation. It provides a forensic guide
to more and less deliberately malevolent attempts to distort debates in
non-Bayesian ways. In a sense, MacCoun does for contentious situations
what Ruth Beyth-Marom and I tried to do for individual deliberations
(Fischhoff & Beyth-Marom, 1983).

MacCoun raises one potential limit to this framework, posed by the observation of persistently non-Bayesian behavior. These biases have long
been used to demonstrate the frailties of human judgment and, with them,
the need for compensatory policies. For example, if people cannot understand risks, then, arguably, they need strong regulatory protections, in
order to keep dangerous products off the market. Arguably, they also
need manipulative public health measures in order to protect them from
themselves (e.g., high cigarette taxes, social marketing of abstinence or
condom use).

However, MacCoun notes that persistent violations also might suggest
a fundamental flaw in the normative model. An extreme position is that
people cannot think in the prescribed way, making it an inappropriate
aspiration. As a result, it is investigators' responsibility to discern the

263

method in any persistent apparent madness. This position runs the risk of throwing out the baby (axiomatically derived rules of rationality) with the bathwater (imperfect behavior). It also turns scientists into philosophers, a flattering role, but not necessarily one for which we are properly trained.

A less extreme position is that alternative modes of thought are more effective, in guiding choices, than is the pursuit of unachievable rationality. For example, "precautionary principles" are often advocated as an alternative to cost-benefit and risk analyses. They prescribe acting cautiously, in situations where uncertainty is so great that analysis produces indeterminate results.[1] Arguably, measures of precaution might be incorporated formally in rational models (DeKay et al., 2002). However, advocates of precautionary principles often mistrust the individuals performing analyses and even analysis itself (Löfstedt et al., 2002). They fear not only the sort of mischief catalogued by MacCoun but also the analysts' intellectual ability to create, estimate, and evaluate models. They see incentives for analysts to formulate policy questions in ways that require the purchase of their services. They fear the disenfranchisement of those without the resources needed to hire analysts (or even to critique their work in a sustained fashion).

BEHAVIORAL RESEARCH CAN GUIDE POLICY DESIGN AS WELL AS ANALYSIS

The spirit of MacCoun's critique might be extended to conditions in which the Bayesian scheme fails by its own lights. Bayesian analysis presumes enumerating the full set of possible hypotheses. In most of MacCoun's cases, that is accomplished by dichotomizing a continuous variable (e.g., the correlation between smoking and cancer, or between patrolling and crime). The threshold value reflects a balance between the costs and benefits of appropriately and mistakenly adopting the two competing policies. In a few cases, the policy question compares a few discrete programs (e.g., condoms vs. abstinence promotion). That situation, too, has a ready Bayesian representation, at the price of some computational complexity.

---

[1] Although typically advanced by environmental and consumer advocates, they also include the Bush Administration's argument for the Iraq War, despite the acknowledged absence of strong evidence of weapons of mass destruction or support for Al Qaeda (Finkel, in press).

Yet, not all policy issues are so starkly drawn. Even in adversarial contexts, partisans may have some feeling that other options exist, potentially superior to those represented by the warring parties. In principle, such situations have a simple Bayesian representation: create a complementary "all other policies" hypothesis. Non-Bayesian alternatives allow reserving some probability for hypotheses to be determined later (Shafer & Tversky, 1985). Cognitively, though, unelaborated options are likely to receive insufficient attention (Fischhoff et al., 1978; Tversky & Koehler, 1994).

In the short term, neglecting unspecified alternatives creates unwarranted confidence in the focal policies. Indeed, achieving that impression may be a strategic goal. It narrows the playing field, to the form described by MacCoun, subject to its familiar opportunities for mischief. It protects the focal policies from additional forms of attack. As a result, they have common cause in restricting the range of options. Policy analysts may faithfully follow their professional standards, while supporting a system rigged to favor a subset of possible options.

A long-term consequence of this restricted focus is failing to develop better alternatives. They are effectively off the table, receiving neither discussion nor research, without which they cannot be viable enough to attract additional resources. Here, too, the policy analyst can be complicit, by accepting the restricted terms of commissioned work. A narrow focus comes naturally to analysts. They are trained to do detailed work on defined problems. There is no end to the amount of detail possible, with greater detail meaning larger contracts and, often, more work to lower level (and higher margin) workers at consulting companies. Defining the analyst's role as technician removes any pressure to challenge policy makers' fundamental problem framing.

POLICY ANALYSTS HAVE INCENTIVES TO RESTRICT DEBATE

At its inception, risk analysis was much less passive. It was seen as part of the design process, an intellectual alternative to destructive testing, especially with systems that were too complex or expensive to test in prototype. Analyses conducted for design purposes focus on the relative reliability (and costs) of competing designs. As a result, they avoid some of the difficult questions that arise when determining absolute reliability (and costs). However, like other design processes, such analyses require early and continuing interaction with the rest of the design team as alternatives are suggested, critiqued, and refined. They also require an attitude of actively "looking for trouble," trying to discover problems in theory, before they reveal themselves in practice (Fischhoff, 1977, 1989).

In the history of risk analysis as a profession, this role quickly became subservient to a probative one. The U.S. space program was required to prove that it exposed astronauts to no more than a prescribed level of risk. Nuclear power, liquid natural gas, and other industries faced similar challenges of demonstrating acceptable levels of risk for technologies that had accumulated too little operating experience to demonstrate their performance empirically (or, in some cases, did not exist at all). Probative analyses invite the turns of mind that MacCoun describes, by creating a zero-sum game with fixed alternatives. Any scrap of evidence that favors one policy undermines its competitors. New designs can frustrate both the analysts, by providing a moving target, and their clients, by suggesting that things could be better. As such, analysis itself can discourage innovation (O'Brien, 2000).

Being treated as tools of vested interests may be an unexpected role for analysts who thought of themselves as dispassionate professionals. When analysts and analysis are inseparable, attacks on one are inevitably attacks on the other. The ensuing discomfort may contribute to their often dismissive attitude toward critics without comparable training (Fischhoff, 1995; Fischhoff, Slovic, & Lichtenstein, 1982). Although viewing the public as irrational may be comforting, it does not resolve the fundamental conflict of interest in needing to accept a client's restricted problem definition in order to secure the analytical contract.

The demand for absolute estimates of risk and benefit creates incentives for claiming to offer such services. The supply of analysts making such claims facilitates framing policy questions in that way. For example, current pressure for widening the scope of cost-benefit analyses presupposes the existence of viable procedures. Thus, policy analysts' interests may run counter to those who need better policies to consider or explicit recognition of fundamental uncertainties. For example, the probative uses of climate models has framed the greenhouse gas debate in terms of "How confident can we be that there is warming?," rather than "What gambles should we be taking with the environment?"

Pressure for a can-do attitude may further constrain the content of policy analyses, often focusing them on the subset of issues that appears readily quantified. Those analysts who take that work may perform their own part conscientiously, while still helping to distort the policy process. For example, before Three Mile Island, nuclear power risk analyses largely omitted human behavior. Faced by an accident attributed to human error, risk analysts found a way to incorporate behavior within their framework, but in a way that largely ignored behavioral research. Rather, they created conceivable models of the more mechanical aspects of human performance (e.g., error rates in inspection tasks, failure to close valves completely), while ignoring (or at least oversimplifying) the complex cognitive processes essential to system operation (and responsible for Three Mile Island, Chernobyl, and most other infamous accidents).[2]

POLICY ANALYSIS CAN OBSCURE POLITICAL MANIPULATION

Another threat to can-do claims arises when analyses can be designed in different ways, each reflecting different values (Crouch & Wilson, 1981; Fischhoff et al., 1981). For example, "risk" might – or might not – include various forms of morbidity, as well as mortality. Auto accidents are the largest death risk to young people, while drugs and poverty may account for much more morbidity, especially when psychological dysfunction is considered. Mortality itself might be measured in premature deaths or lost years of life expectancy – with the latter measure placing extra weight on deaths among young people (with more years being lost with each life). If analysts make these choices without consultation, then they are arrogating important political choices to themselves. If they consult with their clients, then they force explicit consideration of issues that the latter would prefer to avoid. Indeed, one of the more pernicious aspects of much analysis is hiding ethical presumptions (e.g., how equity issues are treated) under the façade of technical neutrality.

A further conflict of interest facing probabilistic risk analysts is whether to accept the rights of science without its responsibilities. Critical among the latter are independent peer review, archiving data in publicly accessible form, and using methods with known (and acknowledged) strengths and weaknesses. These conditions are hard to achieve in policy research. Qualified peers may be uninterested in ensuring that practical work is done to scientific standards, when it has no theoretical interest. Data may be justifiably confidential. Analysts' marketing may depend on proprietary computer programs. Complex analyses may defy conventional review (e.g., PRAs with a million lines of code). Review processes can be stacked to achieve political aims. Reviewers may faithfully perform their role, while abetting a biased process. Review can be used to delay

---

[2] Fortunately, an aggressive program of improved training and redesigning, drawing heavily on the research literature, was conducted in parallel with the probative analysis.

action, making participants complicit. All of these possibilities are being raised in the controversy over OMB's current proposal to require peer review of government analyses.

Cost-benefit analyses, survey research, evaluation research, and educational testing are other pursuits that often constitute semisciences, seeking the rights (prestige, remuneration) of science without its full responsibilities. When practitioners rotate between the worlds of science and practice, there are incentives to resist recognized conflicts of interest, so that they can go home to academia. However, those extrinsic constraints vanish when they reside permanently in the world of consulting firms, litigation research, and politically oriented "think tanks."

BEHAVIORAL RESEARCH MIGHT FACILITATE SELF-CRITICAL POLICY RESEARCH

As other chapters in this volume demonstrate, there are significant psychological barriers to identifying one's own conflicts of interest. That research obligates us to work doubly hard to do so, then to admit having undershot the target. In my experience, behavioral researchers are often invited to the policy table when their research is (perhaps dimly) seen as supporting a preconceived position. Most commonly, what policy makers want is a bold, sweeping statement about human rationality. Liberals might seek evidence of rationality to support participatory processes, evidence of irrationality to support paternalistic regulation. Conservatives might seek evidence of rationality to support market solutions, evidence of irrationality to support technocratic control.

Such rhetorically driven summaries cannot do justice to the complex suite of strengths and weaknesses that people bring to the varied choices that they face. Such summaries frustrate the search for a nuanced approach, affording people the best balance of autonomy and protection. They ignore the details of research into psychological processes that might expand the envelope of autonomy, by designing circumstances better suited to lay decision making. Unless we can bring our science, as well as our status as scientists, to policy arenas, these invitations are more humiliating than flattering.

Analyses like MacCoun's (and the others in this volume) can help us to understand both how we are being wittingly used and how we might be unwitting prey. Attention to policy makers' needs can help us to be ready with properly sensitive analyses and designs, in situations where they are willing to take our science seriously. All too often, we quickly go from being irrelevant to being late, unable to deliver products in a timely fashion. When that happens, semiscientific consultants will fill in for us, sometimes informed by the research, sometimes selling proprietary nostrums. Being ready for serious policy work requires academic disciplines that value both *applied basic* research, testing in reality theories established in controlled settings, and *basic applied* research, domesticating, for systematic study, problems arising from real-world problems (Baddeley, 1978).

References

Baddeley, A. D. (1979). Applied cognitive and cognitive applied research. In L. G. Nilsson (Ed.), *Perspectives on memory research*. Hillsdale, NJ: Lawrence Erlbaum.

DeKay, M., Small, M. J., Fischbeck, P. S., et al. (2002). Risk-based decision analysis in support of precautionary policies. *Journal of Risk Research*, 5, 391–418.

Finkel, A. M (in press). Too much of the "red book" is still (!) ahead of its time.

Fischhoff, B. (1977). Cost-benefit analysis and the art of motorcycle maintenance. *Policy Sciences*, 8, 177–202.

Fischhoff, B. (1989). Eliciting knowledge for analytical representation. *IEEE Transactions on Systems, Man and Cybernetics*, 13, 448–461.

Fischhoff, B. (1995). Risk perception and communication unplugged: Twenty years of process. *Risk Analysis*, 15, 137–145.

Fischhoff, B., & Beyth-Marom, R. (1983). Hypothesis evaluation from a Bayesian perspective. *Psychological Review*, 90, 239–260.

Fischhoff, B., Lichtenstein, S., Slovic, P., Derby, S. L., & Keeney, R. L. (1981). *Acceptable risk*. New York: Cambridge University Press.

Fischhoff, B., Slovic, P., & Lichtenstein, S. (1978). Fault trees: Sensitivity of assessed failure probabilities to problem representation. *Journal of Experimental Psychology: Human Perception and Performance*, 4, 330–344.

Fischhoff, B., Slovic, P., & Lichtenstein, S. (1982). Lay foibles and expert fables in judgments about risk. *American Statistician*, 36, 240–255.

Löfstedt, R., Fischhoff, B., & Fischhoff, I. (2002). Precautionary principles: General definitions and specific applications to genetically modified organisms (GMOs). *Journal of Policy Analysis and Management*, 21, 381–407.

MacCoun, R. J. (2004). Conflicts of interest in public policy research. In D. Moore, G. Loewenstein, & D. Cain (Eds.), *Conflicts of interest*. New York: Cambridge University Press.

O'Brien, M. (2000). *Making better environmental decisions: An alternative to risk assessment*. Cambridge, MA: MIT Press.

Shafer, G., & Tversky, A. (1985). Languages and designs for probability judgment. *Cognitive Science*, 9, 309–339.

Tversky, A., & Koehler, D. J. (1994). Support theory: A nonextensional representation of subjective probability. *Psychological Review*, 101, 547–567.

NINETEEN

Conflict of Interest as an Objection to Consequentialist Moral Reasoning

Robert H. Frank*

Cornell University

In their simplest and most popular form, consequentialist moral theories identify the morally correct choice as the one that results in the best overall consequences. Despite this criterion's sensible ring, it remains deeply controversial. Many critics object in principle, arguing that a choice may be immoral even though it leads to the best consequences on balance. Here, I explore an alternative possibility, that although consequentialist theories in their simplest form might be attractive in principle, they also might suffer from serious implementation problems.

The difficulty stems from the fact that to engage in consequentialist moral reasoning, one must first construct estimates of the costs and benefits of the relevant alternatives. These estimates almost invariably involve considerable uncertainty, with the result that a broad range of values must be viewed as reasonable. Evidence suggests that even people who are committed to doing the right thing have a natural tendency to exploit moral wriggle room, by employing estimates that favor their own interests. There is a natural tendency, in other words, to estimate the personal benefits of an action at the high end of the reasonable range and to estimate the costs to others of the action at the low end of the reasonable range. Social comparisons reinforce these biases, creating a dynamic that extends the range of estimates that neutral observers can defend as reasonable.

The problem, in short, is that consequentialist moral reasoning may fail not because it is wrong in principle, but, rather, because of an inherent

* H. J. Louis Professor of Economics, Johnson Graduate School of Management, Cornell University, Ithaca, NY 14853.

conflict of interest facing those who must estimate the relevant costs and benefits. As a practical matter, consequentialism may not lead to the best results on balance.

Variants of the concern I raise have been acknowledged by consequentialists at least as far back as Henry Sidgwick (1874), leading some to call for a more indirect approach that relies on nonconsequentialist heuristics and ways of thinking. But recent empirical evidence suggests that the magnitude of the problem may be far greater than commonly supposed, and indirect forms of consequentialism entail problems of their own.

CONSEQUENTIALIST VERSUS DEONTOLOGICAL MORAL THEORIES

Consequentialism differs from traditional, or deontological, moral theories, which hold that the right choice must be identified on the basis of underlying moral principles. These principles may spring from religious tradition (for example, the Ten Commandments) but need not (for example, Kant's categorical imperative). Whatever their source, the principles invoked by deontologists have moral force insofar as they accord with strongly held moral intuitions.

For many, perhaps even the overwhelming majority, of cases, consequentialist and deontological moral theories yield the same prescriptions. Both camps, for example, hold that it was wrong for Enron to have lied about its profits and wrong for David Berkowitz to have murdered six innocent people. Even in cases in which there might appear to be ample room for disagreement about what constitutes moral behavior, a majority of practitioners from both camps often take the same side.

Consider, for example, a variant of the familiar trolley car problem discussed by philosophers. You are standing by a railroad track when you see an out-of-control trolley car about to strike a group of five people standing on the tracks ahead. You can throw a nearby switch, diverting the trolley onto a side track, which would result in the death of one person standing there. Failure to throw the switch will result in all five persons being killed on the main track.

Consequentialists are virtually unanimous in concluding that the morally correct choice is for you to throw the switch. Some deontologists equivocate, arguing that the active step of throwing the switch would make you guilty of killing the person on the side track, whereas you would not be guilty of killing the five on the main track if you failed to intervene. Yet, even most deontologists conclude that the distinction between act and omission is not morally relevant in this example, and that your best available choice is to throw the switch.

But even though the two moral frameworks exhibit broad agreement with respect to many of the ethical choices we confront in practice, many deontologists remain deeply hostile to the consequentialist framework. In this section, I examine two lines of objection they raise and conclude that neither appears decisive.

THE STATUS OF MORAL INTUITIONS

Critics often attack consequentialist moral theories by constructing examples in which the choice that consequentialism seems to prescribe violates strongly held moral intuitions. In another version of the trolley car problem, for example, the trolley is again about to kill five people, but this time you are not standing near the tracks, but on a footbridge above them. There is no switch you can throw to divert the train. But there is a large stranger standing next to you, and if you push him off the bridge onto the tracks below, his body will derail the trolley, in the process killing him but sparing the lives of the five strangers. (It would not work for you to jump down onto the tracks yourself, because you are too small to derail the trolley.)

Consequentialism seems to prescribe pushing the large stranger from the bridge, since this would result in a net savings of four lives. Yet, when people are asked what they think should be done in this situation, most feel strongly that it would be wrong to push the stranger to his death. Those who share this intuition are naturally sympathetic to the critics' claim that the example somehow demonstrates a fundamental flaw in the consequentialist position.

Many consequentialists, Princeton philosopher Peter Singer among them, respond that it is their moral intuition rather than their theory that the example calls into question (Singer, 2002). To illustrate, Singer asks us to imagine another variant of the trolley problem, one that is identical to the first except for one detail. You can throw a switch that will divert the train not onto a side track but onto a loop that circles back onto the main track. Standing on the loop is a large stranger whose body would bring the trolley to halt if it were diverted onto the loop. Singer notes that this time most people say that the right choice is to divert the trolley, just as in the original example in which the switch diverted it onto a side track rather than a loop. In both cases, throwing the switch caused the death of one stranger, in the process sparing the lives of the five others on the main track.[1]

Singer's Princeton colleague Joshua Greene, a cognitive neuroscientist, has suggested that people's intuitions differ in these two examples not because the morally correct action differs but, rather, because the action that results in the large stranger's death is so much more vivid and personal in the footbridge case than in the looped-track case:

> Because people have a robust, negative emotional response to the personal violation proposed in the footbridge case they immediately say that it's wrong. . . . At the same time, people fail to have a strong negative emotional response to the relatively impersonal violation proposed in the original trolley case, and therefore revert to the most obvious moral principle, "minimize harm," which in turn leads them to say that the action in the original case is permissible. (Greene, 2002).

To test this explanation, Green used functional magnetic resonance imaging to examine activity patterns in the brains of subjects confronted with the two decisions. His prediction was that activity levels in brain regions associated with emotion would be higher when subjects considered pushing the stranger from a footbridge than when they considered diverting the trolley onto the looped track. He also reasoned that the minority of subjects who felt the right action was to push the stranger from the footbridge would reach that judgment only after overcoming their initial emotional reactions to the contrary. Thus, he also predicted that the decisions taken by these subjects would take longer than those reached by the majority who thought it wrong to push the stranger to his death, and longer as well than it took for them to decide what to do in the looped-track example. Each of these predictions was confirmed.

Is it morally relevant that thinking about causing someone's death by pushing him from a footbridge elicits stronger emotions than thinking about causing his death by throwing a switch? Peter Singer argues that it is not, insisting that the difference is a simple, non-normative consequence of our evolutionary past. Under the primitive, small-group conditions under which humans evolved, he argues, the act of harming others always

---

[1] The looped-track example suggests that it was not the Kantian prohibition against using people merely as means that explains the earlier reluctance to push the stranger from the footbridge, because choosing to throw the switch in the looped-track example also entails using the stranger as merely a means to save the other five. In the original example, diverting the trolley onto the side track would have saved the others even if the stranger had not been on the side track.

entailed vivid personal contact at close quarters. One could not cause another's death by simply throwing a switch. So, if it was adaptive to be emotionally reluctant to inflict harm on others, the relevant emotions ought to be much more likely to be triggered by vivid personal assaults than by abstract actions like throwing a switch.

A historical case in point helps highlight the distinction. Shortly after British intelligence officers had broken Nazi encryption schemes in World War II, Winston Churchill had an opportunity to spare the lives of British residents of Coventry by warning them of a pending bombing attack. To do so, however, would have revealed to the Nazis that their codes had been broken. In the belief that preserving the secret would save considerably more British lives in the long run, Churchill gave Coventry no warning, resulting in large numbers of preventable deaths. It is difficult to imagine a more wrenching decision, and we celebrate Churchill's moral courage in making it. But it is easy to imagine that Churchill would have chosen differently had it been necessary for him personally to kill the Coventry's residents at close quarters, rather than merely to allow their deaths by failing to warn them. Singer's claim is that whereas this difference is a predictable consequence of the way in which natural selection forged our emotions, it has no moral significance.

In sum, the fact that consequentialist moral theories sometimes prescribe actions that conflict with moral intuitions cannot be taken as conclusive evidence against consequentialist moral reasoning. Moral intuitions are contingent reactions shaped by the details of our evolutionary history. Often they will be relevant for the moral choices we confront today, but sometimes they will not be.

THE INCOMMENSURABILITY PROBLEM

Consequentialist moral reasoning says we should install a guardrail on a dangerous stretch of mountain road if the dollar cost of doing so is less than the implicit dollar value of the injuries, deaths, and property damage thus prevented. Many critics respond that placing a dollar value on human life and suffering is morally illegitimate. (For a discussion of this position, see Adler, 1998.) The apparent implication is that we should install the guardrail no matter how much it costs or no matter how little it effects the risk of death and injury.

Given that we live in a world of scarcity, however, this position is difficult to defend. After all, money spent on a guardrail could be used to purchase other things we value, including things that enhance health and safety in other domains. Because we have only so much to spend, why should we install a guardrail if the same money spent on, say, better weather forecasting would prevent even more deaths and injuries?

More generally, critics object to consequentialism's implicit requirement for a metric enabling us to place the pros and cons of an action on a common footing. They complain, for example, that when a power plant pollutes the air, our gains from the cheap power thus obtained simply cannot be compared with the pristine view of the Grand Canyon we sacrifice.

Even the most ardent proponents of consequentialism concede that comparing disparate categories is often extremely difficult in practice. But many critics insist that such comparisons cannot be made *even in principle*. In their view, the problem is not that we do not know how big a reduction in energy costs would be required to compensate for a given reduction in air quality. Rather, it is that the two categories are simply incommensurable.

This view has troubling implications. In the eyes of the consequentialist, *any* action – even one whose costs and benefits are hard to compare – becomes irresistibly attractive if its benefits are sufficiently large and its costs are sufficiently small. Indeed, few people would oppose a new technology that would reduce the cost of power by half if its only negative effect were to degrade our view of the Grand Canyon for just one fifteen-second interval each decade.[2] By the same token, no one would favor adoption of a technology that produced only a negligible reduction in the cost of power at the expense of a dark cloud that continuously shielded North America from the rays of the sun.

We live in a continuous world. If the first technology is clearly acceptable, and the second clearly unacceptable, some intermediate technology is neither better nor worse than the status quo. And we should count any technology that is better than that one as an improvement. Scarcity is a simple fact of the human condition. To have more of one good thing, we must settle for less of another. Claiming that different values are incommensurable simply hinders clear thinking about difficult tradeoffs.

Notwithstanding their public pronouncements about incommensurability, even the fiercest critics of consequentialism cannot escape such tradeoffs. For example, they do not vacuum their houses scores of times

---

[2] The few who did object would likely invoke a variation of the "slippery-slope" argument, which holds that allowing even a single small step will lead to an inevitable slide to the bottom. Yet, we move part way down slippery slopes all the time, as when we amend the laws of free speech to prohibit people from yelling "fire" in a crowded theater in which there is no fire.

each day, nor do they get their brakes checked every morning. The reason, presumably, is not that clean air and auto safety do not matter, but that they have more pressing uses of their time. Like the rest of us, they are forced to make the best accommodations they can between competing values.

From the preceding discussion, I draw two conclusions. One is that critics have failed to offer persuasive arguments that consequentialist moral reasoning is objectionable as a matter of principle. Yes, it does often conflict with strongly held moral intuitions. And yes, it does often require us to compare things that are exceedingly difficult to compare. But as I have attempted to show, neither of these objections is decisive. Moral intuitions are sometimes irrelevant or misleading. And the fact that categories are difficult to compare does not imply that we will choose more wisely by eschewing attempts to compare them.

If these objections against consequentialist moral reasoning are not compelling, why does it remain so controversial? I conclude by considering an alternative explanation, one rooted in the practical consequences of thinking about moral issues in cost-benefit terms.

Deontologists insist that immutable moral principles distinguish right conduct from wrong, irrespective of costs and benefits. They insist, for example, that stealing is wrong not because it does more harm than good, but simply because it violates the victim's rights. The consequentialist resists such absolute prescriptions, confident that there could always be *some* conditions in which the gains from stealing might outweigh its costs.

Yet, even if we grant the force of consequentialist position on such issues, a worrisome aspect of that position remains, which is that people who view their ethical choices in cost-benefit terms must also construct their own estimates of the relevant costs and benefits. The obvious concern is that their estimates will be self-serving. More than 90 percent of all drivers, for example, feel sure they are better than average (Gilovich, 1991). More than 99 percent of high-school students think they are above average in terms of their ability to get along with others (College Board, 1976–1977). Ninety-four percent of college professors believe they are more productive than their average colleague (Cross, 1977). The same forces that make us overestimate our skills and underestimate our weaknesses can be expected also to distort the estimates that underlie our ethical judgments.

Outcome

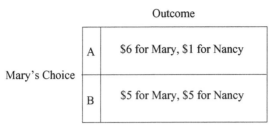

	A	$6 for Mary, $1 for Nancy
Mary's Choice		
	B	$5 for Mary, $5 for Nancy

Table 19.1. Dictator Game with Known Payoffs

My point is not that individuals are ruthlessly self-serving in general. On the contrary, considerable experimental evidence suggests that most people are willing to forego financial gains in an effort to promote ethical goals. Such, at any rate, is the prevailing interpretation of the evidence that has emerged with laboratory experiments such as the dictator game. In this game, one subject ("Mary") is given a choice about how to divide sums of money between herself and another subject ("Nancy"). Confronted with the choice portrayed in Table 19.1, for example, Mary typically chooses B, resulting in a payoff of $5 for herself and $5 for Nancy. The fact that she passed on the opportunity to choose A is typically interpreted to mean that Mary is willing to sacrifice at least $1 on behalf of her preference for the fair outcome (the even split) over the unfair outcome (the one-sided split).

Jason Dana, Roberto Weber, and Jason Kuang caution against this interpretation. They concede that when people are forced to choose in this manner, they usually exhibit an apparent willingness to pay for fairness. But they go on to note that the pattern is also consistent with other interpretations, such as not wanting to be seen by oneself or others as an unfair person. The two interpretations are different, they explain, because in actual experience, we are rarely forced to choose directly and publicly between being fair or unfair. More commonly, we confront situations that enable us to demonstrate that we care about fairness, but in which failure to act simply does not speak to this issue.

In any event, if we really care about promoting fair outcomes, opportunities abound for us to seek ways to act on this preference – for example, by seeking ways to give some of our money to others who have less. Do people seek out such opportunities? Or, if circumstances permit, do they prefer to preserve their self-image as fair persons without actually sacrificing any money in the process?

In an attempt to answer this question, Dana et al. performed a simple variation of the basic dictator experiment described above. As before,

OR

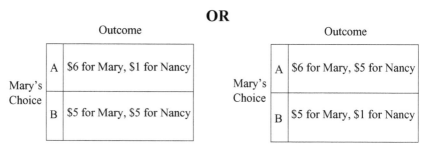

Table 19.2. Dictator Game with Unknown Payoffs

Mary is told that if she chooses A she will receive $6 and only $5 if she chooses B. But this time, Mary is told that no matter which option she chooses, the amount that Nancy actually receives will depend on the results of an earlier coin flip. If the coin came up heads, Nancy gets $1 when Mary chooses A and $5 when Mary chooses B, just as in the original game. But if tails, Nancy's payoffs are reversed: she gets $5 when Mary chooses A and $1 when Mary chooses B. The payoffs are thus as summarized in Table 19.2.

Having been given this description of the possible payoffs, Mary is then told that at no charge she can click on a button on her computer screen and learn exactly what Nancy's payoffs will be under each choice. The choices that Mary sees on her screen in this version of the experiment thus look something like those portrayed in Table 19.3.

Mary can click on the "Reveal Payoffs" button, in which case the question marks in the table will be replaced with the payoffs Nancy will actually receive under each choice (as determined by the outcome of the prior coin flip). Once the payoffs are revealed in this manner, Mary would then choose either A or B with full knowledge of the consequences of each choice for Nancy. But Mary also has the option of choosing not to click on the "Reveal Payoffs" button, in which case she would choose

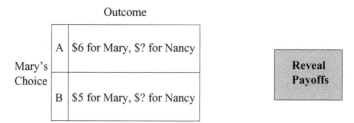

Table 19.3. Dictator Game with Costlessly Revealable Payoffs

between A and B without knowing the consequences of her choice for Nancy.

Dana et al. found that in the conventional version of the experiment (Table 19.1), 74 percent of their subjects chose B. This finding replicates a host of similar experiments that have been interpreted as revealing a willingness to pay for fairness. But if fair outcomes are what these subjects really care about, the prediction is that they should immediately click on the "Reveal Payoffs" button when confronted with the unknown-payoffs version of the game shown in Table 19.3. The logic is that with a preference for fair outcomes, clicking on this button is a no-lose option. If Nancy's payoffs are revealed to be the same as in the original version of the game, Mary will have an opportunity to buy a fair outcome that is worth the dollar she sacrifices; alternatively, if Nancy's payoffs are the reverse of those in the original game, Mary can choose the higher payoff for herself without any pangs of conscience.

What Dana et al. observed, however, was a strikingly different pattern. Only half of their subjects in the Mary role chose to click on the "Reveal Payoffs" button. Among those subjects, three-fourths chose the fair outcome (B) when the payoffs were revealed to be the same as in the original game. The remaining half of subjects in the Mary role declined to click on the "Reveal Payoffs" button, and 100 percent of them chose A (assuring themselves a $6 payoff), even though they knew there was a 50 percent chance that Nancy would only get $1 under that choice.

In discussing these findings, Dana et al. offered the following comments:

> Our subjects appear to have some taste for equitable social allocations when the situation is unambiguous: that is, when they are directly confronted with others' payoffs and there is a direct link between the immediate action and the payoffs for these others. However, this taste for equity is sharply reduced when allocations can be made – if the proposer desires – in ignorance of others' payoffs. If subjects preferred equity, they should have sought the virtually costless information about others' payoffs in order to obtain equity, but they often did not. The subtle change of covering the other party's payoffs breaks the direct link between action and payoffs: the immediate action of the proposer (to reveal or not reveal the payoffs) does not have any direct impact on the welfare of the receiver. By not revealing the true state, subjects then avoid having to make an explicit decision not to give.... [o]ur subjects chose not to know another's payoffs, as this information might only tempt them to forego a small amount of money to help the other person. (2003, pp. 15, 16)

The Dana et al. findings are also consistent with observed behavior concerning charitable giving. If the primary motive for such giving were the utility people experienced from promoting better outcomes for less fortunate others, we might expect most donations to result from donor efforts to seek out the beneficiaries whose needs best match their own concerns. In fact, however, almost all charitable giving occurs in response to direct requests for aid (Freeman, 1993). If a charity does not ask a donor directly, that donor's gift will almost always be zero. An intermediate case is the over-the-air appeal by public radio stations for donations from their listeners. Although the appeal is not personal in the traditional sense, listeners know that it is addressed to them rather than to the general public. Although they cannot pretend not to have heard the appeal, the response rate in such cases typically does not exceed 10 percent.

Other experimental evidence suggests that people are especially quick to abandon moral norms when they can do so by omission rather than by direct action. The economist Robert Piron, for example, conducted the following experiment in an attempt to assess the honesty of students on the Oberlin College campus. Piron ran an ad in the student newspaper describing a test that was to be offered to identify the smartest Oberlin undergraduate. Numerous students responded and sat for the test. Piron then graded the exams with a conspicuous error in each student's favor. Knowing that I had studied the emergence of spontaneous moral behavior, Piron asked me what fraction of students I thought had come forward to report the grading error. Not wanting to appear naïve, I attempted to guess on the low side and said 15 percent. The actual percentage, he told me, was zero.

ADDING SOCIAL DYNAMICS

As the preceding examples illustrate, the problem of self-serving bias in moral cost-benefit estimation can be severe even when subjects make their decisions in isolation from one another. But often these decisions involve a social dimension, and here the tendency toward bias will be even more severe. Thus, when self-serving calculations lead some to disregard the common good, their example will often make others more apt to do likewise.

The problem is vividly illustrated by the forces confronting honest executives as they weigh how to report their company's earnings. They know that many entries in the company's financial statements necessarily entail subjective judgments. Some, for instance, hinge on estimates and assumptions about the future, others on imperfect models for imputing monetary values to nonmarket assets. For any firm, there is thus a broad range of earnings estimates that could be defended as reasonable.

Each company's ability to finance its future growth depends strongly on how its current reported earnings compare with those of rival firms, for it is on this basis that capital markets infer which firms are most likely to succeed. Under the circumstances, it is difficult to see how even the most scrupulous executives could justify calculating their company's earnings on the basis of strictly neutral, let alone pessimistic, assumptions. On the plausible forecast that most other companies will report earnings near the optimistic end of the reasonable range, failure to do likewise would be to understate the company's true prospects.

Worse still, this situation is unstable, because the standards that define acceptable accounting judgments, like those that govern other ethical judgments, are inherently dependent on context. When almost all companies issue optimistic earnings reports, such reports come to be viewed as normal. Even the most cautious executives then feel pressure to report their earnings more aggressively, creating room for their more aggressive counterparts to push the envelope still further.

Needless to say, people may also be prone to self-serving biases in their interpretations of deontological moral principles. But because the deontological approach tends to emphasize inflexible rules grounded in sacrosanct moral principles, it would appear to have a clear edge over the consequentialist approach in this respect. The downside, of course, is that these rules are mute with respect to many moral questions and counsel choices that lead to bad consequences in others.

In the end, which approach entails the greater risk is an empirical question. My point in this chapter is that it is at least *possible* that consequentialist thinking, at least in its most simple and direct form, could lead to a worse outcome on balance. If this were shown to be so, consequentialists would have little choice but to endorse the deontological position (much as an atheist might support fundamentalist religious institutions on the view that threats of hellfire and damnation are the only practical way to get people to behave themselves). They would have to view consequentialism as correct in principle yet best avoided in practice.

Even the most committed consequentialists seem to recognize that statements such as "Stealing is permissible whenever its benefits exceed its costs" are not rhetorically effective for teaching their children moral values. Indeed, like the deontologists, most consequentialists teach their children that stealing is wrong as a matter of principle. As noted at the outset, many ostensible consequentialists have also advocated decision procedures with a decidedly nonconsequentialist bent. Following Sidgwick, for example, some have advocated various forms of indirect utilitarianism that recognize "that an agent is more likely to act rightly by developing the right attitudes, habits, and principles, and acting upon them, than by trying to calculate the value of the consequences before deciding to act."[3] On this view, consequentialism tells us what makes a right action right, but does not prescribe a method of deciding what to do.

There is evident tension, however, in any moral theory that identifies right conduct according to one criterion but prescribes action according to another. It is not clear, for example, how ordinary people might bring themselves to act with conviction according to a principle like "It is never right to kill an innocent person" and yet at the same time embrace a moral theory that endorses killing innocent people in some situations.

My point, I hope it is clear, is not that consequences are always best ignored when making moral choices. As all moral theories acknowledge, consequences count. The question is the extent to which a moral theory should be prepared to embrace general principles whose effect is to diminish the importance people assign to consequences when making moral decisions. Recent psychological research suggests that the gains from relying on such principles may be greater than many consequentialists believe.

References

Adler, Matthew. (1998). Law and incommensurability: Introduction. *University of Pennsylvania Law Review*, 146, 1169–1185.

College Board. (1976–1977). *Student descriptive questionnaire*. Princeton, NJ: Educational Testing Service.

Cross, P. (1977). Not *can* but *will* college teaching be improved? *New Directions for Higher Education*, 1–15.

Frank, Robert H. (2004). *What price the moral high ground?* Princeton, NJ: Princeton University Press.

Frank, Robert H. (2000). Why is cost-benefit analysis so controversial? *Journal of Legal Studies*, 913–930.

Freeman, Richard B. (1993). Me give to charity? Well, since you ask. Paper delivered at the Conference on the Economics and Psychology of Happiness and Fairness, London School of Economics, November.

Gilovich, Thomas. (1991). *How we know what isn't so*. New York: Free Press.

Greene, Joshua. (2002). *The terrible, horrible, no good, very bad truth about morality, and what to do about it*. Department of Philosophy, Princeton University.

[3] Mautner (1997).

Greene, J. D., Sommerville, R. B., Nystrom, L. E., Darley, J. M., & Cohen, J. D., (2001). An fMRI investigation of emotional engagement in moral judgment. *Science*, 293(5537), 2105–2108.
Mautner, T. (Ed.). (1997). *The Penguin Dictionary of Philosophy*. New York: Penguin Books.
Posner, Eric. (1998). The strategic basis of principled behavior: A critique of the incommensurability thesis. *University of Pennsylvania Law Review*, 146, 1185–1205.
Shaw, W. H. (1998). *Contemporary ethics: Taking account of utilitarianism*. Malden, MA: Blackwell Publishers.
Sidgwick, H. (1874). *The methods of ethics*. London: Macmillan. 7th edition, 1907.
Singer, Peter. (2002). The normative significance of our growing understanding of ethics. Paper presented at the Ontology Conference, San Sebastian, Spain, October 3.

TWENTY

Commentary

Conflict of Interest as a Threat to Consequentialist Reasoning

David M. Messick
Northwestern University

Frank's chapter calls into question the vulnerability of consequentialist moral reasoning to the exploitability of the "moral wiggle room" that accompanies consequentialist methodology. Thus, consequentialist reasoning may not produce the best consequences, having been compromised by conflicts of interest, and consequentialists may find that other moral theories are actually superior in creating the improved consequences. This is an interesting thesis, and one with which I completely agree. In fact, Frank may have understated the case for the corruptibility of consequentialist moralizing. I will explain what I mean in the first part of this comment, and then I will make a second point that the processes that threaten consquentialist logic are not only intentional efforts to distort in self-serving directions, but also totally invisible and nonconscious processes that are difficult to eliminate (even if one were to decide they should be eliminated). Finally, I will show that the failure of an explicit maximization process like utilitarianism to maximize is not unique to moral theory.

Frank discusses some of the ways in which self-interest may bias the ways in which people trying to estimate the relevant costs and benefits that need to be calculated to make such a judgment. Surely the issue of commensurability of utilities (can I compare John's pleasure of having a lake in his neighborhood to Fred's displeasure of losing his pasture?) is an issue as is the role of agency, the matter of the equivalence of not of acts of omission and acts of commission. But I think that there are three even more basic problems with this theory. First is the need in utilitarian or consequentialist theories for human preferences to be more or less stable. There is good reason to doubt that this is the case. Take, for instance, the well-known phenomenon of outcome framing. I ask one of our graduating

MBA students if she judges her starting salary of $110,000 a year to be a good or poor salary. Quite good, she replies. I point out that another of our students is starting with the same firm for a salary of $120,000 and I repeat the question. This new benchmark, or standard, or anchor changes the evaluation. Response time shoots up. There is uncertainty because there is evaluative ambiguity. In principle, I could introduce additional standards that could continue to shift the evaluative frame to make the ultimate evaluation of this salary, is it good or bad, uncertain. How can we maximize the greatest good if what is judged good is so inherently labile?

A second problem is that consequentialist theories require that we have accurate means of knowing the future. What will happen if we attack Iraq? If we relax emission requirements for power plants? If we arm pilots of domestic aircraft? Without good guesses about the answers of these kinds of questions, efforts to make the greatest good are silly. So how good are we at predicting the future? This is obviously not a simple question to answer since the answer depends on domains that vary widely. But I think that it is a fair summary of the psychological literature to say that we are much poorer than we give ourselves credit for being. Kuttner (1999) makes a similar generalization about economists when he asked, "What do you call an economist with a prediction? Wrong." Things go sour more often than we expect, but since we are expert at finding "silver linings," we tend not to notice.

Finally, consequentialist methodology is essentially mute on the question of whose consequences do you include in your analysis. It assumes that this has already been specified. But what this means is that you are free to choose. So, in deliberations about NAFTA and free trade issues, most American analysts focused on the consequences for American citizens, not Canadian or Mexican, and certainly not European or Asian citizens.

Taken together, the three factors I have mentioned, the lability of preference, the unpredictability of the future, and inclusion ambiguity, along with the problems mentioned by Frank, lead to the conclusion that consequentialist analyses are inherently strategically exploitable. What I mean is that they can be used to prove nearly anything. One starts knowing the result one wants to get, and one can jigger the analysis with "reasonable" frames, predictions, and inclusions/exclusions to produce the result as the "moral" answer. Moreover, this exploitability is greatest in the most complicated and uncertain situations, where outcomes are complex, the future uncertain, and lots of different people are involved. If I want to go to war with Iraq, I can make up the outcomes, the futures, and the focal groups of concerned people that will prove that war is the moral choice. If I think war on Iraq is wrong, I make up a different set of outcomes, different futures, and different groups to prove my point. And the neat thing is that until a decision is taken, to go to war or not, no one can say which set of scenarios is correct. So, in short, the consequentialist methodology is most likely to fail in precisely those circumstances where it is most needed.

I have made it seem in the previous paragraphs as if the vulnerability of consequentialist ethics is intentional manipulation. This is only part of the problem. A second part is that we are each the accumulation of our experiences, our education, our backgrounds, and our histories. We do not chose our nationalities, our mother tongues, our parents, or our religions (as a rule). Yet, we are influenced by these things. Inevitably, someone born of Muslim parents in an Arabic nation will see the world differently from someone born of Jewish parents in Israel. They will do consequentialist calculations differently. Their frames, forecasts, and focal groups will differ in predicable ways, and they will each think that they occupy the moral high ground and that the other side is biased and wrong. Moreover, it will be hard, if not impossible, for them to avoid this difference. This is not willfully exploiting consequentialist methodology to forward one's agenda; this is the result of the inevitable fact that we are all, in part, the products of our pasts. We cannot help this: we cannot help but to be the heroes of our own life stories. But the "wiggle room" that Frank and I refer to allows us to use the morality of outcomes to prove our virtue and our opponent's wickedness. So, although intentional manipulation is a problem, a perhaps greater problem is the inevitability of moral disagreements and predicable misperceptions.

My final point about Frank's interesting chapter is to note that the potential paradox he outlines in the final section, that explicitly consequentialist reasoning could lead to worse outcomes, on balance, than deontological thinking, has parallels in other areas of social science. Perhaps the most well-known occurs with the famous prisoners' dilemma. This structure is familiar to everyone, I suppose, so there is no need to review it here in detail. The paradox with the prisoners' dilemma is that when each participant chooses to maximize that person's interests, the collective result is a set of outcomes in which the people's interests are not maximized. Adam Smith's "invisible hand," the one that presumably guides individual maximization to social maximization, is a bit unsteady in this class of situations. We have found that prisoners' dilemma situations are common enough to make us uncomfortable with the hackneyed advice to allow individual self-interest to settle our problems.

A second domain in which explicit maximization may not maximize is in the domain of corporate morality and vigor. For decades, some corporate leaders have touted Milton Friedman's thesis that the moral duty of corporate executives is to increase the profits of firm and hence the wealth of the shareholders (Friedman, 1970). Empirical research, however, has cast doubt on the assumption that the best way to increase corporate profits is to try to maximize corporate profits. In their pioneering research, Collins and Porras (1994) present evidence that the most profitable firms are those that have some purpose for being that is different from profit maximization. Indeed, they point out (p. 227) that "none of the core purposes that are discussed in this chapter fall into the category 'maximize shareholder wealth'." Just as the blind pursuit of profits may not be the best way to achieve profitability, the blind pursuit of positive consequences may not be the best way to achieve them.

References

Collins, J. C., & Porras, J. I. (1994). *Built to last.* New York: HarperBusiness.
Kuttner, R. (1999). What do you call an economist with a prediction? Wrong. *Business Week*, September 6, 22.

Index

academia, 2, 204
  scandals and inputs of, 2
academic psychiatrists and the
  pharmaceutical industry, 183
accounting firms, 4, 167
  auditing and consulting not by same, 106,
    107
  disclosure of, 106
  dispute with client by, 60
  incentives in not rendering negative
    option by, 4
  staving off regulations by, 73
accounting industry, 1, 2
  academic accounting department's
    criticism of, 73
  scandals in, 1, 2, 41, 106, 192–193,
    198–199
accruals, 52
  abnormal, 44, 52–54
  expected total, 52
Adelphia, 1, 106
adversarialism, inquisitorism v., 55,
  246–250
advice, 104
  accurate, 118
  biased, 104, 105, 112, 113, 116,
    118
  discounting, 104, 105, 114, 116, 118,
    127–128
  trust and, 117
advice, given, 114
  disclosure distortion and, 114
  disclosure's effect on, 114–116

  moral licensing in, 115–116
  strategic exaggeration in, 115,
    128
advice, received, 108
  disclosure's consequences to, 116–118
  disclosure's effect on, 108–114
  failure of evidentiary discreditation in,
    112–113
  judgmental correction difficulty of,
    108–112
  lay dispositionism and, 113–114
advocacy, 243, 246
advocate, 248
allegiance, researcher, 240–241
Allison, S. T., 85
Allman, R. L., 173
Allport, F. H., 112
altruism, 206, 208, 212, 213, 224, 225,
  226
  selfishness and, 224–226
Alvarez, J., 90
ambiguity, 98–99, 285
ambiguity-specificity paradox, 98–99,
  100–101
American College of Physicians, 137
American Gastroenterological Association
  (AGA), 136
American Institute of Certified Public
  Accountants (AICPA), 50
amplication, 250
anchoring and insufficient adjustment,
  109–112
  disclosure of, 110

For EU product safety concerns, contact us at Calle de José Abascal, 56–1°, 28003 Madrid, Spain or eugpsr@cambridge.org.

www.ingramcontent.com/pod-product-compliance
Ingram Content Group UK Ltd.
Pitfield, Milton Keynes, MK11 3LW, UK
UKHW042211180425
457623UK00011B/165